MANAGING ORGANIZATIONAL INNOVATION
The Evolution from Word Processing to Office Information Systems

CORPS (Computing, Organizations, Policy, and Society) Series
Rob Kling and Kenneth L. Kraemer, General Editors

MANAGING ORGANIZATIONAL INNOVATION
The Evolution from Word Processing to Office Information Systems

BONNIE McDANIEL JOHNSON
RONALD E. RICE

COLUMBIA UNIVERSITY PRESS
New York 1987

0536345   120251

Library of Congress Cataloging-in-Publication Data

Johnson, Bonnie McDaniel, 1944–
  Managing organizational innovation.

  (CORPS (computing, organizations, policy, and
society) series)
  Bibliography: p.
  Includes index.
  1. Word processing. 2. Information storage and
retrieval systems—Business. 3. Office practice—
Automation. I. Rice, Ronald E. II. Title.
III. Series.
  HF5548.115.J64 1987   652'.5   87-307
  ISBN 0-231-06398-9

Columbia University Press
New York   Guildford, Surrey
Copyright © 1987 Columbia University Press
Printed in the United States of America

Book design by Ken Venezio

This book is dedicated to Jennifer Johnson,
Ron Johnson, Ellen Sleeter

Contents

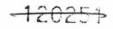

About the Authors

BONNIE McDANIEL JOHNSON recently joined Aetna Life and Casualty in Hartford, Connecticut, as Director, Information and Plans, Corporate Technology Planning. Her responsibilities include coordination and communication for long-range planning of information systems infrastructure. Prior to joining Aetna, she was Manager, Office Systems Development at Intel Corporation. At Intel, Dr. Johnson was in charge of a group that was chartered to promote better use of office tools through establishing programs in end-user training and support, applications development, personal configuration, and interconnection.

Dr. Johnson has also developed and taught seminars on executive communications, organizational development, interviewing, project management, and performance appraisal. She was on the faculty at Penn State University and the University of Oklahoma from 1970 to 1981, after which she was a research fellow at Stanford University. Her B.A. in political science came from Texas Christian University, and her M.A. and Ph.D. in organizational communication came from State University, New York. Dr. Johnson's publications include *Communication: The Process of Organization* (American Press, 1981) and *Getting the Job Done* (Scott, Foresman, 1983).

RONALD E. RICE is assistant professor of communications at the Annenberg School of Communications at the University of Southern California. He received a B.A. from Columbia University, and an M.A. and Ph.D. in communication research from Stanford University. His experience as an operations manager of data processing departments in a statewide bank, as a consultant in statistical and information retrieval programming for the Center for Advanced Studies in the Behavioral Sciences, and as an associate member of Hamlin-Harkins, a Silicon Valley consulting firm, provide the practical background for his academic research. That research has focused on the diffusion of innovations, the social impact of telecommunications, human communication networks, and the implementation of information systems.

Dr. Rice has co-edited *Public Communication Campaigns* (Sage, 1981), co-authored *The New Media: Communication, Research and Technology* (Sage, 1984), coauthored *Research Methods for the Study of New Media* (New York: Free Press, 1987), and published in the fields of information science, communications, and social networks. Professional affiliations include the American Society for Information Science, the Academy of Management, the International Society for Social Network Analysis, and the International Communication Association, of which he is a divisional officer.

Acknowledgments

This book represents the dedicated work of many people spanning the time from inspiration of the idea to the proofreading of the final document. Funding for the research came from the National Science Foundation via Grant 8110791. The opinions and conclusions of this book are, of course, not necessarily those of NSF. J. D. Eveland, NSF's project monitor, provided valuable assistance throughout the project, beginning with helping to focus the project. J. D. was a careful critic and editor of the instruments and all chapters of the final report.

James C. Taylor was a coauthor of the NSF proposal. He contributed to the theoretical basis of sociotechnical systems, and shaped the telephone and survey instruments and collected data on site visits. He was involved in several stages of the data analysis and contributed to the writing.

Timothy J. Cline helped to shape the interview and survey instruments. He trained and led the "Washington team" of interviewers who contacted ninety-six sites by phone and visited eighteen organizations. He contributed significantly to the discussion of communication and continuous learning.

Dennis Smith also helped to construct the interview and survey data. He led the West Coast interview team and collected all of the Kansas data. Dennis was a coauthor of the first report of this study (Johnson et al., 1983). He consulted on the organization of the final report to the NSF.

Larry Browning collected data in site visits on the East and West Coasts. He contributed substantially to the qualitative analysis and to the writing of the final report, particularly the chapter on boundary management.

Several people contributed their talents to instrument design, interviewing, and data analysis: Clare Cummings, John Jessen, Margaret Davis, Patrick Ford, Young Kim, Elaine Huey, Betsy Knight, Georgia Woodridge, and Misty Battles.

We would like to thank the Department of Communication, University of Oklahoma, for their support during the writing of the proposal and for their generous assistance in administering the project. We also thank the Institute for Communication Research of Stanford University for providing Dr. Johnson with office space and access to the fine facilities of Stanford as a post-doctoral researcher, and for training and providing computing resources to Dr. Rice. The Annenberg School of Communications provided additional computer and travel assistance. The Annenberg Learning Center, under the direction of Carolyn Spicer, was exceptionally helpful in retrieving articles and materials. Roger Felder managed to configure a microcomputer and educate the second author on its care and feeding in a few short, but intense, days.

The authors did all their own typing, using a variety of software packages and a variety of microcomputers. Sometimes knowing which diskette version to use was more difficult than knowing what to write.

We thank Sage Publications, Beverly Hills, for permission to adapt pages 158–176 of *The New Media: Communication, Research and Technology,* by Rice and Associates (1984) for use in chapters 1 and 3.

Our special gratitude goes to Everett M. Rogers who encouraged Dr. Johnson from the beginning to pursue this project, who co-authored the article that provided some of the conceptual foundations for the initial proposal (Rice and Rogers 1980), and who was a helpful mentor to both of us during our times at Stanford University.

Chapter 1

Word Processing: A Foundation for Integrated Office Systems

A powerful tide is surging across much of the world today, creating a new, often bizarre, environment in which to work, play, marry, raise children, or retire. . . . Old ways of thinking, old formulas, dogmas, and ideologies, no matter how cherished or useful in the past, no longer fit the facts. The world that is fast emerging from the clash of new values and technologies, new geopolitical relationships, new life-styles and modes of communication, demands wholly new ideas and analogies, classifications and concepts. (Toffler 1981: 1–2)

The Problem

Since 1980, guidelines for managing organizational innovation have become so commonplace as to seem like clichés (for example, Grove 1983; Kanter 1983; Peters and Waterman 1982; Peters and Austin 1985). With rapid developments in computer-based office information systems, innovation in white-collar work has been a particular challenge. "The information age" seems here to stay. The premise that information work somehow demands new approaches to management is reasonably well accepted.

This premise is derived from several fundamental assumptions of management scientists, organizational theorists, and communication researchers: 1. Organizations are more complex than in previous generations and call for more complex models of management; 2. Organizational environments are more turbulent, hence an organization's survival is intimately connected to its adaptability; 3. Information technology provides powerful new ways of processing, communicating, storing, and accessing messages. The increased speed and power of communications is changing options for managers and ultimately the culture of management.

The primary assertion presented here is that *adaptation is an underemphasized and critical outcome of information work.* Information systems provide a way for organizations to adapt more successfully to environments, and indeed to adapt their environments to their own evolution. Managers of information workers should pay increasing attention to adaptation rather than solely to narrow definitions of production.

The book shows by way of the example of word processing implementation how the industrial assumptions about work clashed with the possibilities of new technology and the essential features of information work. Efforts to implement word processing using organizational principles of the industrial bureaucracy *did not work.*

This question from a word processing implementer to the "In-House Consulting" column of *Words* (1982:34) is typical of the sentiments of people disappointed in their word processing installation:

In my organization, which is a major industrial corporation, implementing word processing departmentally produced less than the desired results. Before installing the equipment, we had undertaken a feasibility study. Equipment was recommended, approved, and installed. Outdated equipment and procedures were discarded. Based primarily on her outstanding administrative background, a former executive secretary with over fifteen years of service to the company was selected to be the supervisor. Unfortunately, the result of our efforts was frequent turnover among the operators. Turnaround time was slow; transcription inaccuracies abounded, and retyping of already printed documents was frequent. How could this have happened when our organization followed all the right steps?

Indeed, unsuccessful implementation of office information systems is the rule, not the exception. In one large-scale study, only 10 percent of the 110 organizations had successful implementations of office automation (Westin, Schweder, Baker, and Lehman 1985). Insufficient strategic planning, inadequate and overly narrow training, high employee fears but low involvement, little consulting with human resources departments about job design or work satisfaction, inadequate ergonomics and weak communications about safety issues are all too frequent consequences of efforts to implement an innovation such as an information system.

Those who implemented word processing successfully, therefore, had to forge their own ways. The most successful ones of those reported in this book focused their efforts on *adaptation* using the technology rather than on *production* per se. Adapters often achieved observable and appropriate increases in production, but were not blinded by traditional criteria for productivity. In their experiences, we can see new organizational patterns emerging.

The Argument

Here is the argument explicated in the following chapters: Word processing, as a significant element of office technology, began with the introduction of the typewriter in the 1870s. The typewriter, along with other technologies such as the dictaphone, the copier and the computer, were not isolated events, but part of the social and economic contexts of the times. Thus, office technology and social relations—such as the nature of clerical work and the design of jobs—are inextricably linked and must be analyzed, and implemented, jointly.

With the computer-based systems of the late 1960s, word processing technology was also seen as a way of improving the efficiency of secretarial work—an organizational activity heretofore unsusceptible to "improvement" through industrial practices, which were designed for routinized, manufacturing kinds of tasks. (The origins and implications of these assumptions are discussed in greater detail in chapter 5.) The "code" of industrial design as identified by Toffler (1980) consists of six principles:

- Standardization
- Specialization
- Synchronization
- Concentration
- Maximization
- Centralization

Kanter, for example, observes this about secretarial work in the late 1970s:

The job, made necessary by the growth of modern organizations, lay at the very core of bureaucratic administration; yet, it often was the least bureaucratized segment of corporate life. The product of the rationalization of work and the vast amount of paperwork that entailed, it still remained resistant to its own rationalization. . . . The secretarial job involved the most routine of tasks in the white-collar world, yet the most personal of relationships. The greatest time was spent on the routine, but the greatest reward was garnered for the personal. (1977:70)

In the late 1970s and early '80s word processing technology and the economic rationale of centralizing to utilize an expensive resource intensively provided a reason to reorganize at least one part of secretarial work—typing—in accordance with the industrial model. Word processing *technology* was, for many, synonymous with *implementation* of the industrial bureaucracy.

Word processing equipment was put into large centers (sometimes a hundred or more workstations) where operators worked on shifts round the clock to produce standard, measured lines of text. A secretarial textbook published in 1978 observed that "management is sold on the concept" of word processing because "word processing techniques can usually result in a decrease of 15 to 30 percent in clerical payroll and overhead for every 100 workstations." The authors noted that "this is another indication that word processing systems are feasible only in large companies." They predicted that "no more than 20 percent of today's offices are organized for word processing. Many will never be" (Marshall, Popham, and Tilton 1978).

By the time interviewing for our research began in 1981, there were no large centers in the sampling regions (though there were reports of some in other areas). Large centers did not "work." Large-scale centralization and the other premises of industrial organization were not working as ways of effectively managing information work. At best this approach worked in a marginal fashion to facilitate "production typing"—in which the content of the printed text means nothing to the person doing the typing. In jobs where thinking about the content was required or advantageous, implementations based on the industrial model went out of business amidst great anguish.

Implementations based upon narrow notions of productivity and narrow definitions of word processing also failed to see how word processing could even play a role in planning for automation, much less provide any lessons for implementing such integrated systems. But the functionality/cost ratios are increasing steadily, and integration is becoming more and more feasible—and necessary. Understanding word processing from the generic perspective of information processing—inputs, processing, outputs, transmission—leads to the awareness that well-managed word processing can provide the foundation from which successful integrated information systems will evolve.

This conception of integrated systems is centered around the fact that organizations are becoming more and more information intensive, and work consists of managing information. This change from a focus on industrial manufacturing has raised a serious problem for managers—how to measure productivity of information work, and how to assess the productivity gains from implementing information systems.

The management of word processing—structure, procedures, product, culture—itself evolved through experience into different configurations in each organization. There is no single pattern, but there are some similarities across sites. Four approaches to the management of word processing technology have been synthesized from observations at nearly sixty organizations, and are referred to here as four "word processing systems." The term "system" is used throughout this book as a reference to the management system, not the hardware and software per se. The four systems are:

Low-integration systems: decentralized use of word processing technology with little systematic innovation and little automation beyond typing functions.

Clockwork systems: efficient word processing centers that did not adapt their services to changing user demands and technological capabilities.

Expanding systems: effective word processing centers where supervisors and managers kept in close contact with users and evolved
more productive applications that expanded their services.

High-integration systems: adaptation of decentralized word processing
capability to create integrated information systems through special
attention to user involvement, support, and communications.

The evolution of these systems took place as the result of purposeful
management practices. Managers who were successful in implementing word processing in innovative ways acted purposefully on
a set of sociotechnical systems principles, though few labeled them
as such, influencing their employees to do things that adapted the
technology creatively to accomplish the organization's mission more
productively.

Principles for Managing Innovation in Information Systems

This book analyzes the evolution of management practices in terms
of eleven principles for action:

1. Understand how information work differs from industrial production, and how traditional criteria for productivity misdirect
   management's attention.
2. Promote self-regulation of work groups through autonomy. Locate the decision making at the task requiring the decision.
3. Design jobs so that people can perceive and complete whole
   tasks.
4. Administer policies with flexibility.
5. Design jobs for upward mobility.
6. Involve members in changing the technology and social system
   jointly to accomplish the organizational mission.
7. Provide experiences for continuous learning.
8. Encourage experimentation. Systems evolve; managers must continuously attend to adaptation.
9. Design work units to optimize communication for high performance and quality of work life.
10. Establish boundaries so that recognizable successes can lead to
    claims of expertise and authority.
11. Attend to the environment outside the boundaries.

The Research

Rather than broad social commentary, this book reports a focused study of the early implementation of office technology in nearly two hundred organizations, with special attention to the experiences of sixty of these. The study was funded by Grant 8110791 from the National Science Foundation's Industrial Processes and Management Group. The specific intent of the researchers and the funders was to understand what factors lead some organizations to be more effective than others in the implementation of word processing technology. The more general interest was to describe the general process of implementating successful systems. Representatives of one hundred ninety four organizations that had adopted word processing at least two years prior were interviewed by telephone. In sixty organizations visited after the telephone survey, questionnaires were administered to key decision makers, supervisors, authors, and word processing operators. In addition to the questionnaire data, over four hundred pages of interview notes provided a rich basis for qualitative analysis. Data were collected in 1982 and 1983 and analyzed from 1982 to 1985; inquiries concerned organizational experiences from the late '70s. The Appendix describes the research process in greater detail.

Although we endeavored to conduct this research in accordance with the principles of our training—generating testable hypotheses, administering replicable measures, suggesting tight and conservative conclusions—we found that these research procedures were difficult to apply to the turbulent subject of this study. In the years from 1981 to 1985 the nature of word processing management was changing rapidly. Word processing technology evolved from very expensive dedicated machinery (costing about $25,000 per machine) to software on inexpensive personal computers (costing less than $3,000 for both)."Word processing operators" were no longer clerical specialists, but often presidents of corporations who found it easier to use keyboards than dictating equipment. The tide of word processing management was moving quickly even as we tried to study it. As a result, this study provides only "windows" into a complex and evolving social process. The text provides evidence for its conclusions, but some evidence is missing.

Organization of the Book

The book is organized to highlight the practical implications of the findings for managing innovation in information systems, but couched in a context of prior theorization and research.

The remainder of this first chapter provides a short history of word processing to emphasize the interrelationship of organizational information needs, work relationships, and text processing technology. It also summarizes trends for the near future as evidence of the relevance of word processing systems to integrated office systems in general. Chapter 2 establishes the theoretical foundations for understanding the concepts of information work and office productivity, and adaptation as a prime goal of implementing organizational information systems. It also analyzes the conceptual and pragmatic foundations for understanding the innovation/implementation process. Chapter 3 reviews the trends in initial implementation practices by the two hundred organizations surveyed, in a discussion structured by a five-stage innovation framework.

Each of the following five chapters is organized around a claim from the research that points to implementation and management practices which foster adaptation in word processing work. These chapters may be summarized as follows:

Chapter 4: Technology implementation develops overtime as a process of problem solving. Four levels of adaptation seem to capture the basic results of different implementation practices.

Chapter 5: Principles of job design and sociotechnical systems are reflected in the levels of innovation shown by word processing units.

Chapter 6: High-quality jobs foster adaptation.

Chapter 7: Communication, participation, and continuous learning in work groups foster adaptation.

Chapter 8: Managing the boundaries between work groups and their environments fosters adaptation.

Chapter 9: Lessons learned from word processing sites are applicable to the implementation of microcomputers and to the problems of information centers. The primary principles in fostering innovation that emerged from the research are summarized.

THE IMPORTANCE AND CONTEXT OF WORD PROCESSING

Why Study Word Processing?

Traditionally, word processing (WP) has meant the entry, editing, storage, retrieval, formatting, and printing of text, by means of dedicated computer-based systems. As discussed in much greater depth throughout this chapter, word processing really should be seen as one component of generalized text management capabilities necessary for any organization, and as central to any concept of integrated office information systems. In addition to the significance of word processing derived from this wider definition, there are several good reasons to look at word processing for lessons in how to manage office information systems:

1. Most importantly, WP allows for considerable variety in organizational uses, procedures, roles, and structures. Therefore, the lessons of WP management provide good guides to management choices in other technology areas, such as end-user computing and office automation.

2. Word processing is a fundamental organizational activity. The production of textual information—its creation, processing, storage, retrieval, and communication—is important regardless of whether the organization is a bank, manufacturing plant, public agency, or service provider. Text processing is a significant computer application, representing around 15 percent of the value of all computer shipments (*Fortune* 1985). Already, 14 percent of all jobs involve the use of video terminals (*Wall Street Journal,* September 6, 1985). Further, and one of the central arguments of this book, WP can contribute to organizational performance not only in standalone mode but more significantly as an integrated part of organization-wide information processing (McLeod and Bender 1982).

3. Productive use of WP requires management practices that both standardize operations and inspire creativity. WP is not just typing. Before personal computers became popular, innovative managers and operators used WP equipment to keep databases and provide means of tracking information. To do this they had to develop standard procedures for doing work and they had to "trick" machines

into tasks beyond what the designers had envisioned. They had to invent new ways of doing work. Thus examining the introduction and development of WP in organizations can help us understand what work unit members do that brings about change in ways that are both creative and embedded into organizational practices.

4. WP was the first "end-user" computing application. It presented the first time that significant computer capability was accessible to employees who had no particular training in computing or data processing. Lessons learned here can be useful in understanding the management of microcomputing, which has been listed in one survey as the second most important information systems issue for the 1980s (Dickson, Leitheser, Wetherbe, and Nechis 1984).

5. The history of computer-based word processing has been compact and complete enough to reveal identifiable life-cycle patterns. Although, as this chapter later shows, office text processing technology has a one hundred-year history, WP became an important organizational technology around 1977 (61 percent of the sample had used WP five years or less). During the period from 1978 to 1983 WP units were organized as centers in most major organizations and many smaller ones. In 1983 decentralized word processing began to be the dominant means of organizing this function. By 1985, though many WP centers remained, WP began to become associated with software that runs on microcomputers. Hence in less than ten years WP began and ended as a major unique organizational form.

6. The history of WP is not only compact enough to reveal patterns, it is recent enough that participants can remember the events of that history. In the study that provided the case studies and data for this book, only 22 percent of the respondents were not present in their organizations when WP was first introduced.

7. Changes of work are easier to observe in WP than in more symbolic innovations such as budgeting or counseling practice.

A fuller understanding of the role of WP in office work comes from a consideration of its historical context and its features, functions, and organizational forms.

The Historical Context of Office Word Processing

The steel pen nib, introduced around 1858, was arguably the first step toward the mechanization of office work (Giuliano 1982). But that year also saw the first sales of pencils with attached erasers, so the development of office information technology began at a fairly fundamental level and progressed rapidly (Beniger 1986). At that time, scribing, drafting, and copying text was the domain of gentlemen who had received specialized training in school. Document storage was cumbersome; incoming correspondence was kept in pigeon holes, boxes, or whatever scheme suited the office manager. Copies of outgoing correspondence were kept chronologically in large flat books. Records processing consisted of the keeping of books—large bound ledgers—and making copies by pressing inked sheets between tissue paper. This procedure not only made it physically difficult to search for portions of a client's file, but there was no necessary linkage between incoming and outgoing portions.

On the other hand, internal written office communication (memos, written procedures, forms), with which we are now all too familiar, hardly existed.[1] It was considered the duty of a manager to be knowledgeable enough about business not to require recourse to any record system other than personal memory.

Written communications were encouraged by a vast efficiency in storage and retrieval, made possible by the development of the *vertical file*. Vertical filing is the method of classifying, storing, and retrieving paper documents that has been standard practice in organizations for nearly a century. The vertical file actually combined *three* inventions: a storage medium, an indexing system, and a duplication facility—in other words, storage, retrieval, and distribution functions. The first component was a physical means to store documents and make them easily accessible. Files that could be laid flat replaced bound ledgers, and were quickly improved to become cabinet files by 1881. The loose-leaf ring binder, introduced in 1894, further increased flexibility in office records and led to the idea of interchangeable parts in maintaining records. The second component was a classification system to store and retrieve the documents, specifically the Dewey decimal system accepted in 1876. The third component was the replacement of the typical way of making copies—inking the ledger's tissue sheets—by (a) a roller copier, (b) carbon copying (invented in 1869, it took until about 1910s to be accepted), or (c) Edison's mimeograph, introduced in 1870. Libraries were the first to combine these components; library card indexes diffused much more quickly than did business vertical files. A library supplier introduced the vertical file at the Chicago World's Fair in 1893, and filing of separate, reproduced documents in upright filing cabinets was in widespread use by 1915; the first School of Filing opened in New York in 1914 (Delgado 1979).

These office technologies not only allowed office workers to do more with greater coordination, but they also increased the need for rationalized practices to control the growing amount of records and copies (Rhee 1968). The ability to file materials easily led to information overload and the dissemination of document storage throughout the organization, i.e., decentralized databases. The need for standardization of filable documents for storage, retrieval, and distribution purposes led to written procedures, one-topic memos, specialized stages in text processing, increased internal correspondence, reduced worker autonomy, and "corporate memory" (Yates 1982).

Parallel to the integration of components necessary for the development of office systems was the revolution in information production and distribution. The increasing vertical and horizontal integration in industry (1880 to 1900) fueled a tremendous growth in transactions (Beniger 1986; Chandler 1977; Whalen 1983). Several components came together in the late nineteenth century to spur the mass distribution of information: the telegraph, the linotype, wire services, the photogravure process, the rotary press, and trolleys and railroads. They combined to make the newspaper cheap, attractive, and pervasive: by 1910, the average household received 1.3 daily newspapers, up from .3 in 1870 (Paisley 1985).

The introduction of the telegraph (first demonstrated in 1844) decreased the effect of distance on business, but did not affect intracity communication traffic much. Messenger news services (1882) and the telephone did that. Although direct dialing in switched local networks was available by 1899, operator-assisted service was available soon after Bell invented the telephone in 1876, and desk telephones were available by 1886.

Organizations needed ways to process this growing flood of information. Indeed, Beniger (1986: ch. 6) shows that the vast increase in the transacting and distribution of material and informational goods created successions of crises throughout the second half of the nineteenth century. These "crises of control"—such as passenger deaths due to inaccurate scheduling of multiple trains on a lengthy rail line—required new ways to handle information, new ways to control organizational processes, and new forms of work specialization. In turn, the new organization and information systems— such as bureaucracy and improved regularity and speed of communication—were used to increase organizational efficiency.

The concept of a typewriter fascinated inventors from as far back as Henry Mill in 1714. Over fifty inventors demonstrated writing machines before Sholes patented his version in 1868; it underwent fifty revisions before being bought by Remington. Remington sold 146 in 1879; one year later they sold 65,000 in spite of the fact that not until 1883 was the typed text visible to the typist (Rhee 1968:2). Typewriting led to a dramatic increase in dictation, and hence facilitated the rise of the role of "personal secretary" and the fragmentation of correspondence handling. By the turn of the century, shorthand and touch typing were widely used; more than 100,000 typewriters had been sold (Giuliano 1982). The typewriter was seen at the time as a major revolution equal to the steam locomotive (Bliven 1954; Curley 1981).

A spate of inventions in office systems quickly followed. Edison, in 1878, and Bell (with others), in 1881, developed the forerunners of the dictation machine—which was introduced as the "business phonograph" in 1913. It did not replace the stenographer—that awaited modern office equipment, as stenography jobs declined 50 percent from 1972 to 1980 (Giuliano 1982:154). There were even early "automatic typewriters" based upon the player piano principle, using two rolls (one each for form text and name lists), sold until after World War II (Leffingwill 1926). Due to the Depression and reduced office work during World War II, there was little development in office products.[2]

During this period, however, Chester Carlson worked on an invention that would significantly transform the office in ways that are still not well described or understood: the office photocopying machine. First patented in 1939, and rejected by many companies including IBM, it was nurtured by the Haloid company, which developed into Xerox. The Haloid Xerox 914 copier, first available in 1959, spurred the growth in the number of copies made in offices from "around 20 million in 1955 to 14 billion in 1966 to approximately eleven zillion today" (Owens 1986:66). By making the production of standard, legible copies easy and cheap, photocopying multiplied the effects of the vertical file and carbon copy on office activities and roles. With the advent of intelligent copiers and laser printers, it set the stage for some of the most recent developments in text management, discussed below.

The development of WP as we know it began as the marketing concept of a German IBM products manager, who saw the magnetic tape/selectric typewriter (MT/ST) as an improvement over the paper-tape Frieden Flexowriter automated typewriter (Curley 1981). He convinced IBM of the possibilities, and they marketed the term "word processing" (WP). They also marketed the idea of reorganizing the office around centralized transcription pools so dictation could take advantage of the costly equipment. This approach followed the earlier need for centralization and redesign of transaction processing to fit the constraints and costs of mainframe computing. It also fit in with the set of assumptions derived from industrial work. Centralization as an organizational concept to match computer technology was advocated by IBM early on and made a permanent mark on the use and design of office technology and work.

The MT/ST was introduced in 1964 and used tape cassettes to store short text material. Storage was increased in 1969 with the IBM CMST, or magnetic card typewriter. WP developments followed rapidly, and included Lexitron's introduction of a video display in 1971 that allowed correction of errors before printing—that is, the processing of stored information was separated from the physical material used for its distribution. Vydec's floppy disks, introduced in 1973, offered random access to text. Programmable WP software appeared in 1977 from Lanier; multiple copying functions were soon added by the IBM 6670 in 1979. Electronic typewriters were first introduced in 1978 by Qyx, later acquired by Exxon. The concept of integrating data and text was manifested in Jacquard's offering in 1979. Prime, Wang, Xerox, and Datapoint introduced networking in 1980. Terminals designed for managerial needs were available from Xerox the next year. Also released in 1981, the Wang Alliance system handled data in a variety of forms and provided integrated functions.

With the rapid diffusion of microcomputers in offices—an estimated nine million in 1985—WP software has proliferated and begun to compete with dedicated WP equipment. Fifty-seven percent of the companies surveyed by Dun & Bradstreet that had microcomputers used them for WP, among other applications (*Wall Street Journal* 1985). The availability of software that emulates dedicated WP functionality has rapidly blurred the distinctions between WP systems and microcomputer systems. Thus, while WP and electronic typewriter shipments have held steady, alphanumeric terminals and microcomputers continue to show considerable growth. Table 1.1 summarizes the history of office word processing, while table 1.2 shows the relative trends for these recent technologies.

Word processing, then, has developed within an historical context. An increasing need to manage information and an increasing interdependence with other organizational systems characterizes the evolution of WP. It is appropriate to ask, then, what functions does the current generation of WP systems perform? And how important is WP to future forms of organizational information management? The following section reviews some of the primary capabilities of WP, its basic organizational forms, and near-term trends.

WORD PROCESSING FEATURES AND FORMS

Word Processing Features and Configurations

The configuration of WP system components can generally be classified into three types: standalone, multiterminal, or nondedicated

TABLE 1.1

Summary of Events in Word Processing History

Year	Development
1844	Telegraph demonstrated
1858	Steel pen nib
1870	Mimeograph in Development
1874	Sholes' typewriter marketed by Remington
1876	Telephone demonstrated
1876	Dewey decimal system
1878–81	Dictation machine in development
1881	Cabinet files introduced
1882	Urban messenger news services
1890s	Heavy growth in industrial transactions; Mass distribution of information
1894	Loose-leaf ring binder introduced
1899	Direct dialing telephone
1900s	Photostat machines developed
1914	First school of filing, New York
1920s	"Automatic" piano-roll typewriters
1938	Chester Carlson begins development of photocopier
1950s	3M's Thermofax and Eastman-Kodak's Verifax
1959	Haloid Xerox 914 office copier
1961	IBM Selectric's "golf ball" element
1964	IBM's MT/ST typewriter
1969	Magnetic card typewriter
1971	Lexitron's video display word processor
1973	Vydec's floppy disks
1977	Lanier's programmable software
1978	Qyx's electronic typewriter
1979	Jacquard's integration of text and data
1980	Laser printing, networking of word processors
1982	Widespread acceptance of microcomputer
1984	Integrated office systems software; Text-oriented retrieval and database software For microcomputers
1985	Desktop publishing spurred by low-cost laser printers
1986	Mass storage from CD-ROM

(Datapro 1984). These systems span the range from electronic typewriters to minicomputer-based multifunction workstations. Table 1.3 lists the main features of word processing systems. *Standalone* WP

TABLE 1.2

Office Terminal Units Shipped, in Millions, Estimated

Year	Word Processors	Electronic Typewriters	Display Terminals	Microcomputers
78	.0			
79	.0			
80	.1			
81	.1			
82	.2			
83	.2	.5	1.6	1.7
84	.2	.7	3.2	2.3
85	.2	1.1	2.7	4.4
86	.2	1.1	3.5	5.2
87	.2	1.2	3.9	5.4
88	.2	1.2	4.5	6.5

SOURCE: *Dataquest*, January, 1985. Numbers estimated, rounded. *Fortune* Magazine (1985) reports considerably higher figures. For example, 2.5 million WP units were sold in 1985, microcomputers will grow from 7.5 million in 1984 to 59 million in 1989, display terminals from 12 to 36 million, and word processors/electronic typewriters from 2.5 to 10 million.

systems have one workstation with accompanying control logic, and include electronic typewriters and display-based WP systems. *Multiterminal* word processors consist of two forms—shared-logic systems and shared-resource systems. Shared-logic systems have multiple terminals which jointly use the processing, storage, and printing resources of a central computer. Shared-resource systems locate intelligence and often storage at each terminal. *Nondedicated* systems is a catch-all term which includes the use of time-shared WP services from an external vendor by means of telecommunications networks as well as a microcomputer and word processing software.

Organizational Forms of Word Processing

There are three primary alternatives to structuring the organizational form of WP units: WP centers, decentralized WP, and distributed WP.

The concept of a *center* is derived from the stenograph/typing pool tradition, from the early model of centralized computing, and

TABLE 1.3

Features of Word Processing Systems

1. General configuration: Number of stations and printers supported (for multiterminal systems); storage capacity and storage media; file organization (page, frame, document for storage and display; keyword, inverted file, relational or free-text for retrieval).
2. Display: Screen type, size, capacity, resolution; color; scrolling; cursor movement; portrayal of formatted text (to what extent does it display spacing, margin formatting, highlighting, fonts, sub- and superscripts, etc.).
3. Printer: Resolution; speed; buffer; fonts; forms handling; width and length; page-feeding; multitasking of printing and processing; handling of formatting options.
4. Operation: Default and alternate formats; user interface and help files; queueing and prioritizing of print jobs; diagnostics; file indexing and security.
5. Input: Device support (such as "mouse," "cat," voice input, optical character reader interface); automatic formatting (such as headers, pagination, footnoting, centering, etc.).
6. Editing and merging: Moving, copying, linking, merging text; column manipulation; global and controlled search and replace; multiple levels of deletion; real-time formatting, including pagination and widows; customizing of spelling verification; sorting.
7. Communications: Display and alteration of protocols and configuration; transmission and receipt of variety of forms of information; standardized or proprietary interfaces.
8. Mathematical support: Calculations; symbols and equations; interface with spreadsheet.
9. Data processing: Use of microcomputer operating systems (CP/M, MS-DOS and UNIX); multitasking; compilers; interpreters; applications packages.

NOTE: Adapted from Datapro 1984.

from industrial assumptions about structuring of work and principles of division of labor. A quote from a Datapro report illustrates this rationale:

By establishing separate job positions for correspondence and administrative secretarial personnel, improvements in efficiency through functional specialization can be achieved. A standard method of achieving this specialization has come to be the company-wide dissolution of the private secretary position in favor of a centralized word processing center plus one or more administrative support positions in locations near executive personnel requiring such service. (1984: WP11-040-104)

A WP center, then, is a distinct work unit (though not always physically separate from other tasks) whose members are wholly dedicated to the processing of text and often organizational records, using WP systems as described above. Centers typically have at least one supervisor who monitors performance and schedules tasks. WP jobs generally have several grades within the category of WP operator or specialist.

Decentralized WP is at the other end of the continuum of WP unit forms. In the extreme, WP systems are obtained by individual offices or work units, and WP is considered one of several components of the unit's tasks.

Distributed WP places the equipment in separate physical locations, but is managed centrally to a greater or lesser extent. It may perhaps include a multiterminal system where entry and editing is distributed, but storage and processing is centralized. One hybrid form of WP is the "word processing team" where a primary WP unit provides services to the distributed sites (Krois and Benson 1980).

TRENDS IN WORD PROCESSING

Precisely because word processing capabilities are extending into so many areas that will eventually be integrated, lessons learned about effective ways to manage WP will provide some of the tools for organizations to evolve their own integrated office systems.

But this claim may seem abstract. How, specifically, can word processing be seen as a source of expertise, a testing ground, a foundation for implementing more complex systems? The next sections briefly review the near-term trends for WP in terms of generic information processes—input and storage, language processing and retrieval, output, communication, and integration.

Input and Storage

Currently, WP input takes the form of hardcopy drafts (prepared by hand, typewriter, or microcomputer), dictation delivered over the telephone or by audiocassettes (sometimes in combination), drafts stored on tape or diskette media, text communicated from micro-computers or mainframes, or pages captured by image processors. It seems likely that several developments in input and storage will increase the functionality and integration of WP.

"Image processing" has been used to mean methods for capturing text, graphics, or visuals directly into a system without rekeying or hand-digitizing the image. If the images are captured as text characters by means of *optical character recognizers* or *readers* (OCR), the text may then be edited by WP software. If the images are captured as video or digital signals by means of *picture processors,* they may then be edited by computer "paintboxes" that can alter form, color, placement, and perspective. Digitizing the text—either during input or processing—allows typeface design and visual effects to become part of the process of document handling (Bigelow and Day 1983; Gilheany 1985; Knuth 1979; Labuz 1984; McNeill 1985; Stewart 1985). The imaging market has grown over 60 percent per year recently (McCartney 1985), with revenues from scanners rising from $15 million in 1984 to $300 million by 1990 (Bridges 1986).

How the material is entered or captured is related to how it is stored. Digitized visual and textual material stored on optical las-erdisks or CD-ROM (compact disk—read-only memory) is already an established storage and retrieval medium in the information industry (see *Information Today* 1985; Lerner, et al. 1983; Melin 1983). Images, data, and text can be combined in one "document" for full viewing, indexing, annotating, browsing and zooming. The original document may be scanned and archived; all subsequent activities manipulate only the document image. Office tasks using this system are process-oriented "virtual offices"; there are few if any shadow costs or media transformations, and each task has immediate access to all interdependent information (Giuliano 1982).[3]

Language Processing and Retrieval

The laborious, routine, and error-prone aspects of proofreading and copy-editing are essentially unproductive shadow costs. Already, so-phisticated packages offer functions such as spelling correction, synonyms based upon the current context, readability scales, alternate phrasings, punctuation suggestions, and abstracting and indexing (Akiba, Ehrlich and Munson 1982; Cherry, et al. 1983; IBM 1983; Rosenthal 1984; Winograd 1984).

Familiar word processing capabilities for merging of blocks of text files are necessary but very limited when compared to outline processors and text databases which allow for Boolean searching and alternate views of document structures. Eventually, text database management systems will support unstructured entry of text which could then be indexed by keywords and searched using the full array of information retrieval tools. Text segments related to a particular topic could be retrieved, prioritized, sorted, and structured in several formats and media for comparison and ongoing composition (Nelson 1974; Perry 1985; Salton and McGill 1983; Shapiro 1984).

Another application of computer processing to textual data is software to filter, gatekeep, process, and manage electronic communications. Such procedures can search for semantic content or other cues which would indicate how the message should be processed (Hiltz and Turoff 1985). Soon, users will be able to manage their text as powerfully as they analyze numerical data.

Output

WP products have often been used as the content for a typeset or photocomposed final product. There is a growing trend, however, toward bypassing the intermediate transformations of rekeying the text or entering specific typesetting codes (Labuz 1984). The "desktop publishing" market is expected to grow from $300–$473 million in 1985 to $1 billion in 1989 and $4 billion in 1990, possibly replacing up to 80 percent of manual material processing by 1992—clearly not a minor development in WP (Buell, Bock, and Lewis 1986; Chartock 1985; Leddy 1986; *Poplar Computing* 1985; Pytka 1986; Scott 1985; Smith 1983). The desktop laser printer market grew over 350 percent between 1984 and 1986 (Austin, 1986).

Desktop publishing software allows the use to either embed codes in, and integrate graphics with, text, or to view the form of the final output directly on the screen. Thus, the entire composition process from outlining to page layout to final printing can be done using a desktop computer. Benefits for information work include cost savings, flexible and last-minute modification of copy, control over the quality, and confidential content of the output.

Readers of output supported by WP seem to find it superior: two studies have reported that documents that are set in type and/or prepared using end-user WP can be read faster and are considered to be more readable, professional, credible, and persuasive than documents produced in traditional ways (pen, paper, and typist or printed on dot-matrix printer) (Bennett, Durand, and Betty 1986:1; Sargent 1984:A40).

Indeed, the advent of the office laser printer may be a relatively inexpensive and simple but significant development in WP systems output. The convergence of digital facsimile, intelligent copiers, and laser printers is expanding the utility, functionality, and acceptability of what has typically consisted of machine sound and operator fury, signifying jammed paper and higher stacks of unread reports (Arnett 1981).

Aided by laser printers but also by color printers and slide-processors is the rapid growth in the use of computer-based business graphics. As of 1984, nearly all of 200 companies surveyed by Lehman, Vogel, and Dickson (1984) had some computer graphics capability. Forty percent of the DP managers surveyed felt that the use of business graphics would grow to a great extent in the near future, primarily for decision support, written reports, and data analysis.

Communication

Data processing departments, which have typically controlled data communication, are finding out that nontechnical wordsmiths have crucial transmission needs and are connecting communicating word processors to mainframe computers. Electronic mail, initiated through communicating WP machines, mainframe terminals, or microcomputers (with modems), provides a fast, distance-independent way to transfer data and text at both the sender's and receiver's convenience (Rice and Case 1983; Steinfield 1986). Telephone lines, PBXs, value-added computer networks, and local area networks are providing the channels for this increasing amount of text transfer (Dordick and Rice 1984).

Communicating with WP is no longer a "trend"—it is an important reality, as shown in table 1.4. Sixty percent of the organizations surveyed are using, or plan to use, WP communication within buildings, across buildings, and interconnected with data processing facilities. Soon, WP will be one of many devices sharing documents via document exchange or publishing interface standards. By means of such architectures, mixtures of data, text, graphics, image, and voice can be managed, programmed, and communicated across different systems (Cordell 1984; DeSousa 1981; Lum, Choy and Shu 1982).

Integrated Office Systems

Table 1.5 shows the plans that organizations currently have for their WP systems. International Data Corporation estimates the growth in integrated office systems to rise from less than $1 billion in 1984 to $3.5 billion in 1988. Thus, WP is not just the entering, storing, editing, and printing of words: it represents one component of a complex set of office activities that will eventually encompass all forms of information, will be communicated through multiple channels, and will be used in a variety of media determined by designers

TABLE 1.4
Word Processing Communication Plans

WP Communication	In Use	Planned	No Plans	Total
Between WP in same building	41%	20%	40%	101%
Between WP in different buildings	36	23	41	100
Between WP and DP units	34	31	35	100
WP and electronic copiers/printers	21	18	61	100
Using local area network	14	27	59	100

NOTE: Source of raw figures is Datapro 1984; percentages were calculated by weighting vendor-specific percentages by the number of organizations using each vendor; then these percentages were summed, and divided by the total number of responding organizations (N = 3,451).

and users alike. WP functionality is diffusing through, and becoming an integral part of, office automation—in terms of hardware, software, capability, job design, management issues, and employee concerns. Lessons learned from the implementation of WP can help organizations evolve toward successful integrated office systems.

CONCLUSION

This brief history of the word processing components of office information systems emphasizes the following points:

1. Office technology, job design, and organizational roles have always been linked. For example, the typewriter brought hundreds of thousands of women into organizations, fragmented the job of text handling but made it more effective, and standardized the forms of textual communications.
2. Office technology has been a cause of, and a response to, the rapidly growing amount of information that organizations must handle—either to generate more business or control current operations.
3. Assumptions about work design and organizational structure based upon industrial practices were applied early on to the implementation of word processing in the hope of improving secretarial productivity.

TABLE 1.5

Planned Expansions for WP Systems

Type of WP Expansion	Percent of Organizations
Microcomputers	51%
Local area networks	43
Additional software	21
Electronic mail	20
Workstations	19
Laser printers	16
Typesetting	7

NOTE: See note for table 1.4 for source and transformation of percentages taken from Datapro 1984 (N = 3,451 organizations).

4. The continuing development of computer-based word processing is bringing pressure to bear on not only the boundaries of text management but also on traditional ways of doing work.

An increasing need, then, to manage information, work, and interdependencies with other organizational systems has characterized the history of word processing—and must guide the future of integrated office information systems.

Chapter 2

Foundations: Information Work and Innovation

Information work is unlike industrial work in ways that require a new look at concepts of productivity, value, and innovation. Information work is contextual, integrally linked with the process of communication, often unstructured, and difficult to evaluate. Yet in complex and changing environments, organizations need access to just such nonroutine, situational information in order to develop and diffuse innovations.

So the traditional criterion for productivity—more of the same product for less cost—misses the point. Efficiency does not, in this situation, improve an organization's chances for adaptation. Rather than more information, different kinds and more processed kinds of information are needed. That is, "value-added" and "adaptive" information are productive outputs.

Thus, how information systems are implemented is important for more than just technical reasons. The approach to innovation taken here is that there are attributes of organizations and attributes of innovations that foster earlier adoption, but that political and cultural aspects of organizations—such as role modeling by leaders, and an organizational climate that encourages innovation—are equally powerful influences.

Communication—both mediated and interpersonal—is crucial to the diffusion and implementation process. However, interpersonal communication is more important for changing attitudes and increasing the perceived salience and relative advantage of a complex innovation such as an information system. Different managerial actions are important at different stages of the innovation process. For example, rationales for resistance should be identified and resolved before they become counter-implementation strategies.

Overall, implementation policies should encourage, yet control, the adaptation of the initial form of the innovation. In this way, the system will better fit the needs of the users and the organization, will avoid unintentional consequences, and will build into the organization's procedures the ability to generate alternative ways of achieving organizational goals.

Successful, active management of the evolution toward innovative organizations and integrated office information systems requires, then, an understanding of two crucial aspects of information systems: the nature of information work and the complexity of implementing information systems in organizations.

INFORMATION WORK VS. INDUSTRIAL WORK

The Value of Information Is Contextual

According to Shannon and Weaver's classic information theory, information is that which reduces uncertainty. The ability to precisely measure "noise" vs. "information" has enabled engineers to make tremendous advances in information systems. But, as ordinary people experience and require information, it is not measurable in this fashion. Rather, the context of the information establishes the value of information. For example, Zmud (1978) reported eight different dimensions by which users evaluated the information from a Management Information System (MIS): relevance, readability, reliability, timeliness, reasonableness, quantity, accuracy, arrangement, and factualness. Only a few of these can be precisely measured, and their particular value depends on the situation in which the MIS is used. Moreover, establishing the value of information is problematic largely because it does not follow the rules of classical economics (Hall 1981).

Constrained only by the physical markers used to transport its symbolic content, information can be diffused over time and space in ways that material products can never be. On the one hand, its utility may expand the more that it is used by more people; on the other hand, it may lose all worth when other people obtain it. The quality and timeliness of information may be critical to its use; yet quality may be largely subjective and determined separately by the producer and the user. (Rice and Bair 1984:187)

Unlike material goods, information may be sold yet still kept by seller and buyer; some information products may be infinitely produced. Further, because information is not the same as the materials used to create, distribute, and use it, and organizations have not yet learned to manage the costs and pricing of information, it is difficult to establish or enforce accountability for its use (Strassman 1976).

Communication Is Central to the Use of Information

Communication processes are fundamental to achieving performance in information work. Information work combines verbal and numeric symbols: justifications, reports, budgets, requests, logistics. Nearly thirty studies of how managers and clerical workers allocate their time show that people in offices spend most of their time communicating (Rice and Bair 1984). Managers spend about 75 percent of their time communicating, and most of that in oral exchanges (about 60 percent in discussions, meetings, or telephone conversations). Clerical workers spend less time communicating, but proportionally more of their time writing and reading. Due to these differences, information systems are likely to have greater immediate *applicability* to clerical tasks, but greater organizational *impact* on managerial tasks (Ginzberg 1978; Rice and Bair 1984). So, the context of the job influences the value of the communication channel used to accomplish information work.

Information Work Is Both Routine and Complex

The industrial assumptions about work are particularly misleading when blindly applied to information work. This is because information work has often been conceived of as similar to the repetitive, routine transaction processing handled by mainframe computers. But information varies along dimensions of predictability, instrumentality, and analyzability, as table 2.1 summarizes.

These dimensions suggest that there are two very different kinds of information work. One kind focuses on finding the right information to satisfy a well-defined need. The other kind of work emphasizes context and interpretation, leading to adaptations to current and future situations. One kind of work can be facilitated by batch-oriented, fixed-field data processing systems and text-based communication systems; the other can better be aided by information retrieval systems with fourth-generation application languages and relational, multimedia databases. That is, what is productive use of media and content in one situation may be wasteful in another.

Productivity Concepts Appropriate to Information Work

Much of the current interest in office information systems is centered around the concept of increased productivity. But what is productivity with respect to an information task or its associated information system? And what forms does productivity take for organizations attempting to survive in an information economy?[2]

Measuring productivity in ways that capture the value, communicativeness, and complexity of information is not a simple matter. Traditionally, productivity is measured in terms of efficiency or effectiveness.

Efficiency measures divide partial or total inputs by partial or total outputs. That is, increased productivity is indicated by a lower input/output ratio. The simplest way of measuring the productivity gains of an information system, then, is to determine whether it now costs *less* to do the *same* job as before. Or, improvements could lead to producing *more* output for the *same* cost.

Effectiveness measures may emphasize ratios of actual to intended outputs, achievements compared to objectives, and accomplishments relative to resources. That is, increased productivity is measured at the group or organizational level, and indicated by a higher ratio of output value to production costs (Strassman 1985).

Assuming these approaches are appropriate, choosing which variables to use is still not necessarily straightforward. Campbell, for instance, found thirty different measures of organizational effectiveness (1977).

TABLE 2.1
Dimensions of Information Work

Routine versus nonroutine (Pava 1985; Perrow 1967). Routine work tends to be linear and sequential, performed by lower-level staff, guided by rules and procedures. Nonroutine work tends to be simultaneous, involving multiple goals and unclear performance criteria, and performed by upper-level managers.

Programmed (structured) versus nonprogrammed (ad hoc) (Martin 1976; Simon 1960; Strassman 1985). Structured information problems can be predicted, since the type of question, the source of the information, the scheduling of the request, and the form of the answer can be programmed into an information system.

Uncertain versus equivocal (Daft and Macintosh 1981; Daft and Lengel 1984; Weick 1979). Uncertainty can be resolved only if sufficient facts are available. Equivocal problems involve intuition, judgment, context, symbolic value and the like. Face-to-face channels are more effective at reducing equivocality than are text- or computer-based channels.

Signal versus symbol (Feldman and March 1981; Keen 1981). Information that serves as a signal in organizations is content used to accomplish work related to its content. However, information may be collected for symbolic purposes even when there is too much information already available, after the decision has already been made, without relevance to the particular decision, and as conspicuous consumption of "facts."

Type B versus type A (Christie 1981). Type B information involves a "functionally significant store of some kind"—filing, retrieving, organizing, and editing materials. Type A information is person-to-person communication involving dyads or groups, telephone, meetings, and teleconferencing, where there are no substantial storage and retrieval processes.

Office versus knowledge (Englebart 1962; Gregerman 1981). Knowledge work involves more nonrepetitive activities, control over what methods to apply to a task, large gaps between activity and feedback, etc. Knowledge worker systems are designed to support, and job evaluation is oriented toward, group activities.

Type I versus type II (Panko 1984). Type I office work involves routine information tasks, single products, assembly or batch processing, and is organized by procedures. Type II work involves non-routine policymaking, diverse products, batch as well as custom processing, and is largely nonprocedural.

Task versus socioemotional (Short, Williams, and Christie 1976). Task information is more objective, quantitative, and unambiguous in nature; socioemotional information requires more interpersonal cues, such as to resolve conflict, or to get to know someone (Daft and Macintosh 1981; Rice 1984).

TABLE 2.1 *Continued*

Object versus process (Paisley 1985). Object knowledge focuses on objects and their properties, such as who, what, where, and when. Process knowledge focuses on understanding and predicting how things happen. Process information is necessary to achieve adaptability and formulate strategic actions.

Traditional productivity measures come under other attacks. Many of the accepted measures (a) cannot be applied to custom or small-batch activities, (b) cannot be compared across products where style or consumers' taste or perceptions determine the market price, (c) overemphasize outputs relative to outcomes or impacts, and (d) require generally arbitrary decisions about data interpretations, such as quality or trends (Packer 1983).

Over and above difficulties in measurement and definition, productivity concepts such as efficiency are challenged by the complex and ambiguous nature of information work. The value of information cannot be equated with the number or amount of physical outputs. Managers have different information needs than clericals. Adaptivity is necessary to respond to environments. Thus, many of the traditional notions of the role of information in organizations can be questioned.

For example, in WP applications, the problem of emphasizing cost displacement rather than added value can be seen by considering programmable function keys, called "glossaries" or "macros." The use of these keys may easily reduce the lines of input and the time necessary to produce information. Yet fewer lines of input means less "productivity" by some standards. Those who operate and manage WP systems recognize the paradox of less is more, as indicated by these quotes from the on-site interviews:

"Measurement of work activity gets to be a little strange sometimes. You can take an hour and a half to write a glossary that will do the job; another person will take three hours each time to do it manually. It doesn't make any difference to the administration because it only sees the number of pages and the number of lines. No account is made of the time required, or time saved."

"Monitoring output is ridiculous because it is so easy to write a program that will keep the CPU constantly counting lines."

"In data processing we have always worked on a theory that we know only approximately what the user needs and so we give them a dump of information—often hundreds of pages of output—and let them figure out if there is anything in there they can use. It suits our purposes because all we have to do to show we are productive is to count our lines of output."

Another example of the flaw of strict cost displacement is the oft-repeated benefit of "increased communications." However, one way to improve organizations is not to produce *more* information but rather to *reduce* the amount that any one subsystem must process (March 1978; Simon 1973; Strassman 1980, 1985). That is, information overload, misunderstanding, delays, incorrect distribution, inadequate matching of the production costs versus usage benefits, and symbolic uses of information resources all are symptoms and byproducts of excessive or *irrelevant* information, rather than *insufficient* information.[4] The truly scarce resource in information work is *attention*. Information systems should be managed to allow organizational members to pay more attention to crucial and strategic tasks, and less attention to processing unnecessary information.

When information processing enables organizational members to attend to critical organizational tasks, and thus to manage them better, the information system "adds value" to the organization's outputs (Edelman 1981; Meyer 1982; Strassman 1985). Porter and Miller (1985) forcefully argue that competitive organizations are not only adding value to a product by expanding its information content, but also adding value to the organization by using information to extend, improve, and protect the total product environment. For example, many electronic products now contain self-diagnosing microchips that make repair or replacement of the primary product easier. Or, some companies have extended their competitive boundaries by means of "distribution chains," such as by placing a customized inventory and ordering terminal, with connections to the company's mainframe computer, inside the client's organizations so that the client will tend to make most of its orders from this company instead of from others who do not offer such service. The *value added* to all the various inputs becomes the product for evaluation. The environment (other departments, customers, competition) determines the output value. Efficiency, effectiveness, and added value are all necessary for organizational survival and growth.

Value-added applications naturally pose problems for determining workers' productivity. Some alternative performance evaluation criteria for knowledge workers include task competence, judgment, innovation, action orientation, flexibility, communication, interpersonal relations, professional status, general business perspective and leadership (Gregerman 1981). Some indicators of individuals who achieve high performance in using new office systems are: a dislike of external controls, continuous learning, discovery of unpredictable new capabilities, elaboration of initial system features, development of new applications, and ongoing redesign of their jobs (Strassman 1985: ch. 4).

There are five specific areas where information systems and job redesign can improve even narrow definitions of productivity, because they take into account the nature of information work (Rice and Bair 1984:189):

1. Control: requiring less information to perform a task; understanding better the consequences of specific information; anticipating of environmental changes; structuring communication activities to conform to organizational needs and goals; improving accountability for resources used for the benefits obtained from information; developing alternative ways to process information or arrive at a decision. For example, WP can provide authors more control of their material, to the extent that they can affect and revise input, edit, retrieval, processing, output, and distribution activities.

2. Timing: reducing "information float," or the delay between creation and use of information; reducing response time; reducing time spent in decision making, and initiating action; increasing flexibility of work schedule. For example, WP can be used to experiment with "textual what-ifs."

3. Automation: augmenting the information activities of office workers by improving access to, and processing of, information through various computer-based technologies; off-loading routine of-

fice work and programmed decisions to an information system; applying algorithmic and processing capabilities to members' tasks and needs. For example, WP can integrate data analysis with form letters to provide relevant and readable exception reports.

4. Media transformations: reducing time, energy, and errors in transferring information from one medium or mode to another (such as transcribing a telephone call to a message form which is then entered into a printed calendar). For example, WP can coordinate and facilitate the redesign of joint projects involving several managers and analysts, thus reducing intermediary forms of information.

5. Shadow functions: reducing unforeseen, unpredictable, time-consuming activities that are associated with accomplishing tasks, but that do not contribute to achieving outcomes and goals (such as telephone tag, waiting for the late meeting participant). For example, WP can bring the cycle of report generation into "real time," avoiding multiple delays between dictation, transcription, printing, and proofing.

The positive outcomes of WP, then, are based upon an understanding of information work and added value—not solely on reduced costs—and upon the management of benefits and people—not solely on technological details.

INNOVATION AND IMPLEMENTATION OF INFORMATION SYSTEMS

As Heraclitus wrote, the only unchanging fact of life is change itself. This reality is reflected in the vast literature on innovation, the study of change: Rogers (1983) claims that approximately four thousand articles exist on the topic of innovation diffusion; Kelly and Kranzberg (1978) include four thousand entries on technological innovation alone.

The concept of an *innovation* covers considerable territory: an innovation can be the invention of an idea, behavior, or product never before conceptualized or seen by others; the item when first adopted by any social unit; the item adopted early relative to comparable social units; and the item perceived as new to the adopter regardless of its relative newness to other social units. The diffusion of an innovation has been defined as the spread of an idea, product, or practice perceived as new by the adoptors, through communication channels to the members of a social system, over time (Rogers 1983).

To establish the terms and analytical perspectives used in later chapters, the following sections review literature on the basic components of organizational innovation in information systems: (a) how communication channels affect the diffusion of innovations, (b) what makes innovations diffuse, (c) what makes organizations innovative, (d) what stages organizations go through in the process of adopting and implementing systems, and (e) how the traditional adoption model has been revised to include reinvention and adaptation.

Communicating About Innovations

The medium (print, electronic, or interpersonal), source (friend, vendor, consultant) and type of information (persuasive, educational) all interact to determine the role of communication in diffusion of an innovation. For example, the classic diffusion study by Coleman, Katz, and Menzel (1966) showed that drug vendors and medical magazines were used as sources of information by doctors deciding whether to use a new antibiotic in their prescriptions, but that opinions of valued colleagues were particularly significant in making the final decision.

Communication *media* are generally thought to be more successful in providing information, or setting the agenda for evaluating which issues are salient, rather than actually changing opinions. In particular, *print* media are more successful in transferring information, say when a potential adopter is interested in a possible set of alternatives, or in detailed technical or cost information. *Electronic* media are more successful in establishing an image about the product, and aiding in the formation of new opinions, but do not transfer much detailed information.

Interpersonal communication about innovations is more successful than print media in actually changing opinions and persuading reluctant adopters to change their behaviors. Implementations of information systems tend to be more successful, for example, when there are regular project meetings and extended face-to-face training sessions (Sheposh, Hulton, and Knudson 1982), in work groups with greater cohesiveness (O'Keefe, Kernaghan, and Rubenstein 1975) and with greater prior communication contacts (Kerr and Hiltz 1982). Interaction between the person who represents the organization's desire to adopt the innovation and the person who promotes adoption from the users' perspective has been shown to be crucial in determining how a technology will be used (Stolz 1984:242).

Other than the necessary awareness about an innovation that is increased by the exchange of information, why is interpersonal communication so important in the diffusion process? Communication helps develop shared appreciations which "are necessary if group members are to generate a sufficiently common view of reality to formulate and to implement a plan to achieve a shared objective" (Cummings and Srivastva 1977:113; Vickers 1965). Open communication—which allows criticism and revelations of failures as well as successes—is crucial to the development of innovative solutions to problems (Kanter 1983; Peters and Waterman 1982). Users of tools—both internal and clients—generate the bulk of new ideas about products, but only if the communication channels allow this (Peters and Austin 1985).

The primary interpersonal communication role in the diffusion of innovations has been the *opinion leader*. This person influences the opinions of others, and is sought out for advice when others are considering the merits and costs of innovations. The opinion leader typically shares the norms of the network, but is slightly better educated, better traveled, better informed, and communicates with more people than others in the network. Such people adopt innovations which are compatible with the social norms fairly early on, and others model their behavior accordingly. However, if the innovation is "taboo" or counter to the social norms, the first to adopt are typically "isolates," those who are outside the social network and do not communicate much with social members. Because of their isolation, they (a) have access to kinds of information that are rejected by the majority, and (b) they have less social status to lose by adopting risky innovations. For example, in organizations such as Xerox Palo Alto Research Center or Bell Northern Research, organizational norms emphasize flat hierarchies and low numbers of clerical staff, with consequent high levels of managerial use of terminals. In more traditional organizations, managerial use of a keyboard is a "taboo" activity left to programmers, clerical workers, and the professional working at the office on the weekend.

Thus, supervisors and managers serve two powerful communication and political roles in facilitating the diffusion or organizational innovations. First, they serve as opinion leaders, providing task and socioemotional information about the innovation and appropriate adoption behaviors.[5] In general, subordinate satisfaction and quality of decision making is higher with more interaction with supervisors, with more openness between supervisor and subordinate, and greater accuracy of information from supervisors (Klauss and Bass 1982:29-30).

Often, organizational norms for information sharing greatly influence how much imformation is actually shared (Dewhrist 1971). Thus, the role of the highly influential factor of communication in any particular innovation effort depends on organizational and managerial support for such communication and information sharing.

Second, they provide the organizational resources, both political and material, required to implement the innovation.[6] "Top management support" is a rallying cry for implementation researchers and change agents.

Thus, if the innovation would be readily accepted if only potential adopters knew more about it, then this informational function would be better served by print media. If potential adopters are more resistant, due to personal opinions or norms against the innovation, or if the innovation is risky, then interpersonal communication is more appropriate to effect change. Typically, diffusion occurs more readily when media channels are used in conjunction with interpersonal channels, to provide both informational and persuasive effects.[7]

What Makes Organizations Innovative?

Stepping back from the level of the individual communicating about an innovation, the following organizational characteristics have been proposed to *explain* organizational innovation.[8]

1. Organizations that are more flexible and consensual ("organic") are more likely to innovate than structured and authoritarian ("mechanistic") organizations (Burns and Stalker 1961; Lawrence and Lorsch 1969). They are more decentralized and flexible; they tend to be smaller. Norms and practices in organic firms emphasize advice over commands, commitment to mission over loyalty, and the design of tasks by interpersonal relations over formal procedures. These and related characteristics facilitate the sharing of information and the acceptance of change. This proposition has received the greatest empirical support of all the alternative explanations, but it does not indicate directions of causality. For example, constant technological or economic change may force a company to reduce its levels of authority (Daft 1982).

2. Organizations that have separate units in charge of each stage in the innovation process will be more innovative overall. The reasoning for this proposition is that each stage requires different resources and decision making units. For example, complex organizations may generate more proposals for innovation because of the increased diversity of needs and information, but larger, older, and more centralized organizations have the mechanisms and political traditions to reduce conflicts and actually make the innovation work (Duncan 1976; Hage, Aiken, and Marrett 1971; Robey and Zeller 1978; Wilson 1966; Zaltman, Duncan, and Holbek 1973). There seems to be little to support the idea that early innovators are slow implementors, however, and the practicalities of managing multiple organizational structures for innovation and implementation seem quite difficult.

3. Organizations that match the structures, needs, and environmental demands of their predominant unit—the technical or administrative core—will be more innovative. If, for example, changing regulatory policies affect the administrative core, then "mechanistic" characteristics of organizations facilitate such changes better than do "organic" characteristics, due to the typically high centralization, formalization, and authoritarian norms for implementation in administrative units (Thompson 1967). Daft argues that this proposition is ambiguous about how to identify which types of innovation to initiate or which core is predominant.

4. Organizations (particularly if they are fairly informal and in conditions of high uncertainty) are more likely to be innovative when compatible streams of problems, solutions, choices, and participants come together. Innovation in these organizations does not necessarily have much to do with rational, planned interactions of these forces. That is, different streams collect in "garbage cans" until they meet or are brought together in organizations identified as "organized anarchies" (Cohen, March, and Olsen, 1972). Although this proposition emphasizes the political processes and the roles that individuals play in innovation, the proposition is too general and does not identify when organizations are "organized anarchies" (Daft 1982).

5. Organizational innovation is strongly influenced by prevalent expectations and shared meanings. Implementation is a socially constructed process that happens as people's actions take shape over time. The relationships among variables result from *meanings* that people attach to their own and others' actions (Silverman 1971:141; Yin 1978). Actors take cues from what they are told, from what they see others do, and from the formal system of rewards and constraints in which they work (Salancik and Pfeffer 1978). Thus, when communication and reward systems support innovation, organizations are more likely to innovate.

6. Organizations do not generally *search* for innovations, but instead respond to perceived *performance gaps*. Inertia is not due to resistance, but due to a lack of convincing evidence of the need for change (March and Simon 1958). Herbert Simon argued that people and organizations not only are limited in their ability to process information, but that they essentially satisfy only pressing demands, rather than develop optimal or maximal solutions. Crucial to this proposition is the development of standards or criteria which make relevant performance gaps salient, and mechanisms for finding a satisfactory innovative solution.

Attributes of Innovations That Influence Adoption

The propositions about organizational innovation focus on what characteristics of firms and their environments lead to innovation action. While these characteristics indicate whether an *organization* may adopt an innovation, actual acceptance emanates from *individuals* within the organization. Thus, how innovations are perceived by the ultimate adopters is a crucial factor in determining the success of organizational information systems.

Innovations have many attributes that affect the rate of adoption.[9] The five most common categories include:

1. *Relative advantages:* the degree to which the innovation is perceived as superior to the practice it replaces. Criteria for evaluation include economic factors, adopter's status, decrease in discomfort, and incentives for adoption. That is, part of the increased advantage does not necessarily have to come from the innovation itself—the sheer act of adoption may be costly or advantageous from a political or incentive perspective. The symbolic value of the system may outweigh the functional values. Other criteria may include: perceived accessibility of information source; perceived organizational need for the innovation; unmet expectations after the innovation has been adopted; and technical performance and reliability, which is necessary but not sufficient.

2. *Compatibility:* the degree to which an innovation is perceived as being consistent with the potential adopter's prior experience, beliefs, and values. Aspects of compatability include the metaphors used in marketing the innovation, its actual name, and its positioning with respect to other familiar products, ideas, or practices. For example, the slow diffusion of medical information systems can be partly explained by norms of doctors that favor their own individual experience and expertise, government intervention in the form of regulations and subsidies, and the public's expectations of personal treatment (Brenner and Logan 1980). Unsatisfactory experiences with past change efforts may be associated with a subsequent innovation, and be included in the potential adopter's perception of compatability.

3. *Complexity:* the degree to which an innovation is perceived as difficult to understand. The difficulty may reside in the meaning of the innovation as well as in its actual use. For example, "intelligent" telephones (PBXs) are not particularly complex to use, but when they are perceived as computers, instead of the familiar telephone,

then their perceived complexity may increase (Manross and Rice 1986; Rice and Manross 1986).

4. *Trialability* or *divisibility:* the degree to which the innovation can be tried out in a phased or experimental fashion. The idea here is that the need to reduce uncertainty interacts with the need to avoid risk in the adoption process. Risk and uncertainty can be reduced by means of small-scale pilots or incremental adoption, or by trying a few components at a time. Implementation that is too formal or slow can prevent adopters from gaining early benefits and from experimenting with the system to create their own compatible applications; "turnkey" implementation can increase the system's perceived complexity, thereby making it more difficult to observe real benefits. Trialability seems more crucial for early adopters, who have few other sources upon which to rely.

5. *Observability* or *communicability:* the degree to which potential adopters can experience or find out about the innovation, or the degree to which its attributes and outcomes are easily perceived. Some aspects of an innovation—software, outcomes, and benefits—are less observable than others—hardware, operational procedures. In general, the greater the innovation's perceived relative advantage, observability, trialability and compatability, and the less its complexity, the more rapidly it will be adopted.

Phases in the Innovation/Implementation Process

Organizational adoption of innovations has been modeled as a five-stage process (Eveland, Rogers, and Klepper 1977; Rice and Rogers 1980; Rogers 1983). Those stages include:

1. *Agenda setting:* a common recognition of a problem or an idea by interested organizational members. The problem is typically only generally defined. Further, the problem may not be a performance gap, but a perceived need to be innovative. In more extreme cases, the simple accessibility of an innovation may create an agenda for change.

2. *Matching:* the general problem on the agenda and a possible (set of) solution(s) are brought together. The initial innovators may

be top management, or may require its support to establish some sort of match. Innovation attributes are initially identified.

3. *Redefining:* attributes of the innovation are defined relative to the problems on the agenda. However, the problems and even the agenda may be altered here, as deeper understanding of several innovations, and of the problem, may change members' perceptions and uncover more fundamental problems. Incremental implementation may facilitate the process, while aroused pluralistic values and needs may make the process more lengthy and complex.

4. *Structuring:* the innovation is established within the organization's structure, often generating resistance and requiring negotiation, bargaining, peer pressure, and conflict. Interpersonal communication facilitates the diffusion of the innovation through the social system.

5. *Interconnecting:* the innovation becomes a routinized component of the organization, embedded in practices and procedures, budgets and behaviors. The wider organization must respond to, and resolve, consequences and impacts of the innovation.

There seems to be no clear consensus on the distinction between innovation and implementation. Innovation may be defined as the decision to change. The common definition of an innovation in the diffusion literature is any practice or tool perceived to be new by a potential adopter (Rogers 1983). Implementation may be defined as the operations necessary to effect that change. The operational aspects of implementation are indicated by Nutt's definition: "a series of steps taken by responsible organizational agents in planned change processes to elicit compliance needed to install changes" (1986:230). Innovation generally focuses on the process of adoption, and the variables that facilitate this decision. Implementation focuses on issues of system management, bureaucratic processes, organizational development, user resistance, and conflict and bargaining. It emphasizes operational and administrative details of actually installing the innovation, the political aspects of negotiating or mandating the form and application of the innovation, and the explanatory models and guidelines of management scientists and operations researchers (see, particularly, Lucas 1981; Schultz and Slevin 1975; Sheposh, Hulton, and Knudsen 1982; Tornatsky et al. 1983; Zaltman et al. 1973).

A phased approach suggested by Kolb and Frohman (1970) has been frequently used to organize normative descriptions of implementation efforts.[10] Those phases include:

• Scouting (identifying needs, finding the entry point).
• Entry (establishing goals, trust, felt need).
• Diagnosis (describing data and resources).
• Planning (defining operational objectives, alternative solutions, implementation plan).
• Action (implementation and adaptation).
• Evaluation (satisfaction of objectives, agreeing upon closure).
• Termination (establishment of new behavior patterns, users take over).

The different stages in the five-stage innovation model and in this implementation model help to identify at what point some factors are more conducive to successful adoption than are other. For example, Ginzberg (1981a, b) found that the variables that best predicted successful information systems (extent of project definition and planning, organizational commitment to the project, and organizational commitment to change) all arise early on in the implementation process. Lucas (1981) also used the model to analyse how the implementation process should consider management and users as two sets of equally important clients. For example, scouting would investigate the motives and resources of both parties; the action phase would set user acceptance of the system as the primary goal.

The Kolb-Frohman model is conceptually based on Lewin's proposition that there are upward forces favoring change, and downward forces resisting change. Implementation consists, then, of unfreezing the current situation by altering the presence or weighting of these forces, restructuring the situation, and then re-refreezing it by organizational interconnections and group reinforcement. Resistance is reduced by increasing the salience of the desired outcomes, and providing the tools and behaviors for achieving those outcomes.

While user resistance is a focal point for many implementation studies, its role may be overemphasized. Much resistance is evidence of something actually gone wrong, or of perceived outcomes that would not be acceptable to a particular user group. Resistance in these cases is a diagnostic aide for improving the social and technical aspects of the system (Keen 1981; Sheposh, Hulton, and Knudsen, 1982; Zuboff 1982).

Lucas (1981) has summarized the research on implementation factors in an interactive model which includes (a) technical system quality, (b) client actions, (c) user attitudes, (d) decision style and (e) personal/situational variables. The final mediator leading to successful use of an information system is user attitudes.[11] User involvement in the implementation process has the strongest influence on user attitudes, so it should be a part of adoption and implementation activities. The topic of user participation will be discussed in greater detail in chapter 5, with respect to principles of job design.

Various authors (Cummings and Srivastva 1977; Keen 1981; Walton 1975) identify other contingencies that explain why information system and job design interventions have frequently failed:

1. The organization fails to sustain the initial success.
2. The pilot systems or sites are poor choices, as they lack validity or credibility.
3. Implementation actions are not diffused along with the system.
4. Top management decreases its level of support, often for reasons unrelated to the project itself.
5. Unions oppose job restructuring.
6. Employees perceive their preferred work roles as threatened.
7. Complex experiments may generate hostility about their status in the organization.
8. Approval channels are excessively bureaucratic.
9. Ambiguity in and lack of control mechanisms for defining the scope of the implementation.
10. Resistance (counter-implementation) is ignored, particularly when it is justified.
11. The assumption that all potentially affected units share the same values and norms concerning the innovation.

Developing the Concept of Adaptation or Reinvention

The preceding sections have briefly reviewed the role of communication channels in informing or persuading potential adopters about an innovation, characteristics of an innovation that make it more or less "adoptable," characteristics of individuals and organizations that make them more or less "innovative," and interactions of these characteristics that predict how rapidly an innovation will diffuse.

However, participants in the 1977 Northwestern Conference on Innovation, sponsored by the National Science Foundation Office of Policy Research and Analysis, critiqued the assumption that innovation is merely an "invention" created by experts, "diffused" to users who then "adopt" it. They called for investigation of the development of technology as a system of work rather than a tool, and for the study of adaptation or reinvention. *Reinvention* is "the degree to which an invention is changed by the adopter in the process of adoption and implementation after its original development" (Rogers 1978:12-14; Rogers 1983:16-17; Rice and Rogers 1980:501).[12]

In general, reinvention or adaptation has been measured as a deviation from a standard or "main-line" form of the innovation. That is, the standard innovation consists of a set of components or practices that constitute a "main line"; additions, deletions, or alterations from that main line are indicators of reinvention. For example, the configuration may be the same, but the innovation may be put to a different use than intended; conversely, an entirely different innovation may be chosen for the same use. Further, the configuration and use may be kept, but the intended outcomes may be altered.

What influences adaptation or reinvention? Table 2.2 presents a typology of the causes of reinvention. A social unit may directly adapt an innovation, may learn from other sources, may have to adapt because the initial form of the innovation was not matched to the unit (or caused unintended consequences) or may have to adapt the innovation because the consequences from some other unit's adoption are creating problems for the adapting unit. Certain conditions increase the likelihood of reinvention: little contact with the change agent, a complex but not tightly packaged innovation, local pride of ownership, social and professional norms for original development (such as software development in data processing departments), incomplete or ambiguous description of the innovation, and slack resources (Hall and Loucks 1978; Rogers 1983).

Given the argument of the first half of this chapter—that adaptation should be encouraged in order for organizations to perform well in changing, complex environments—we argue here that intentional reinvention should be encouraged. A fundamental assumption in policies that support reinvention is that the user in some way knows best how an innovation should be fitted to the local situation.[13] The typology of table 2.2 suggests that knowledge and communication of the wider context for implementation, and of others' approaches to a perceived problem, will lead to intentional rather than unintentional reinvention. However, there is still considerable controversy on the desirability of reinvention (see Stolz 1984). Clearly, organizations should avoid situations leading to secondary reinvention, and carefully manage the development of intentional reinvention. However, implementation that focuses solely on technical aspects of a fixed, standard version of the system will likely lead to dissatisfied users and noninnovative applications.

CONCLUSION

Emery and Trist (1965), in their classic discussion of organizational environments, argued that increasingly complex environments generate increasing uncertainty. Katz and Kahn (1978) similarly called for "adaptive mechanisms" in organizations to absorb and integrate information from the external environment—including information

TABLE 2.2
Typology of Reinvention

Choice	Source	
	Direct	*Indirect*
Intentional	Planned (choosing to reinvent)	Vicarious (learning from others' mistakes)
Unintentional	Reactive (solving problem generated by the innovation)	Secondary (solving consequences of reinvention elsewhere in the organization)

SOURCE: Adapted from Rice and Rogers 1980.

on trends, research on procedures, plans for the future, and scanning environmental demands.

In changing environmental conditions, simply doing the same thing more efficiently will not likely lead to long-term survival. As Weick argues, "Doing what you have always done is necessary in short-term adaptations. Doing what you have never done is necessary in longer-term adaptations, and both need to be done simultaneously" (1977:42). Practical managers know this: a survey of 256 top managers in 195 organizations found that management identifies excessive concern with short-term results as one of the two top reasons for declining productivity (Judson 1982).

The fundamental alternative to doing something faster, cheaper, or better is to do something different. That is, adapting the nature of the output, focusing on another market, or redefining the goals of the organization may be an appropriate response to a changing environment. Innovating and managing the process of implementation lead to improvements in organizational performance.

Crucial to this approach toward organizational performance is having access to new ideas about how to conduct one's activities; adaptiveness depends on different, rather than more, information. Decision making, information acquisition and distribution, self-regulation and innovation will be increasingly significant influences on organizational survival (Huber 1984). Office information systems in general, and WP in particular, then, have great potential for improving the productivity and adaptability of organizations. But they must be explicitly managed to foster innovation.

The conclusions of two studies of office technology support this position:

The only alternative to a process of emergent design is a future shaped by uninformed default. (Pava 1983:vii)

There is no evidence to suggest that evolution toward more successful implementation occurs in the absence of a specific strategy to increase managerial effectiveness . . . it seems to require the active intervention of management who view the technology as a catalyst for a variety of job and organizational changes which ultimately bring about the more widespread productivity gains promised by OA technology. (Curley 1981:243)

In a complex and changing environment, nonroutine, nonprogrammed, equivocal, symbolic, and process information becomes more necessary and relevant. But by definition these kinds of information are more difficult to acquire, interpret, evaluate, and use. So the organization's internal mechanisms themselves must be innovative, adaptive, and protected. Establishing inflexible rules and procedures for responding—such as narrow criteria for productivity based on industrial assumptions—will constrain the kinds and forms of information produced (Lynton 1969; McFarlan and McKenney 1983; Weick 1977).

Productivity is increased with information systems through a heuristic process of adapting technology, work groups, and resources to accomplish tasks that contribute substantially to organizational goals and survival. Such tasks include those that are impossible, impractical, more difficult to coordinate, or less effective without the technology. Implementation, then, must include as its primary goal the encouragement and management of adaptation.

The next chapter describes how the innovation known as word processing was implemented in nearly two hundred organizations.

Chapter 3

Implementing Word Processing: Ready, Fire, Aim

This chapter examines the history of WP in two hundred organizations during the period from the mid-70s to 1983. Adoption of WP technology in these organizations spread widely in the years from 1978 to 1984, as table 3.1 shows. Implementation of word processing took the form of problem solving as people figured out how to be most effective with organizational structures, technical capabilities, equipment costs, job designs, and skill levels. The proper route to implementation was not always obvious or easy.

The two representative cases that begin this chapter provide a contrast in scope. The first, "Big Bank," describes attempts to implement WP "rationally"—that is, by analyzing clerical tasks and creating very large WP centers to do the typing of the organization. Over time this approach of large-scale implementation did not work. The organization has recently moved to a decentralized approach.

TABLE 3.1

Year of Organization's First Experience with Word Processing

Year of Adoption	Cumulative Percent of Organizations (N = 172)
before 1975	22%
1975–76	39
1977–78	63
1979–80	97
1981	100

NOTE: As of January 1982.

The second case, "District Office," represents implementation on a small scale. The description looks at one department of a large, geographically dispersed organization where the central WP coordinator influenced district offices to create WP centers. It highlights the importance of individuals in the history of WP implementation.

The five-stage model of adoption outlined in chapter 2 is used as a descriptive framework to summarize the process by which WP was implemented in these organizations. The chapter then assesses the extent to which there is a "typical case" by looking for a quantitative definition of the "standard adoption" of WP—that composite of procedures, roles, and uses that constitute a main-line adoption.

REPRESENTATIVE CASES

Implementation on a Grand Scale: The Case of Big Bank

Big Bank epitomizes the history of WP implementation in very large organizations. This organization has hundreds of branches in its home state, and provides multinational financial services. Wherever the trend of information system usage and management goes, Big Bank seems to go a little sooner and a little more intensely. Management of the bank says that while their cultural image is not that of the automation leader in banking, they are very advanced: "electronic banking is a major part of the company's facilities."

In 1974 a task force from administrative units formed to study how the bank might benefit from WP. The task force concluded that it was easy to use, but that few understood its operations and that each unit was too expensive to be assigned to secretaries. They set up a center that continued in existence until 1979. The rationale was to optimize the use of the equipment by specialists who had WP skills. They justified the center by arguing that it would lead to displacement of present staff through attrition. Thus its rationale was based upon the cost-displacement form of productivity. Included in the justification were the results of many kinds of studies—for six weeks they logged all the activities of secretarial personnel and compared activities to staffing levels. A single brand of WP equipment is used throughout the bank to assure compatibility—thus enabling an electronic mail system to connect departments across the world— and to "leverage the maximum cooperation from the vendor through bulk sales."

As the center grew, the bank set up a department of WP that managed five centers. But "the centers just got too big and with bigness came diminishing returns." The center managers studied the effectiveness of WP centers and found that with more than thirteen operators in any one center, output per operator dropped dramatically. Therefore, they began to decentralize into smaller centers.

Eventually the centralized WP operation went out of business. The core of the WP department combined with a systems research group and an acquisition group to become the Central Planning Group (CPG). CPG's mission was consulting, not center management. Some users, for example in the legal department, run their own centers of seven or eight operators. According to CPG's manager: "Centers should be the users' responsibility—the responsibility should be squarely on the managers of the departments."

What motivated the change from centralization to decentralized word processing?

"Key users who said, 'We want our own systems.' And others who threatened to get their own. We were so busy handling center operations that we had a hard time seeing what was happening. Planning suffered because of immediate demands."

In 1982, CPG's mission changed. Its new goal was to "respond to the substantial demands for computer resources in branch levels, and that is for WP." CPG provided information about how to determine what kind of equipment was best for an operation. CPG was in the business of "wholesaling" office automation to the rest of the bank. Their approach was to develop workbooks that offices could use in implementing office automation. Information in the workbooks came from CPG's evaluations of vendors and their understanding of generic bank needs. The workbook continued the initial rationale by outlining stringent "cost-displacement" bases for acquiring equipment. It detailed the study of keystrokes and pages of typed material. A requesting department filled in the needed information which was then sent to CPG who read the material and, when appropriate, delivered and maintained the equipment. Courses on how to use the equipment were offered in-house.

Typically an operation would ask for an upgrade after about six months of operation. CPG pointed to this demand for upgrade as an indication of the proven effectiveness of WP in banking operations. So, for subsequent expansions of WP capability, effectiveness demonstrated by demand replaced effectiveness demonstrated by cost displacement. The CPG philosophy was that the cost of equipment had become so low that a department could afford to have enough terminals for everyone to have access. The evolution in CPG philosophy from effectiveness through detailed analysis of tasks to effectiveness through end-user ownership and learning exemplifies a trend found in most of the surveyed organizations.

Although planning and research continued as CPG activities, their principal activities became more user-centered. Their attempts to influence a large number of users with a small number of resources centered around being a conduit for information about adaptations:

"We tried to pull together all the glossaries compiled by the end users. We have about 350 such applications."

After assuring that the applications conform to standard banking practices, they filed them and sent them out to all users, periodically upgrading their file by seeking information and new applications. This approach to encouraging productive adaptations of WP capability was motivated both by a lack of resources (pressure to keep overhead low) and an assessment that centralized WP operations had low credibility with users:

"If we developed uses here and sent them out, it would be the kiss of death for us. The innovation must be user-oriented and user-driven."

The CPG philosophy, evolved from a time of strict controls and rational procedures, had become "the user is right."

In the long run, the centralized research activities and diffusion program were seen as economically unjustifiable and organizationally inappropriate. Sometime shortly after our visit to Big Bank, CPG was disbanded. One interpretation is that in spite of CPG's energetic role in diffusing WP innovations, it was still resisted as a centralized operation by users and as an unnecessary expense by management. Another interpretation is that, except for its function as an innovation clearinghouse, CPG had successfully managed its way out of a need for its services.

Implementation by Individuals: District Office Case

Around 1977, a division director of a federal agency's District Office saw an IBM memory typewriter and was struck with the notion that such machines could drastically improve the typing efficiency of his office. The main work there revolved around preparing forms for approximately six hundred cases handled by the office. They bought one machine and soon had the operator swamped with work. The director's secretary, Mary, suggested that a WP center would make the whole organization more efficient.

The early operations of the center were full of problems. Employees felt that the director had crammed the idea of a center down their throats. He assigned the lowest-level staff members in each unit to the center; the center operator with the highest seniority was made the working supervisor. She hated the job. They had one VDT-style machine. No one would touch it. Everyone in the center was looking for another job. The work piled up because the supervisor, a fine secretary, was "nitpicking the operators to death." Work came in, but did not go out.

The center came to the critical point frequently mentioned in interviews at other sites: "We tried a center, but it didn't work here." In the first installations of WP, few could distinguish between lack of management and failure of the technology. In some cases, WP equipment sat unused; in other cases, centers were disbanded.

The District Office began the process of establishing an efficient center by appointing a good person to supervise it. At the point of undeniable failure, Mary said she could no longer stand watching "her baby"—WP—being mishandled. She asked to become the center supervisor. Like some of the supervisory respondents, she had little managerial or WP experience, but did have two things that seem to make a difference in managing WP services: vision and influence. She took several actions to improve WP services. She concentrated first on turning back the work quickly and with high quality. Next, she enlisted the help of key opinion leaders as liaisons with each department. She experimented with new procedures. She concentrated on visible accomplishments to win others' support. She developed communication channels with department heads by going to department meetings and working to alleviate problems discussed there, even when others did not view them as "WP problems."

Mary and her WP operators were not content with succeeding at their initial aim of efficient typing. As soon as they were regularly turning out the work, they realized how the flow of work could be improved. They began to take some initiative in controlling information flow. For example, when two different departments were each requesting that the center input information from a form they filled in by hand, Mary suggested that they already had the information to fill in the form for the analysts from data about the cases stored on the system. They set up procedures for tracking each case from its entrance into the agency until its disposition. The result was substantial savings in man hours and more accurate information because it was not copied by hand anymore. Mary established career ladders for operators. She was eventually promoted to a federal position directing WP and office automation activities for the agency.

These two cases illustrate the following principles of WP implementation found throughout the sample:

1. Evolution rather than rational planning characterizes WP history. This history can generally be understood in terms of the five phases of implementation: agenda setting, matching, redefining, structuring, and interconnecting.

2. Managing WP was a learned skill. WP was indeed a new kind of technology for most organizations. Metaphors of typing and data processing, viewed in the context of narrow rationales based upon cost displacement, proved to be inadequate to explain what kind of management was required.

3. Conflicts between users and central providers of WP services shaped implementation. Like data processing, word processing re-

quires skilled professionals. Users of services, however, often prefer control of their own work even if it is done less efficiently than it might be by specialists.

4. Single individuals, most notably supervisors and executives, shaped implementation. The history of WP in most organizations is very much a history of individual vision and accomplishments. Good managers understood, early on, the potential of the technology and worked diligently to sell its benefits to skeptics.

THE PROCESS OF ADOPTING WORD PROCESSING

The following sections examine how WP evolved through the five phases of implementation—agenda setting, matching, redefining, structuring, interconnecting. The discussion focuses on the kinds of decisions made in each phase and how these decisions reflected assumptions and shaped potential adaptations of WP.

Agenda Setting: Initial Actors and Rationales

Although the details of implementation varied from organization to organization, the initial stage in the adoption process was quite similar. In 62 percent of the organizations, an executive, sometimes with the approval of a committee, initiated the idea of securing WP capability. Only 11 percent of organizations reported that office services or clerical employees introduced the idea. Table 3.2 shows the kinds of organizational members who were the first and second initiators of the idea of WP.

A survey by the journal *Word Processing and Information Systems* (1981; based upon 2,164 *WPIS* readers, a 19 percent response rate) and another by Curley (1981; based on completed questionnaires from twenty-one organizations out of thirty) asked similar questions. The *WPIS* survey found that 77 percent of those deciding initially to buy word processors were chief officers—fully 25 percent were the organizations' CEOs. Curley reported less of an influence of top management—only 38 percent were top executives; 46.7 percent were individual managers. However, her definition of managers seems to be a higher level than the supervisor/manager category used here.

TABLE 3.2

Initiators of Word Processing

Job Classification	First Initiated (N = 168)	Second Involved (N = 70)
Executive	62%	21%
Clerical	11	23
Authors	10	14
Data processing	5	17
Dept. manager	7	4
Others	6	20
Total	101	99

Curley does note that subsequent purchases, or companies deciding on WP later than average, were more likely (61.8 percent) to have top management make the decision.

Another survey of 230 secretaries (79 percent response rate) on their attitudes and beliefs about office automation (OA) reported that only from 53 percent to 73 percent ever actually participated in decisions about OA, but over 96 percent felt they *should* be involved (Hicks 1984). Involvement in this study included all phases of OA implementation, not just the initial decision, but there was still a considerable gap between secretarial preferences and organizational behavior. Similar results were found in the *9-to-5* study (1985) of over two thousand users of OA: only 25 percent of clericals reported that they were able to influence design, choice and use of OA equipment, while 38 percent of professional and technical workers were, and 53 percent of managers were.

WP in the present sample seems to be initiated by a "godfather" who then delegates the idea to lower levels, where support may be less visible or real. On the one hand, this explains the strong work-reduction rationale behind initial WP justification, but it also explains why these rationales rarely considered changing the nature of work: high-level managers are not sufficiently involved in the work process to suggest those kinds of changes.

And what were those initial rationales? They were quite utilitarian but in the long run possibly limiting. The first rationales, in order of frequency of mention, were repetitive typing (66 percent), improving work unit (14 percent), reducing or maintaining staff (11 percent), being innovative (7 percent) and other (2 percent) (N = 163).

Two of the other surveys found similar rationales: document preparation, documentation, and some data manipulation in the *WPIS* survey; and faster output, keeping up with increasing paper volume, and better quality output in Curley's. The latter found that 84 percent of organizations reported their initial use of WP was for form letters or extensive revisions.

These are quite important rationales for justifying the first plunge into an expensive innovation, but as chapter 2 suggested, these uses do not change, and likely do not much improve, an organization. As McFarlan and McKenney write, "it is often impossible to foresee and plan for the full range of consequences before introducing information systems technology. . . . excessive control and a focus on quick results in the early stages can inhibit learning about a system" (1983:92).

As described in the previous chapter, innovations may be characterized by their perceived attributes. The initially perceived attributes of WP are likely to influence both the rate and success of that innovation—and sometimes in opposite directions. Though the innovation's attributes may be identified more completely in the matching stage, the most obvious attributes—whether inherent to the innovation or projected by potential adopters—play a strong role in agenda setting. Consider how each attribute is associated with initial rationales.

With respect to *relative advantage*, the reduction of repetitive typing makes WP clearly superior to current practices. However, this focus on repetitive typing may obscure advantages relative to other, non-typing tasks.

With respect to *complexity,* early WP was seen as quite similar to typewriters and thus conceptually simple. However, early WP technology was limited in functionality and not easy to operate. The "windowless" WP typewriters certainly did make it difficult to devise alternate formats for text. Current WP systems are highly functional and easy to use for certain tasks, but they also offer highly complex procedures. Indeed, the median number of months the operators reported needing to become competent was a short 1.6 (mean = 2.7) but 72.4 percent reported that they were still learning "some" or "much" about ways to use WP.

With respect to *compatibility*, placing WP operators into steno-like centralized "pools" reduced the initial perceived incompatibility of WP. This served to place WP in existing procedures and operations. However, the potential of WP was often constrained by preexisting procedures that could not take into account the computer's capability.

With respect to *communicability*, the final product is quite visible—rapidly produced, correct, formatted, clean copy. Thus, this quickly becomes the standard for demands by authors. However, the process of WP is nearly invisible to clients, so tensions can rapidly arise between authors' expectations and WP unit/operator capabilities.

With respect to *divisibility*, there is often a large leap to the first WP equipment, so divisibility is not a strong attribute of WP. This limitation encourages risk-adverse organizations to emphasize clear cost-benefit justifications. Further, attempts to keep initial WP simple also work against developing managerial expertise and effort in designing the unit's structure and procedures.

Thus, many of the initial attributes of WP that facilitate preliminary adoption may operate in the long run either to suppress its potential or to generate organizational conflicts that must be resolved in later adoption stages: "We had no idea what we were doing then. No idea of shifts or equipment. Things have just evolved here." This statement characterizes much of how respondents remembered the early stages of WP. When they look back on early operations, they are amazed at how much they did not understand about the equipment, its potential, or its management.

WP was an infant whose potential was unknown. In most sites, WP management was not a matter of conscious design. There was little consciousness of how social factors might relate to technical factors and little understanding of what the initiators were doing besides bringing in a high-tech typewriter. Though there existed literature describing procedures for managing WP centers as early as 1972, few organizations used consultants or did much planning or analysis. Agenda setting was typically simple and fatefully narrow in scope: use word processors to eliminate repetitive typing.

Matching: Early Planning

Most organizations did not even attempt to rationalize the introduction of WP as much as Big Bank, though most tried to implement the technology in what they considered the "right way"—paying attention to a narrowly defined need and choosing an appropriate brand and configuration of equipment.

Approval for acquisition usually came from an executive; generally, administrative personnel were involved in decisions about uses. Those who had the most influence in initial installation decisions were executives and top managers. Table 3.3 shows respondents' answers to questions about the first and second most influential decision maker.

WP was brought in as the idea of a rather high-level executive. The installation was rather casual; clerical supervisors had some influence in most organizations. There were very few organizations where office engineers were involved. Median planning time was about six months. Table 3.4 shows the kinds of analyses conducted. The general pattern following the initial idea for WP was to acquire equipment

TABLE 3.3

Who Was Most Influential in Implementation Decisions?

Job Category	Most Influential (N = 194)	Second Most Influential (N = 194)
Executive	33%	11%
Clerical	28	22
Clients/authors	5	10
Data processing	10	8
Other	10	7
No answer	15	42
Total	101	100

with clear but narrow rationales with a moderate amount of planning, and turn it over to others. Then, either machines were set out for shared use or a WP center was begun. Twelve organizations mentioned that site visits to comparable organizations using WP played a role in shaping their definition of what WP might do for them. Others mentioned trade shows and vendor presentations as important. Vendors often did work flow analyses and cost-benefit analyses for them.

In most organizations WP was introduced on a small scale, often only one or two scattered machines. By far, the most common first machines were "magnetic card" typewriters developed by IBM in 1969, though many respondents were quick to point out that they thought WP "really began" when they acquired some kind of video screen. The person put in charge of this WP idea and equipment was typically a secretary, or WP operator (73 percent). In many cases it was the executive's secretary, or an operator in the original WP unit, who felt that someone had to take charge. Table 3.5 shows that approximately 60% of the managers and supervisors who were in charge of the units in the organizations surveyed had some or much previous experience in WP supervision, coordination, or design, or coursework in WP or computing.

When matching activities *were* planned and organized, particularly in nonprofit organizations, they typically emphasized procurement. For example, "in our examination of over 70 studies for word processing and office automation systems in the four agencies reviewed, the justifications were often merely reviews of different types

TABLE 3.4

Analyses that Preceded WP Installation

| Kind of Analysis | To What Extent Was Analysis Performed? | | | Total N |
	Much	Little	None	
Work flow analysis	46%	13%	41%	162
Cost/benefit	48	16	36	159
Lease/buy	50	18	32	164
Employee attitude	27	16	58	147

TABLE 3.5
Previous Experience of WP Supervisors/Managers

Level	Supervision, Coordination, Design (N = 80)	WP or Computing (N = 80)
None	33%	23%
Little	8	16
Some	19	39
Much	38	19
Missing response	4	4
Total	102	101

of equipment" (Comptroller General 1984: 39). Federal policies are becoming more sophisticated at procurement, however: they now encourage agencies to procure large numbers of machines at one time to secure favorable bulk prices and compatibility among machines. Moreover, justification is no longer based solely on hours of equipment use or pages of output. In a federal standards document (NBS 1980) managers are directed to determine the "key products" of their units and to measure the level of effort required to complete them by various kinds of employees. Level of effort and level of employee grade are key factors in determining whether automation is justifiable. One report (GAO 1981; 1) states, "Office automation is not likely to produce significant benefits when equipment is installed as a general purpose tool, or to compensate for basic systems deficiencies."

In the federal government (and in other organizations) there are incentives for procurement. The incentives for day-to-day management are less clear. The need for good day-to-day management is mentioned, but few guidelines are provided. Yet, WP history shows that management is far more important than prior justification. Generally, though, with little knowledge of who would use WP and a moderate amount of expertise in analysing office systems, the justification was "soft." Organizations that used WP more effectively than others were not necessarily more rigorous than others in their initial justification. Quite the contrary, those sites that have continually adapted their WP typically began with a little more faith and charity and a little less control than others. However, they emphasized notions of learning, value-added functionality, and risk. Here are some typical remarks about initial justification from some of the most adaptive users:

"If I had to justify, I never could have gotten it. You probably never can justify before you have one. How many people could justify a TV the first time they bought one? I got it to learn."

"Word processing was not justified in the usual company manner (20 percent return on investment), but rather in what they could do with word processing that they are not now doing. For example, a commonly used engineering report could have an additional column with computed measures added. It would take a long time to do by hand and input, and the cost in time could not be justified without word processing."

"We don't have to cost justify. We got terminals for secretaries primarily on the basis that it was the first step toward OA; secondarily because we are developing an electronic newsletter."

"There is no bottom line return on investment policy. To get something here, you have to convince the partners to take the risk."

Redefining: Beyond the Typing Pool

Once the unit was established, experience with equipment, capabilities, or task needs led to changes in WP systems, with a different set of rationales. Those reasons were upgrading of functions (34 percent), dissatisfaction with current equipment (27 percent), adding new features (23 percent), increasing demand for WP services (13 percent), or other (4 percent). This may be interpreted as a slight redefinition of the original concepts of WP, developed through actual use.

The WPIS survey also reported what functions users wanted to acquire (thus their question is biased toward functionality). The most mentioned functions included more work stations, communication, additional software, electronic mail, and photocomposition interface. All except the first-mentioned reason imply redefinition of the initial role of WP as a way to reduce repetitive typing. Curley also reported a shift in top uses among her responding organizations: broad correspondence was ranked first by 55 percent, word and data processing by 30 percent, and forms typing by 15 percent. In general, she concluded that there were no overall differences in initial and subsequent purchase rationales, although five organizations (24 percent) did argue for "soft" dollar savings, greater managerial productivity, and increased effectiveness as changes in cost-benefit criteria.

Another indicator of how WP was redefined within an organization was whether WP units altered their initial ways of performing or offering services. Table 3.8 includes a column indicating that about a fifth of the organizations indicated that they did alter their services. Much of the change had to do with how the services were provided, and some of the changes involved increased formality of procedures for managing the boundaries between the WP unit and authors or external departments, as shown in table 3.6. Thus, while there was a general redefinition of the kinds of reasons for which WP was acquired, and reasonable amounts of effort were expended to match and redefine the innovation in a relatively short period of time, the initial ways in which WP was used to perform services typically did not change greatly.

TABLE 3.6
Client Contact—Procedural Formality and Change

Amount	Formal Procedures (N = 194)	Procedures Changed? (N = 194)
None	18%	30%
Few	45	38
Many	25	17
Missing response	11	15
Total	99	100

Structuring: The Evolution of Centers and Procedures

In most organizations, structuring involved two primary decisions:

• The decision to form a word processing center.
• The decision about who will manage the center.

Centers or Distributed Word Processing? The impact of the ideas about the "right way" to structure WP within organizations began to redefine WP about 1978. Prior to that time organizations that had WP capability (about half of the sample) had equipment that looked like typewriters. Equipment was used by people who were already full-time typists; sometimes in typing pools, sometimes in corners of offices. With use of WP being pushed by over twenty vendors in the fledgling market, organizational decision makers began to search for appropriate administrative practices, particularly with regard to uses, procedures, and roles. The conventional wisdom promoted by WP vendors and consultants was to establish "separate job positions for correspondence and administrative secretarial personnel with company-wide dissolution of the private secretary position in favor of a centralized WP center" (Datapro 1984:104). This arrangement appealed to many.

About 80 percent of the organizations had WP centers or centers with satellite units. However, this percentage does not represent a static condition: when asked what was the growth pattern for WP, 25 percent of the organizations were remaining the same, 21 percent indicated changes toward decentralization and 14 percent were moving toward centralization (41 percent did not know or respond). Curley found about the same shifting, but she commented that the direction tended to be away from whatever structure was devised initially. She concluded that any change in organizational structuring was "reactive" and not necessarily directed by conscious choice or managerial planning. The data from the organizations sampled here provide reinforcement for that conclusion.

Hence, the content of most redefinition decisions concerned whether the organization would have a WP center or whether equipment would be dispersed for scheduled (people sign up for hours to use the machine) or shared (first come, first served) use. As in the District

Office case, many early WP operations—both centralized and dispersed—were not managed well. On the one hand, machines set out like pencil sharpeners for occasional use by uninformed users constituted the path of least resistance. When word processors were dispersed, early horror stories told of machines gathering dust. On the other hand, reorganizing office work and requiring that documents be sent to a centralized service or, sometimes, phoned in and dictated to a machine, violated many people's sense of self-importance and control of their work. When WP was centralized, horror stories usually described resistance to WP resulting from early, clumsy attempts to change people's office habits by fiat. Here are two examples:

A hospital department started out with a dictation system. According to the current supervisor: "A consultant recommended the system, the supervisor and administration forced it onto the buyers without preparing them for it, and they resented it. They didn't use it. The buyers rebelled and the system was removed."

In a consulting organization, even the idea of using word processing was resisted at first. "They conducted orientations to explain the equipment. One person said he made no revisions and therefore would have no use for it. Three secretaries refused to learn. They were told to learn or leave. That department is still resistant."

Those that had the most difficulty in introducing WP seem to have been those in which a consultant analyzed what would constitute "efficient" use and recommended a rigid set of procedures for setting up a WP center. As one WP supervisor in a consulting firm responded when asked to critique the consultant's study of the firm's word processing:

"I totally disagreed. The report just didn't understand the equipment. Consultants don't understand that accuracy is still important with word processing."

Although many said that "the greatest problem is getting people to change their behavior," most talked of how WP eventually proved itself through the efforts of the people doing it. Resistance was not to WP as it evolved in most organizations, but to an idealized concept of what constituted "efficient" management of clerical resources.

Advocates of WP centers often had a naive understanding of the nature of clerical work. They ignored the "value added" by a good typist. They ignored the importance of good relationships between typists and authors. Mostly they ignored authors' insistence of control over their work. Hence, the centers that thrived were those in which management understood WP technology, the system of human relationships in which wordsmithing is done, and the potential of text editing for contributing to the mission of the organization.

Who Will Manage and How Will They Manage? Decisions to create WP centers usually resulted from compromises about efficiency and from resistance to the new work patterns centers required of operators and authors. These compromises were usually resolved by WP supervisors. For this reason, the second decision, "who will manage the center," was often more important than the decision to form centers. Procedures for administering WP, whether in a center or not, largely depended upon the supervisor. This considerable range of supervisory outcomes is a direct result of (a) the abdication of responsibility for WP by most initiators, and (b) the lack of managerial and technical training of many supervisors. Thus, while some supervisors were free to devise appropriate WP structures, many managed according to "default" assumptions and practices.

As an author described the WP operation in an organization where he formerly worked:

"The critical part of that operation was selecting the right person to manage the center. If you don't get the right personality as supervisor for a center, it probably won't work. The supervisor must orchestrate priorities of work, and enforce strict rules on operations in order to make it work for everyone."

There is another reason for the importance of the supervisor's role: as described earlier, upper managers brought WP into the organization and quickly ceded it to a secretary or other subordinate. Keen (1981) claims that this is a common practice because managers' emphasis on upward mobility puts a premium on early results. This eagerness often prevents establishment of explicit goals or specific commitments, and later managers do not have an understanding or mandate about what they must support. So, supervisors must take up the slack without guarantee of upper support.

A consistent theme of authors and upper-level managers was the importance of the supervisor's or coordinator's attitudes and management style. This issue is illustrated by an example from a hospital where a new supervisor had to overcome problems of slow turnaround and high turnover left from a predecessor:

"Problems in WP are due to attitudes of supervisors. Many supervisors are petty and protective. Possibly they are afraid of their own job security and therefore make everyone else afraid of theirs."

The skill involved is one of balancing the need for procedures with the flexibility required to keep job satisfaction high and meet the needs of diverse authors in a field where everyone was new to the game. Many of the comments at site visits concerned this balancing of procedural rigor with administrative flexibility. Some of the most important structuring decisions concerned how flexible the formal structures would be and reflected the supervisor's assumptions about the nature of human motivation.

The supervisor of a center in a financial institution emphasized this point: "Remember that it is a service, and that you are in a service department. That means that you are always friendly and cooperative. You must have strict rules and regulations governing use and interfacing users and operators. People can't just come in and say, "do this." Don't believe everything is a rush. At first we had so many of these, everything was a rush. I got around that by having the department manager sign for any rush job. We eventually used the rush requirement as a way of getting additional equipment— that was early on. Now the needs are pretty well understood."

The supervisor of a WP center in a legal office was quite strict—so it seemed to the researchers. For example, personnel worked three days a week, a practice in place when she was hired. But unlike the former supervisor, she insisted that the three days a week could not be in sequence. Yet the operators and proofers praised her zeal and her flexibility; she was flexible in ways that were important to them.

Some of the least flexible managers were not supervisors at all, but were coordinators of WP in decentralized systems. These people have responsibility to make the system function, but no authority to manage users. Some of them see rules—backed by threats to cut people off the system—as their own means of insuring that the system will work for everyone. For example, the coordinator of a shared-logic system in a consulting company where equipment is dispersed for use by secretaries and occasional authors said:

"I laid down the law and said if they didn't get training, I'd take their keys away. They (secretaries) ignore training. They feel they know how to use the OCR, then they mess it up and it's down for a week. I don't let them use it after hours. People also have to file off every night. That rule is for the system and their own good. With twenty people using the equipment, if you screw up, you go to the end of the printing line. If I schedule you to print at 9:00, you have to be there." One secretary described her reactions to such inflexible procedures: "I've learned to do only what I'm told."

Inflexibility results in strained relationships between the coordinator and secretaries. By its very nature, inflexibility works to reduce adaptations. The important point here is that this structural consideration results from a perceived necessity for control. In the example above, a shared-logic system necessitated coordination among many users, but the coordinator had no managerial authority. That lack of authority (because author/consultants resisted having a WP center) led the coordinator to resort to rules about the property she managed. Inflexible procedures only made the situation worse.

Interconnecting: Managing Authors

Interconnecting requires attending to largely nontechnical issues, such as turf, social benefits, control, and access. Solutions may be dictated, negotiated, or evolved, but they strongly determine the success of the innovation and its eventual form. As discussed in chapter 2, adoption resistance is likely to be influenced by "features of the information system's design which represent a loss in power for affected users" (Markus 1981).

The most common rules in WP operations are those that regulate contact with authors or users. At the extreme, some authors lost their personal secretaries upon the implementation of WP, and thus felt a keen need to maintain contact with their documents and the operators. On the other hand, supervisors quickly became wary of easy access to their operators, and devised ways to protect the operators who were not in a position to negotiate authors' demands. For example:

The supervisor of a center in a manufacturing firm talked about the firm rules she enforces for authors, indicating implicitly what she told us at another time: "There are almost no rules in the center itself. It's the author's responsibility to pick up material when completed unless they have special requests for delivery or the operator may just want to take a break and take it over to them."

Effective WP supervisors, especially those in charge of expanding centers, were good boundary managers (see chapter 8 for greater detail). That is, they were good at managing relationships with relevant others outside the center to win support; they kept internal operations open to new possibilities while protecting internal operations from diversions and attacks.

Table 3.6 shows that in about a quarter of the organizations, there were many formal procedures concerning client contact; in nearly half, there were few formal procedures. The majority of changes in these procedures occurred in organizations with procedural formality (55 percent). The most mundane of formal regulations concerned procedures for checking in material to be processed; there were occasional complaints, but for the most part intake and delivery had been routinized.

Setting of priorities is an early issue that must be resolved if an installation is to continue to exist. When a WP center cannot establish a reputation for turning around material quickly, the center is vulnerable to being disbanded. Installations that have succeeded in establishing a reputation for good service—fast turnaround, reasonable accuracy—often go on to influence more directly how authors do their work. Two different philosophies about the relationship of WP units to the authoring process were voiced:

The supervisor of a manufacturing firm has a philosophy of minimum storage. If material is not used regularly, she does not want to keep it. "We are not the filing cabinet for the department. I make people be realistic about what they want to keep." This supervisor wants authors to do their own filing. She resists record keeping as an activity for word processing.

Another supervisor, again in a manufacturing firm, has a philosophy of minimum rekeying. She keeps exact figures on what kinds of documents are produced. Seventy-five percent of her output is "pre-stored." She aims to eliminate as much original keying as possible; hence her center becomes a records department.

Some supervisors were more explicit that WP should not only store, but also control, documents. In effect, their attitude was that "documents belong to word processing." Nowhere was this more evident than in the District Office case at the beginning of this chapter.

IS THERE A STANDARD FORM OF WORD PROCESSING?

As chapter 2 mentioned, it is not always clear just what constitutes adoption. Both the process and the object of adoption are rarely distinct enough to allow explicit theoretical definitions or operational measurements. This section attempts to identify what constitutes— or whether there is—a common form of "word processing."[1] Data from the telephone interviews are used to examine the extent to which the adoption of WP followed a standard or "mainline" pattern. Forty-six questions about the organizational form of WP (structure), about the roles of those involved (role/procedure), and about uses for WP (services) were analyzed. A straightforward measure of standard adoption is the number of innovation components adopted; in particular, if at least 50 percent of the organizations regularly used a component, that component can be considered part of the standard form of the innovation.

Table 3.7 lists the level of usage of each service component and the respective number of organizations which reported that usage; table 3.8 provides similar information with respect to roles and structure. The standard service components include draft copies, proofreading, indexing files, and using boilerplates (frequently used forms or paragraphs). Role and structural forms of standard adoption include centers (perhaps with satellite units), staffed by operators or specialists, working for a supervisor/manager. The initial rationale was repetitive typing; the unit was begun at the initiative of top management. Only lease buy assessment is performed. Analysis of standard role forms show that there is considerable contact between operators and authors, though the WP unit has its own location and does not share it. Changes are initiated primarily by the supervisor/manager.

Another criterion for detecting a standard form is to inspect the distribution of the number of components adopted by organizations.

TABLE 3.7

Word Processing Service Components, Ranked by Frequency of Organizational Adoption

| | Does Organization Provide Service? | | | |
| | | | | Was Service |
Uses	Never	Occasionally	Regularly	Changed Much?
Draft copies	7	26	158	23
Proofread	24	41	125	28
Index files	25	20	145	24
Boilerplates	42	49	99	25
Develop forms	53	51	85	14
Edit and rewrite	55	50	85	22
Fill out forms	61	47	83	20
Keep activity log	65	25	96	13
Maintain inventory	71	25	92	18
Maintain data base	76	27	85	26
Deliver work	69	44	65	4
Process records	82	36	66	15
Write original material	94	42	56	15
Telecommunicate	102	22	60	22
Provide admin. support	110	23	53	6
Provide photocopies	120	20	46	9
Phototypeset	153	9	26	6

NOTE: Figures are *numbers* of organizations giving that response, rather than *percentages*, to avoid comparisons involving unequal response sizes. Service components are ranked according to total of "occasionally" and "regularly" responses. The question asking whether the unit had changed how it performed or delivered its service allowed the responses "none," "some" or "much."

For example, a bi-modal distribution would indicate two different types of WP installations—one concentrating on a few basic services and the other providing a wide range of services. Or, a negatively skewed distribution would indicate a rapid dropoff in the number of WP sites offering more customized or difficult services. The service

TABLE 3.8

Word Processing Role and Structure, Ranked by Frequency of Organizational Adoption

Rank	Role/Structure/ Procedure	Response/Number of Organizations		
2	WP unit	Center	Distributᴇᴅ	
14	Operators' title	147	35	
		WP specialist/ tech.	Secy./typist	
		94	94	
		Other	Supervisor/Mgr.	
			89	
15	In charge	104		
	Initial idea			
9	Rationale	Repetitive typing	Other	
		108	55	
11	Source	Exec./top management	Other	
		104	84	
	Assessments	None	Little	Much
8	Lease buy	53	29	82
12	Cost benefit	57	26	76
13	Work flow	66	21	75
17	Employee attitudes	85	23	39
	Client boundaries	None	Little	Much
4	Amount of contact	32	31	108
5	Procedural formality	35	88	49
20	Chargeback	Never	Depends	Always
		121	30	17
	WP unit evaluation	No	Yes	
16	Line/page/doc. count	120	66	
17	Turnaround time	125	62	
17	Client satisfaction	120	62	
18	Lead to changes	100	61	
21	Errors	151	35	

TABLE 3.8 *Continued*

	Physical boundaries		No		Yes
7	Others share WP place		68		120
10	WP personnel in one place		84		105
	Involved in changes	None	Some	Often	Usually
1	Supervisor	17	15	25	119
3	Execs./top admin.	37	68	28	49
6	Clients	49	72	29	28
19	Data processing	103	29	8	21

NOTE: Ranks based upon combined positive responses, or upon most frequent category of response.

variables, and the role/structure variables, were dichotomized and summed for each organization. The mean and median sum for the sixteen service variables were 9.3 and 9.5; for the role/structure variables, 10.4 and 10.2. Both distributions are quite normal, indicating no typical threshold in the number of components typically adopted.

Another approach is to identify interrelationships among the role, structure, and service variables which would represent a main-line WP innovation.

Factor analysis of the *service* components resulted in two factors, explaining 40.9 percent and 17.9 percent of the variance, respectively. (Making draft copies was not included, as it was such a commonly adopted WP service.) The first factor consisted of boilerplating, developing forms, keeping an activity log, maintaining inventories, and maintaining a data base. These services combine a strong capability of computing—the handling of repeatedly used or updatable material—which can be used either as a passive sort of warehousing or an active automation of information processing. The second factor was a "writing" factor: the WP unit is actively involved in the creation and editing of text. These two factors represent standard WP components, but in fact this analysis does not show much differentiation: only two factors resulted, and less than half of the variables loaded on these factors. Further, only boilerplating is done regularly by at least 50 percent of the organizations.

Factor analysis of the *role/structure* components revealed somewhat more differentiation. Six factors explained a total of 89.3 percent of the variance. The first factor indicated that early planning and assessment activities were likely performed together, and comprised lease buy, cost benefit, work flow and employee attitudes assessments. However, these assessment activities were typically done externally to the WP unit and organized from above; internal changes perhaps do not follow easily in such a structured environment. The second factor represented just such a change: a variety of WP unit evaluations occur together (line/page/document, count, turnaround time, client satisfaction, and errors), and these evaluations tend to lead to changes.

The third factor constituted the general identification of WP in the sample: centers, staffed by workers titled as "operators" or "technical specialists," with changes initiated by the supervisor, who was clearly in charge. Factor four perhaps was the type of WP installation that characterized the "default" way to organized WP: personnel located in the same place, initially justified to reduce repetitive typing. Factor five presented a managed, but not participative form of WP: initiated by top management, which continues to be involved in change, that change often following from unit evaluation. The final factor was a "client" factor: clients are involved in changes, and have much contact with operators, but all this is regulated by formal procedures.

Cluster analysis did not find any clusters. Along with the low differentiation of the service components in the factor analysis, this result indicates that the components seem to be rather loosely associated—that there are few sets of variables that represent subsets of a standard configuration of WP.

Another, rather simplistic, indicator of a standard form of the WP innovation is the extent to which the *number* of service components can be predicted. The total was regressed on variables measuring structure and change. These variables were number of employees, public or private organization, amount of operator contact with clients, executive involvement in change, influence on change of evaluation of the WP unit, and presence of formal procedures for dealing with clients. Only increased operator contact with authors had a significant coefficient ($N = 107$, R-square increment of .14, significant at .001).[2] More communication with authors, which presumably indicates more potential for cooperatively designed services, is associated with more WP services.

Overall, the analyses indicate that there is no obvious "standard" configuration of the innovation called "word processing," and the extent of WP services cannot be predicted by the variables included here. One implication is that WP is a flexible concept comprising a diverse set of services, roles, and structures. Managers can thus take advantage of a flexible technology by adapting and redesigning to fit their organization's goals and the needs and preferences of operators and authors. Indeed, this insight leads to an analysis of just how WP has been structured and designed in the sample organizations—the topic of the next chapter.

CONCLUSION

Managing office technology has developed heuristically since WP first became popular in the late 1970s. WP entered organizations largely through executive decree and over the protests of both operators (who, often rightly, felt that the intent was to control and demean their work) and authors. Early vendors described large gains to be made from the centralization of typing in WP centers. Managing such centers was no easy task, however, for the technology is far more complex than typewriters if used for its processing capability.

Supervisors assigned to WP centers had to appreciate human resistance to the technology; such resistance is not surprising given that the technology was sold on the basis of its ability to control and reduce clerical labor. Those who succeeded in managing WP work—whether in centers or in distributed settings—were those who envisioned the capability of WP to make real productive gains in an organization's ability to process textual information.

The critical stages of implementation were not the early ones of planning and matching, but rather the later ones of redefining needs in light of technological capabilities, of flexible structuring of WP units, and of interrelationships among operators, authors, and upper management. This history of implementing WP was consistent across organizations only in a general way. Quantitative analysis failed to identify a clear "standard adoption," which indicates considerable potential for flexibility and adaptation in WP application structuring. The next chapter considers in greater depth the different levels of WP organization that manifested this flexibility and displayed different patterns of control and the awareness of value-added information work.

Chapter 4

Four Word Processing Systems

As organizations went through the process of adopting and implementing WP, they developed different ways of providing WP services, managing jobs, structuring units, and influencing diffusion. A four-level typology of WP systems provides a framework for understanding differing organizational processes and how they are associated with differences in adaptation. The four levels are divided into adoptive and adaptive systems.

Adoptive systems are work units that adopted the innovation of word processing, but are using it only to perform preexisting information work more efficiently.

- Low-integration systems are unsuccessful adoptive systems.
- Clockwork systems are successful adoptive systems.

Adaptive systems are work units that not only adopted the innovation of word processing, but are adapting the innovation to add value to, or redesign, preexisting information work.

- Exanding systems emphasize localized adaptations.
- High-integration systems emphasize organizational adaptations.

Though all sites contained some aspects of each category, most sites fit remarkably well into one classification. The discussions throughout this book of these four systems are based upon case studies at twelve, eighteen, twenty-one, and nine sites, respectively, from the sample of sixty case study organizations, but this distribution is not necessarily representative, or important, per se. The Appendix discusses the procedures and frequencies used in categorizing the sites.

Subsequent sections of this chapter explain the name chosen for each system and describe how these four kinds of systems differed with respect to

- Adaptations of word processing uses.
- Monitoring of performance of those who provided WP services.
- Diffusion of innovative applications among system members.
- Future direction of word processing within the organization.
- Management decisions about how to coordinate and control the unit.

Chapter 8 considers possible transitions from system to system in greater detail.

To place this fourfold typology in a wider context of the relationships between organizational structure and technology, several assumptions of organizational contingency theorists are noted.

CONTINGENT CONDITIONS AND THE STRUCTURE OF SUBSYSTEMS

Contingency theorists in general argue that no one organizational structure or even job design is best fitted for all environmental conditions.[1] The two fundamental assumptions behind this approach are that (a) organizations are open system and (b) organizations operate in changing environments. As open systems, organizations must use inputs (resources, constraints) from their environments, and return outputs (products, new industrial arrangements) to those environments. Yet environments vary in the degree to which change is rapid and unpredictable. Environments include raw resources, external information, competitors and allies, regulations, labor, etc.

Therefore organizational structures, departmental interdependencies, and organizational capacities for processing information influence how well organizations respond to, are selected by, occupy, and survive their environments by matching environmental changes through reductions of environmental uncertainty or improvements in performance. One of the fundamental questions of contingency theory is the extent to which organizations can determine their own fate—the managerial perspective—or are shaped primarily by environmental forces—the ecological perspective.

The Managerial Perspective on Contingencies

The central question in the managerial perspective is to what extent do organizational size and technology affect structure. *Structure* is the coordination and control of subsystems, and includes complexity, span of control, formalization, centralization, and administrative intensity. Structure affects the flow and diversity of information, which is necessary to (a) respond to environmental change and complexity, (b) maintain internal conversion processes, (c) facilitate participation, and (d) foster innovation. *Technology* is the mechanism used to transform inputs into outputs. Technology includes the extent of automation, relationships among tasks, adaptability of work flow, means for evaluating operations, and the degree to which search procedures are analyzable. Depending on how technology influences structure—does its effect vary, is it linear and immediate, is it largely an effect of the organization's size—management can more or less directly influence how an organization matches its environment.

An example of this debate is Aldrich's (1972) reanalysis of the Aston group's study of forty-six organizations (Pugh, Hickson, Hinings, and Turner 1968) to test the relative effect of size and technology on structure. Pugh et al. had rejected any "technological imperative," or a direct impact of technology, and instead had argued that organizational size was the predominant influence on the nature and structure of technology. The reanalysis showed instead that technology is a strong independent variable.[2] Automation may create more interdependent tasks and remove some jobs (leading to smaller organizations), decrease the cost per unit (allowing more employees), or increase the division of labor (requiring a greater diversity of employees).

Although technology's effect seems to be independent from that of size, the subsequent question is whether its effect is deterministic, that is, inherent in the nature of technology.

The first analyses of the impact of computers in organizations argued quite strongly for technological determinism (see Dunlop 1962 for an example of the approach, and Rice 1980 for an abbreviated review). These studies concluded that implementing mainframe computers for transaction processing (such as in insurance companies) directly led to increased centralization and job fragmentation. Davis and Taylor (1979) examined the validity of this particular perspective by testing the methodological soundness and consistency of the results of over a hundred investigations of relationships between technological characteristics and job design, group structure, and organizational structure. They found considerable direct evidence of flexibility in the design of technology and much reason to doubt technological determinism as an explanation of organizational structure or administration.

For Davis and Taylor, an apparent deterministic relationship between technological characteristics and administrative features turned out, upon closer examination, to be a manifestation of a self-fulfilling prophecy. The psychosocial assumptions of planners and managers were more important than technological characteristics in shaping the development of procedures, jobs, and uses for the equipment. In investigating the structural effects of computerization, Simon (1979:227) came to a similar conclusion: "Whether we employ computers to centralize decision-making or decentralize it is not determined by any inherent characteristics of the new technology. It is a choice for us to make whenever we design or modify our organizations."[3]

Technology does, then, affect organizational structure and performance independently of size, but not in a linear, deterministic fashion. A major implication is that the meanings and assumptions of decision makers at all stages of implementation shape the use and outcomes of technology. Hage, Aiken, and Marrett (1971) suggest that there are two opposing strategies for achieving the necessary coordination and control of subsystems to influence organizational performance: *sanctions* such as planning, standardization, and programming, which are forms of control *external* to the work unit, and *socialization* such as feedback, adjustment, and acquisition of new information, which are forms of control *internal* to the unit.[4]

The Ecological Perspective on Contingencies

The organizational ecology perspective argues that environments are the major "external constraints in explaining or designing organizational structures and processes" (Aldrich, McKelvey, and Ulrich 1984). From this perspective, organizational designs are the joint products of the form of the organization in the environment and characteristics of the environment. Meaningful change occurs at the level of a *population* of organizational forms. The matching of organizational actions and environmental outcomes must be random in order for selection and retention of designs to occur at the population level. Fundamentally, the organizational ecology perspective says that selection and survival of organizations are largely independent of individual managers' intentions (Hannan and Freeman 1977, 1984).

These forces operate locally as well:

Selection also takes place within subunits or organizations. As loosely coupled systems, organizations may be transformed through the selective survival or elimination of particular structures, processes, or subunits (Weick 1979). Past observers have tended to attribute such changes to the deliberate manipulations of peoople within organizations, rather than to the effect of negative selection through external competitive measures. (Aldrich, McKelvey, and Ulrich 1984:75).

While this seems on the face of it rather discouraging for individual managers and work units, organizational population theorists do not argue that it is pointless for managers to take action; they do argue that individual action unlinked to a wider understanding of the above processes is insufficient to affect organizational survival. For example, if the environment is highly uncertain, then innovative behavior and entrepreneurship should be encouraged by reducing learning costs and avoiding formalization of early results (Aldrich, McKelvey, and Ulrich 1984). Rogers and Larsen (1984) show that the turbulent environment of Silicon Valley created norms of proprietary information sharing that were at once formally quite strict and interpersonally quite flexible; networks of individual software and hardware designers were more important than the formal networks represented by organizational affiliations. Or, organizations may create collective strategies and thereby exert more control on the environment (Astley 1984).[5]

Word Processing Subsystems in Information Environments

The major thrusts of these two perspectives are brought together by an "organizational assessment" approach (Van de Ven and Drazin 1985). This approach emphasizes a fundamental aspect of open systems theory, that of equifinality—the ability to arrive at a final state by diverse paths. That is, organizations can choose to respond to one or a few strategic contingencies, but those responses must be consistent. Because environments are complex and therefore consist of "multiple and often conflicting contingencies," no one specific interaction between enviromnent and organizational design can be deterministically successful. Further, matching and selection occur at several levels—population, organization, and work unit. Thus, work units are less affected by environmental pressures and organization-wide designs, and instead "tend to reflect the particularistic style and discretion of unit personnel" (p. 359). Individual managerial choices *do* affect organizational survival, but only when those choices are part of a consistent organizational strategy which focuses on selected environmental contingencies.

FOUR TYPES OF WORD PROCESSING SYSTEMS

The sections that follow integrate an awareness of these perspectives with the concept of adaptation developed in chapter 2. As the introduction noted, WP systems—the configuration of technology, organizational structure, employee involvement and communication, and the nature of work—are categorized into four levels. These levels are well identified, insofar as representative indicators of organizational and managerial practices typify each level, but they are not well operationalized, insofar as they are not quantified by a set of discrete, measured variables. The systems identified below are not deterministic outcomes of fits between organizations and environments, but attempted solutions, sometimes conscious, often not, that created opportunities for matching organizational and environmental needs. It is very likely that adoptive systems are well suited to the short-term needs of organizations in a stable, narrowly defined environment; but it is also likely that adaptive systems are well suited to the long-term needs of organizations attempting to survive in an information-based economy.

Low-Integration Systems

Representative Indicators of Low-Integration Systems

<u>Typical quote:</u>	"This office has a weak administration. There are forty-five cowboys and cowgirls here doing their own thing."
<u>Uses:</u>	"Cadillac of a typewriter"; little automation of routine.
<u>Monitoring:</u>	By hours in use.
<u>Diffusion:</u>	Pockets of cleverness.
<u>Future:</u>	Planning electronic mail.
<u>Management of system:</u>	Weak or no supervisor/coordinator. Little communication about word processing or adaptation. Little participation in decision making. Little impact on jobs.

The most common original rationale for acquiring WP in the organizations surveyed was to reduce repetitive typing: wordprocessors were seen as "no problem" typewriters. When a new technology is first introduced, people tend to perceive it—and justify getting it—as a more efficient replacement for a current practice or technology. That is, a conceptually simple, immediately implementable and convincingly justifiable application of the innovation is adopted. By such strict criteria, these systems are "adoptive."

Low-integration WP users had yet to develop a shared appreciation of it as a technology with its own unique and useful functions. Low-integration systems have not even automated routine. At these sites basic functions of WP software such as boilerplating, global search, math, linear graphics, and simple records processing functions were seldom used because their utility was not appreciated. Few sites had developed procedures such as forms books for repetitive letters and reports that would require the use of such functions.

There were few references to using WP "programming languages" such as glossaries or program functions. Typical attitudes are reflected in these comments by a secretary in a private organization where WP is left to secretaries with little training on the equipment, and by a programmer in a public organization.

"Sometimes secretaries will play with the machines." For example, one secretary experiments with glossaries to set line formats for a 130-page table with horizontal lines. "But most secretaries never use glossaries."

"Clerks have learned to emulate IBM typewriters and never go beyond that."

The programmer who made the latter statement also described how she occasionally develops advanced applications for clerks to use, for example, a procedure for tracking correspondence on word processors in response to a request by a U.S. senator to know how long it took to approve a deviation from certain federal regulations. Clerks are taught how to use the commands to track correspondence, but not how the procedure worked or how they might develop similar applications. The attitude—shared by professionals and attributed to the vendor—is that clerks couldn't and wouldn't develop applications, so trying to teach them is wasted effort. According to the programmer:

"They just do the minimum they need to get the job done. I don't see how clerical people could use it as a computer. [The vendor] just sends someone to set it up. Someone who just uses it for typing could not use it for advanced applications."

In part this attitude seems justified. Operators and secretaries at low-integration sites were quite content to use word processors as typewriters, ignoring possibilities for integrating the innovation with other tasks or technologies. Operators who use few of the special functions of the electronic equipment are no less enthusiastic than those who use all of its capability. They sing the praises of word processors, emphasizing their remedial effects—word processors make them competent typists. The attitude of this secretary is typical of most of those who work in low-integration systems:

"I can't see retyping anything. I used to work on an IBM typewriter. If I made a mistake, they were all over me."

Most respondents in low-integration sites were vague about the productive impact of WP. Although most respondents in these sites were generally favorable about the impact of WP, all of the sites where the operation was described as "poor" (7 percent) by the supervisor were low-integration sites. Although many did some kind of line count to estimate need in the justification for procurement, none had a systematic way of monitoring the impact of WP on their organization. The typical way of estimating the value of WP was an informal survey of how many hours a day machines were in use.

Respondents who were the most negative about the impact of WP tended to be procurement officers rather than managers in these organizations. They understood that users are enthusiastic, but they were skeptical of real benefits. For example:

"I can find machines gathering dust, but you need steel-toed boots to get equipment from people even if they never use it because they think sometimes they might need it."

"In branch offices, office automation developed in an unstandardized way; some vendors made a fortune selling at the branch level. Central office is an example. They don't put them to much use."

"Seventy-five percent need only the simplest writing equipment, probably electronic typewriters, though they get more. They want full-page screens because the guy next to them has one. Managers have big egos. Sometimes they get away with it because I [person who approves procurement needs] have learned not to sleep on railroad tracks."

An analyst in one agency summarized the findings of his group about WP usage in the federal government; these observations are relevant to all low-integration sites:

- Word processing increases the unit cost of producing documents.
- The majority of procurement is for the typing function.
- There is no training. People have no conception of how word processing is different. It takes thinking as well as finger dexterity.

- It should be used for what it was designed for. It is not a general purpose machine.
- No one ever goes back to evaluate what they are doing for corrective feedback.

In low-integration sites, individuals, usually secretaries but increasingly professionals using either WPs or PCs, are left to their own initiative to figure out how to use the equipment and for what. Thus, for the most part busy clerks, secretaries, or sometimes writers simply use the equipment as typewriters that save them some retyping with corrections. Of course, some users become enthusiasts and develop brilliant applications on their own—pockets of cleverness did exist at many of these sites.

Although access to WP equipment and therefore some experience in how it works is somewhat shared in these sites, there was little reason to believe that system-wide adaptations are in the offing. Some of the uses of WP equipment other than straight draft and final typing are: (a) writing and editing—secretarial support for typing is scarce; writers and editors seek any help they can get, often violating organizational policies that forbid them from using the equipment; and (b) electronic mail—although only 33 percent of the telephone sample regularly used telecommunications in 1982, the number is growing rapidly. Electronic mail seems to be a favorite idea for expansion in low-integration organizations. In many cases electronic mail seemed to be a panacea for the lack of person-to-person coordination in these organizations.

A critical factor in the low performance of these systems seems to be their lack of WP management. None of these sites had a supervisor or coordinator of WP services.

Clockwork Systems

Representative Indicators of Clockwork Systems

<u>Typical quote:</u>	"The supervisor must orchestrate priorities and enforce strict rules of operations."
<u>Uses:</u>	Batch typing.

Boilerplating.
No ties to professional users.

Monitoring: Lines/pages of output.

Diffusion: Emphasis on volume and efficiency precludes expansion of variety in users and purposes.

Future: Dead-end careers/operations.

Management Procedurally oriented supervisor/coordinator.
of system: Little communication about adaptation.
Little participation in decision making.
Closely supervised word processing operator jobs.

Clocks are highly efficient mechanical systems for doing one job in a stable environment. Analogously, clockwork WP operations are very efficient at doing one task—typing—in stable organizational environments. The emphasis at these sites was on developing efficient procedures for reducing the number of keystrokes required to put out documents. WP was successfully adopted at these sites. However, clockwork supervisors, unlike those in adaptive systems, were not ambitious about expanding or adapting the services they provide through WP.

The attitude expressed by one manager is typical in clockwork systems:

"My job is to see that this office operates as efficiently as possible. The measures of this would be low turnaround time and turnover, and a high volume and quality of work."

Clockwork sites aimed to maximize efficient machine and human resources. Use of keystroke-saving procedures such as boilerplating, math functions, search and replace, and records processing were fairly common features. Such sites provided authors with forms books to use in constructing correspondence and other repetitive documents.

Thus, clockwork sites are adoptive and reap productive benefits from WP. But the following comments by *interviewers* about site visits indicate that creativity—continuously developing new uses and procedures to better serve author needs—is not a topic of concern in these sites:

The supervisor of two centers on separate floors spends much time running up and down between them. She has a desk in each center. She describes herself as "a working supervisor and problem-solver" but couldn't think of any "ingenious ways for using the equipment" that either she or her operators had discovered.

When we asked about new uses or procedures in this insurance company, we got puzzled looks from operators. They were hired to do their job in a certain way, and they do it that way. Lilly's response was typical: "Everything we do has to be done according to some kind of form—form letters, charts, procedures, memos, dictation."

The operator identified for us as the most inventive at this manufacturing site could only think of one example of an adaptation: she does several documents as one to save set-up time.

To say that little or no adaptation was occurring within these WP centers does not mean that none was happening within their organizations. In several organizations with clockwork centers there were pockets of WP use by professionals that were often creative, but not tied into the center; in fact, some supervisors told of ways they had fought outsiders in getting WP equipment:

In one organization, while the supervisor was explaining that engineers would never be interested in keying in their own documents, on the other side of a glass panel was an engineer who had brought in his microcomputer and was explaining a word processing program to a group of eager colleagues.

In another organization, a vice president used a microcomputer to create agendas for his meetings and then "reprocessed" them into minutes right afterward. This way, he says, "minutes are out in a half-hour instead of the several days it might take to get it typed officially."

Both of these efforts are WP activities carried on outside the clockwork WP center. Managers who provide their own WP often spoke with disdain about WP centers, dismissing them as "batch shops" that cannot meet their needs.

The tendency in clockwork systems is to monitor by pages of output. These WP units use the equipment at least eight hours a day; many have second shifts that keep equipment in use sixteen or even twenty-four hours a day. For the most part, volume is used to justify the number of operators and the prior purchase or lease of equipment rather than to acquire new equipment. No clockwork systems monitored their impact on organizational functioning. Instead, supervisors' attention was turned entirely inwards—it focused on the question of whether or not they are maximizing units of output with the amount of resources they had.

Clockwork sites tend to keep their equipment longer. They establish procedures for doing typing work; they develop large catalogs of boilerplated material. Therefore, changing equipment is more trouble than it is worth. One site was only changing from nondisplay magnetic card equipment in 1983, long after almost all others in the sample. When the supervisors talked of desired equipment upgrades, the features they wanted were spelling verifiers and software that measured keystrokes.

Adaptation may be suppressed either deliberately or through lack of encouragement to adapt as these examples illustrate:

In one of the larger centers, an operator told how authors used to be allowed in the center. One day an author saw her using the global replace function and asked if she could do a special kind of revision that required global search. She showed him how she would do it. The author then asked the supervisor to use global search for a report he was preparing; he complained that the supervisor had told him previously that such a procedure was impossible. After the author left, the supervisor told the operator that she was not to tell authors what the center could and could not do. Soon after that the center adopted a policy prohibiting authors from entering the center.

A client asked an operator to create a column of numbers using the math function of the word processor. The operator did not want to do that, preferring to work from verbatim copy only. She complained to the supervisor who complained to the client's manager. Afterward the center adopted a policy that it would only type verbatim copy.

The future of clockwork systems is a limited one. Supervisors have merely lived up to the expectations of those who installed WP in their organizations. They have developed sub-optimal operations when viewed in the context of the potential for WP. Their limited assumptions of what might be done limit their own and others' appreciation of potential adaptations.

Expanding Systems

Representative Indicators of Expanding Systems

Typical quote:	"Eight months ago I went to my boss complaining I was too bored to go on. Now I'm working with the computer people to go on-line."
Uses:	Evolving applications. Attempts to service professionals.
Monitoring:	By production and new applications.
Diffusion:	Through supervisors' salesmanship.
Future:	Sophisticated applications.
Management of system:	Boundary spanning supervisor/coordinator. Considerable communication about word processing or adaptation. Little operator participation in decision making. Sophisticated word processing operator jobs.

Expanding system sites have WP centers with ambitious supervisors who are largely responsible for adaptations of the innovation after it has been successfully adopted. Although most of these organizations have developed procedures for efficient boilerplating and other means of keystroke saving, the supervisors did not emphasize procedures or their efficiency. Instead, they told of changes—expansions they are initiating in their services. For example, the WP supervisor of a law firm reviews all documents to see if the same basic text is coming in from different authors. In these cases, she suggests a form to the attorney. Although the practical effect is to reduce typing, there is a conscious effort shown here to understand the nature of the work that generates the input. Here, management of technology directly affects organizational structure.

The law firm supervisor pointed out that they provide better service to the professionals by saving them effort. Unlike the rushed supervisors in clockwork sites, supervisors in expanding sites invest time in adaptation, even when it means taking longer to accomplish the initial task. The supervisor of a consulting firm is always looking for better ways. A theme of her talk is "spend energy to set things up right because it will save time later." For example, she scheduled a task with "extra keystrokes"—an extra half-space after titles—so columns of numbers would line up when entered later. The reason? "It saves time in the long run." This attitude is in sharp contrast to supervisors of adoptive sites who often confided that they knew there were better ways of doing their work—glossaries for example—but that there was never any time to learn them.

Supervisors in expanding sites pay attention to the needs of authors, often generating new ideas from conversations with them. For example:

Working closely with the sales division of a manufacturing firm, a word processing center uses math and automated function keys to update a catalog of several thousand products and send material with typesetting codes directly to the printer.

Although the office automation planners out of the headquarters of a Fortune 500 manufacturing corporation have been trying to push a new system that will allow for text and data transfer between word processors and the main computers, the word processing supervisor in the finance department is not impressed because she has been "communicating with the host" for a couple of years. It started when they needed documentation for financial data systems. They also do auditor reports which internal auditors key in from the field. Auditors input their report; word processing accesses it, cleans it up and prints the final form.

The success of WP in expanding systems is monitored both by production *and* diffusion of applications. These sites do not use the equipment to measure time keying; they interpret production figures with care. They use production figures not only to justify their *current* resources, as in clockwork sites, but also to justify *expansion*. The following comment represents one supervisor's attitudes about methods and purposes of monitoring performance:

"When the OA people were looking at printers that would only do 152 characters to a line, I showed them that 48 percent of our work required more than 152; I clobbered them with my figures."

In most expanding systems, feedback about workers' performance is quick and definitive, for they operate on funds made by charging departments for their services rather than being carried as administrative overhead. Overall, 67 percent of the units did not use chargeback, 16 percent always did, and 17 percent did on special occasions. If centers are not providing good service, customers use their own equipment and personnel. The operation of "chargeback" and its relationship to the evaluation of a WP unit is explained by one supervisor:

"The chargeback system is tied very closely to how the system works. Local managers operate on a budget and they watch very closely where their budget goes and what they are getting out of it. Their chargeback costs are clear to them. WP exists only to the extent that local managers vote with their purchase power to use our services."

Because the WP supervisor is the primary source of adaptation, the diffusion of WP applications depends upon the supervisor's enthusiasm for certain projects. Supervisors and coordinators of these sites are careful about the extent to which they take on new adaptations. For example:

The supervisor in a community college convinced the dean to add typesetting capability to their word processor. Now they save the college substantial money by setting the type on quarterly bulletins, catalogs, and publications required by departments. But typesetting work is tedious and boring for operators. In order to maintain morale and high output, the supervisor limits the amount of typesetting her center will do. She "oversold typesetting to the president and now he thinks (she) can do anything." She does not have the personnel or the financial resources to meet the demand that she could easily generate.

WP systems often expand to fill service needs that data processing cannot or will not fill:

Data processing in the community college is poorly staffed. They use their word processor for file and math functions that might have been done on the larger computer if there had been time and programming resources available. The WP supervisor knows they could do much more of the work on the WP if they added a BASIC compiler, but she is not pushing it because she is uncertain what might happen.

The word processing supervisor at an Eastern college described one of her most clever adaptations—an alumni file. It started as a list of three or four donors they wrote to. "We kept adding to the list. The secretary was still manually typing a list when we had one. I told her we could do it. Then when someone wants to know who gave over one hundred dollars, we know. We make a visit list when someone goes to New York, they know who there contributes to the school and whether we have any proposals out to them at the time." We asked if that is a use that could be done by computer services. "In data processing it takes a month to get a listing. Unfortunately, people accept that."

Because the diffusion of WP technology predated that of personal computers, its history is filled with the kinds of events that since 1983 have characterized personal computer usage: people used the technology to do what they needed, even if it was not the ideal solution. Adaptive systems demonstrated examples of how supervisors and operators applied WP to a variety of database, communication, and even spreadsheet uses. WP technology was available to them and they used it to define their information needs.

The typical case is one where typing purchase requisitions evolved into a database of purchasing needs kept on the word processor. The logic of the database then became the basis for developing a more integrated and powerful system on a minicomputer or mainframe. Supervisors of expanding sites spoke often of the past ways of doing work and how their vision of improved methods led them to find new ways of using whatever technology they had at the time until they could justify more suitable equipment.

Ambitious supervisors have much respect for the ability of operators, but see themselves, not their operators, as the locus of change and adaptations. For example:

The supervisor of a center in the finance department of a manufacturing firm put it this way: "I believe every operator needs to know how software functions with hardware. They have to choose appropriate software. It takes intelligence. Operators have been here four to six years with no turnover. I would be bored doing their job. Most of them love it because no one is standing over them. If a user is giving them trouble, they come to me. I let them do their own little quirks. No one does a job the same in terms of format, etc." Do they share ideas with each other? "Sometimes. They aren't good at sharing. They feel that others might be insulted if they told them how to do a job."

The supervisor in a college administrative office said: "It is hard to find anyone with experience. People are very nonassertive. I interviewed thirty people. I wanted someone who could set up formats, and who wouldn't be intimidated by the faculty or who would think this is antiquated equipment. Typing speed was really not a factor."

Expanding systems had WP supervisors who instigated and sold WP adaptations. In effect, they are "boundary managing" supervisors (that important activity is discussed further in chapter 8). While maintaining efficient operations, they direct much of their attention outside the center itself. They are typically in close contact with authors. They seek to move their operations into more sophisticated applications.

In a time of falling microcomputer prices when more authors and secretaries have access to their own equipment, many expanding systems are getting stronger. The supervisor of a center in a large manufacturing company claimed that as authors and others get access to their own terminals, the center's business has grown. They now understand what WP can do, but they don't have the time or the skills to do it.

Most supervisors of expanding systems were somewhat bored with their jobs. They had built up operations over the past five years to levels beyond anyone's expectations, taking on services such as worldwide communications, typesetting, records processing, database management, and even some data processing. They were also servicing a wide variety of users. In some cases such as the District Office case in chapter 3, they had become the center of information processing for their office or department. They were bored with their own success and found little to move up to in their organization.

At two sites supervisors were decentralizing their operation, widening or removing the boundaries of their units. These units were attempting to move from expanding to high-integration systems.

High-Integration Systems

Representative Indicators of High-Integration Systems

Typical quote:	"We are definitely a service, not a center here."
Uses:	Adaptation as a way of life. Focus on professional productivity.
Monitoring:	Focus on increased capability.
Difussion:	Organized decentralizing (often with microcomputers).
Future:	High risk—career and operational uncertainty.
Management of system:	High-status line manager. Extensive communication about new uses and procedures for WP. Participation in decision making about uses and procedures. Impact on many kinds of information jobs.

In high-integration systems, adaptation has become a way of life.

These systems make productive use of distributed equipment. Unlike low-integration systems, they are well-organized to expand capability using the technology. Idea sharing leads to idea development, and then to system development, not in the narrow sense of hardware and software use, but in the broader sense of people working with technology to accomplish organizational goals. Interaction is an important route to innovation as these examples suggest:

"We also do a lot of proposals. I said to myself, 'what would I do if I had a lot of home computers and wanted to do a proposal.' I worked out a concept. I shared the idea with other people. They had an idea of where we could get the computers."

One operator in the documentation department of data services of a large insurance company described work there: "I always find easier ways of doing my work. With a system this complex, there are lots of ways. We are always telling each other to come over and see a new technique we have figured out. If it is something that has to be standard, we take a vote and the majority rules."

"We trained ourselves, even to use programmable keys. We took four hours a day for a full week and shut the door, played the tape and practiced what it said. We would help each other until we had it figured out."

In high-integration systems, success is monitored by its impact on the operation of the unit. As one manager put it, "We didn't start out to do WP, we started out to get our work done." That is, they have not just adopted an innovation, but the idea of innovating—they focus on organization-wide adaptations. Two cases illustrate this:

The communication department of a large manufacturing firm has terminals distributed for use by writers, but the system is used for more than on-line composition. "When I first came here people were complaining that they had to go downstairs to use the computer to do the budget. It seemed to me that our word processing terminals should be useful. We found a way to use them as timeshare terminals. The beauty is that we can bring everything onto a desk. We also had a lot of invoices. No one knew who they were from or when they were being paid. We couldn't keep track of the amount paid for various things. Now we use the word processor to track and pay the invoices. We do a lot with information bases like Dow Jones, *New York Times,* Dialog, and the transportation database."

In the corporate offices of a bank, word processing equipment is used to keep several kinds of data bases. "We use WP as an information/filing system rather than just typing. We looked at everything we had stored on paper and decided it is cheaper to store on disks. The executive secretary did a study of the Rolodex system. She discovered they had almost two million cards. Now they are putting all that information onto WP system disks. These were hand-written information cards being transformed into data entries by six people working eight hours a day just doing this job. But it is streamlining the office and providing better information."

Low-integration and high-integration systems might look the same to the casual observer insofar as equipment is dispersed for use by both clerical and exempt employees. The principal differences are that in high-integration systems, (a) decentralization is *organized* and *managed* and (b) the product is added value as well as efficiency. These sites were sometimes directed by a WP supervisor who decentralized by progressive steps, making it easy for marginal users such as secretaries, analysts, and managers to use the equipment. Two cases illustrate this.

The word processing supervisor and personnel in the procurement office of a hospital created a "master draft sheet" for the word processor combining a number of formerly separate operations to assist food buyers in using the equipment themselves. Buyers are responsible for the purchase of over a million dollars in food every month. Most of the work is highly repetitive requests for proposals, but numbers need to be altered, names, and so forth. Work that used to take two days a week is now done in fifteen to twenty minutes. When the supervisor needs comparison sheets to let contracts, bids are entered into the machine and items sorted. The machine calculates the comparisons and puts an asterisk by the lowest bid for each item, then prints out the information in several different ways—once by item with vendors' bids in columns and another by vendors who submitted the low bids. The operators in the center support buyers first by programming the machines to work simply for them, then by teaching them how to adapt the system for themselves.

The supervisor and the operators in a legal department of a pharmaceutical company regard their principal job as assisting the lawyers to make the best use of their time. They have the individual needs of each attorney put into a glossary so that all an attorney has to do is enter the code for the kind of document he/she wants and the system automatically formats it and prompts the author through the writing.

In any system, with any technology, some people will be "early adopters" that invent uses and improve their own work. These people are "pockets of cleverness" in low-integration systems. They are leaders in high-integration systems. They understand their system enough to make sure that adaptations are diffused and that people who want to be only marginal users of the technology get assistance in learning to do their job better with the equipment. This writer's sentiments reflected what many people said:

"I don't want to know any more than I absolutely have to to use the system. The supervisor does the maintenance, is the expert, and knows how to make the equipment do what people need."

The future of high-integration systems is promising, but risky. They aim to change organizational information work by means of changing jobs and procedures, as well as by adapting the technology itself. Many places with such ambitions have failed. There are political risks involved in attempting to alter how professionals in other, more established departments do their work. There are employment and career risks as adaptations may make their jobs superfluous. And there are operational risks in rejecting routinized procedures, standardized applications and cost-displacement productivity criteria. But the various management practices, assumptions, and decisions discussed in this and following chapters increased the chances of success.

CONCLUSION

The purpose of this chapter has been to describe operationally some differences in the outcomes of implementation processes in WP. Four kinds of systems have been described: two "adoptive" systems: Low-integration and clockwork, and two "adaptive" systems: expanding and high-integration. For each system, how the technology is used, how success is monitored, how diffusion of adaptation takes place among organizational members, what actions management takes, and what directions the future implementation may take, were discussed.

These four categories can be used to describe many kinds of organizational services. The distinctions and applicabilities are most clear between clockwork systems that strive for efficiency through tighter internal management—based largely upon external sanctions—and expanding systems that strive for effectiveness through understanding and responding to the needs of clients—based primarily upon internal socialization.

Clients want new services; they resent "going hat in hand to beg at the door of the WP center." Consider the following comment by the head of a high-integration system explaining why the clockwork WP system in his organization could not meet his needs:

"Our former method of developing work was to write it out by hand. We couldn't send it to word processing because they couldn't read it. So we had typists do it. Then we would edit and cut and paste a version to send to word processing. About three weeks after we started we would be semi-finished."

A WP center that needs readable input (quite justifiable from an efficiency perspective) cannot meet his needs. Supervisors of clockwork systems are unable to respond appropriately to this new environmental demand. They do not understand that being more efficient in producing lines of text will not keep the center in business.

A consistent theme throughout interviews with users was "we want to do it ourselves." The extent of demand for personal control over WP can be seen in the author survey; 62 percent of the respondents said they wanted a word processor (or PC to do WP) on their desks. In fact, there was a highly significant relationship between authors' doing any of their own typing and wanting WP capabilities on their desk (Kendall's tau = .395, p < .001).

In 1982 WP centers became an endangered species for four reasons. First, lower equipment costs made it easier for managers to justify their own equipment. Second, microcomputers were invading offices and providing WP functionality directly to the user. Third, distributed WP became a means for high-integration systems to diffuse through the organization. Fourth, the concept of information centers—centralized sites that provide resources for decentralized information systems applications and innovation—was becoming more popular in organizations. Thus, successful managers began to develop WP applications *and* WP operators as organizational resources, to be decentralized and diffused throughout user departments in the organization.

Regardless of the exact future of WP, many principles learned about the management of work can be applied to improve WP jobs, and many lessons from the management of WP can be applied to improving other office information systems. The following chapters discuss some of those principles as applied to, and specified by, WP work.

Chapter 5

Principles of Job Design and Sociotechnical Systems

This chapter briefly summarizes some of the concepts and models used in chapters 6, 7 and 8 to explore how organizations designed and managed WP jobs and work units:

- Basic assumptions about work that have influenced the design of organizations and jobs.
- Aspects of jobs that have been hypothesized to affect worker motivation and subsequent outcomes such as satisfaction and productivity.
- Participation, a central concept in job design.
- An overview of the sociotechnical systems approach, a set of principles and practices used to improve the fit of technology and social systems in organizations.

ASSUMPTIONS ABOUT WORK

In the United States, the systematic study of work and attempts to improve it began with the Scientific Management theorists (especially Taylor 1911). This movement was a reaction to an overemphasis on tools and technology stimulated by developments and successes of the industrial revolution, which was grounded in the basic principles of economic reward, the division of labor, and control of the means of production. The Scientific Management theorists were radical for their time because they analyzed the tools currently used and studied how to make the best use of them, rather than taking them for granted (Drucker 1979). A complete approach to job design and implementation recognizes that while some components—material technology, task, organizational design, work group structure, and personnel traits—are perhaps more or less easy to redesign, all are possible and influential areas of intervention (Cummings 1981; Lucas 1981).

Thus, rather than simply giving workmen larger tools (e.g., bigger shovels) or merely adding more men with shovels to a job, scientific management directed workmen to work more efficiently with the tools at hand based on studies of the workers' movements. Unfortunately, this approach proved to be an incomplete paradigm for the complex systems and turbulent environments of more recent years. For the basic assumptions still held: that the only significant motivation for workers was pay, that jobs should be designed strictly for efficiency (by fragmenting, simplifying, and supervising jobs), and that hierarchical organizational structures built up by levels of functional supervision were most efficient. Humans were not seen as particularly efficient information processors; so organizational control, stability, and efficiency were emphasized. One could say that workers were just part of the company's technology, and management viewed workers from a perspective that emphasized technology and rationalism (Kling 1980). Further, a particular way of performing tasks became institutionalized, and organizations were not capable of adapting to changing situations.

By 1950, Scientific Management work systems—with their fragmented, overdetermined factory jobs, where workers take specific individual direction from their foremen—were proving too cumbersome, rigid, and slow to adapt to changes in the consumer market, the labor market, technology, and values of workers and organizational researchers alike.

Alternative perspectives had, of course, been developing for some time, starting with the landmark "Hawthorne" studies by Roethlisberger and Dickson (1939). One of these was the Human Relations school. This perspective looks at workers as individuals who function within a group setting. If individuals' motivations and needs were important to organizational performance, the argument went, then the individual's group must also play a large role. Thus, the psychology of individuals and the communication processes within groups became the focus of research and intervention strategies (group communication is reviewed by Davis 1969 and Moreno 1960, among many others).

JOB CHARACTERISTICS AND WORKER MOTIVATION

Subsequent theories about job design and organizational change have placed more emphasis on the effect of employees' jobs on their motivations and subsequent satisfaction and productivity. The *job characteristics* approach first assumes that workers can be self-motivated and mature; that they respond to complex jobs with motivation, satisfaction, and performance if they have such higher needs; and that motivation is a result of the perceived outcomes of behavior and the perceived satisfaction derived from those outcomes (Hackman and Lawler 1971; McGregor 1960; Vroom 1964). Second, it argues that a core set of job characteristic dimensions—skill variety, task identity, task significance, autonomy, and job-related feedback— affects an employee's psychological states—meaningfulness of the job, responsibility for work outcomes, and knowledge of results. Improved psychological states lead to higher individual growth, motivation, and satisfaction, and eventually to better performance, lower absenteeism, and less turnover (Hackman and Oldham 1976; Rousseau 1977; Turner and Lawrence 1965).

While this focus on the characteristics of jobs has received considerable empirical support, it makes a crucial, but vulnerable, assumption: that job characteristics are an objective aspect of tasks, and that individuals' perceptions of those characteristics are accurate. If neither of these is true, it is not easy to see how objective job aspects can influence employee reactions and work outcomes in any systematic way. One review of ten such studies concluded that both objective *and* socially influenced cues affect workers' perceptions of job characteristics (Thomas and Griffin 1983).

The *social information processing* approach posits that personal motives and values, organizational rewards, and social influence processes are more significant than objective job characteristics (Salancik and Pfeffer 1977, 1978; Shaw 1980). These sources of social information indicate to workers how much attention and importance they should ascribe to specific dimensions of job characteristics. Social cues are especially salient if the stimulus is unfamiliar (there is no prior experience to refer to), ambiguous (as in using an innovation), or if behavioral modeling is occurring (such as when supervisors introduce new applications of technology).

Two conclusions follow from these studies of job characteristics and worker motivation. The first is that a relatively well identified set of job characteristics influences workers' motivation and subsequent satisfaction and productivity. The second is that the surrounding context of social information about jobs—norms, current practices, communication with peers and supervisors—affects motivation and outcomes over and above the objective characteristics of jobs.

PARTICIPATION

The participation of workers in management in general, and the more specific involvement of users in implementing information systems in particular, have been advocated by a wide variety of consultants and researchers.[1] Worker participation in management may include activities ranging from having union representatives on directors' boards and being involved in investment decisions, to placing ideas in a suggestion box. Involvement in implementation to increase productivity and worker satisfaction is just one aspect of worker participation (Strauss 1982).

Reasons why participation and involvement should be encouraged include the following (Ives and Olson 1984; Mumford 1981):

1. Workers have a right to contribute to the design of their work.
2. Involvement leads to a more accurate knowledge of user needs, the organization, and the relevant tasks.
3. Unimportant system features can be identified in the initial stages of implementation.
4. The user gains increased understanding of the system.
5. The user develops realistic expectations of the system.
6. Design issues can be resolved before the system becomes "fixed."
7. Users develop commitment to and ownership of the change.
8. User resistance is detected and diagnosed early in the implementation process.

9. Participation in communication about job or system design leads to increased job satisfaction.

These rationales for participation are, in a more general sense, derived from theories of democracy, socialism, human growth, and organizational efficiency (Dachler and Wilpert 1978; Locke and Schweiger 1979; Strauss 1982). *Democratic* theory assumes that workers are capable of responsibility and learning, and that participation develops these abilities; direct or representative approaches to democracy are founded on issues of pragmatics and the extent to which people are assumed to have equal abilities. The *socialist* approach argues that true participation frees workers from control and domination, leading to liberation and egalitarianism. The *human growth* approach argues that opportunities for self-actualization lead to increased satisfaction, psychological and physical health, and, by implication, organizational stability and performance. The *organizational efficiency* approach argues that participation allows workers to have and exchange better information which will increase the productivity of the organization.

The framework for explaining the likely outcomes of participation on worker satisfaction and productivity is somewhat similar to that of the job characteristics theory. Three causal models have been proposed for the hypothesized role of participation in increased productivity and efficiency, and decreased costs and conflict:

1. The first model emphasizes *values*. Participation leads to the attainment of values that are salient to workers, leading to increased job *satisfaction*, and a resultant improvement in *performance*.

2. The second model emphasizes *cognitive* factors and *motivational* factors. Assuming that workers have relevant information that supervisors lack, participation increases communication, better use of information and better understanding of the job, all of which generate better and more creative *ideas*. Also, participation is hypothesized to improve supervisor-subordinate trust, group support, and identification with organizational goals, leading to decreased resistance to change and increased *commitment to changes*. Better ideas and greater commitment to change then lead to improved *performance*.

3. A third, less frequent model posits that effects of participation are *contingent*, as are the effects of job characteristics, upon indi-

viduals' psychological traits and needs. For example, the assumption in the human relations approach that all workers *prefer* the job characteristics of diversity, wholeness, etc., has been moderated by the awareness that differences in personality traits such as cognitive complexity and dependency lead some workers to prefer nonparticipatory, structured, programmed, and nonambiguous jobs. High performance in these kinds of jobs for these workers is an intrinsic challenge just as accomplishing complex, whole jobs is an intrinsic challenge for workers who are cognitively complex, autonomous, and self-motivating (Cummings and Srivastva 1977; 94).

SOCIOTECHNICAL SYSTEMS

Like other work design interventions, the introduction of information systems has the potential to reduce gaps between employee needs and job rewards, and between work group structures and information processing demands. But technology often increases these gaps, at least for a while. Why might that be so?

Cummings and Srivastva (1977) argue that human and technological change processes occur simultaneously, and in opposite directions. Social systems (work groups) evolve and develop, by adapting and learning. However, this learning process is relatively slow. Poised against these two traits of social systems are two traits of technological systems. Technological change can be quite rapid, particularly if a turnkey system is installed or a system is imposed upon potential users. Yet "technology depreciates in the hands of those who use it" (p. 101). That is, groups change slowly, but learn, while technology changes quickly, but becomes obsolete. This dynamic tension between social and technological systems is generally overlooked in implementation efforts that treat new technologies and its users as a fixed, instantly matched system. Systems are not clocks to be wound and run. They are gardens to be grown; system design and planning are important, but the process of tending them shapes what they become over time.

Increased gaps, tensions, or problems are often blamed on "user resistance" or "inappropriate technology." However, the sociotechnical systems (STS) approach argues that difficulties arise primarily when management decisions about work design, implementation, and evaluation do not pay attention to the dynamic relationship between social and technical systems. "Since our knowledge of [creativity, complex problem-solving, motivation, and social interaction] is not well formulated, we often opt for simplistic work structures accounting for only well-known aspects of social behavior and hope that the other parts will somehow sort themselves out" (p. 102).

The STS perspective emphasizes the importance of job characteristics developed by human relations practitioners and analysts, and the significance of the participative process, but goes beyond these approaches to alter the fundamental perceptions about the importance of interactions among technical and social systems.[2] The STS approach attempts to "jointly optimize" technical systems (tasks, processes, and technologies that convert inputs to outputs) and social systems (relationships, attitudes, communication networks, individual needs, skills, and values).

The STS approach forces the implementation process to identify and consider assumptions held by designers, managers, implementers, and users about the nature of workers, systems, goals, users, and change. Typically, assumptions held in each category lead to narrowly defined systems that do not take into account the interaction among organizational, technological, and human systems (Bostrom and Heinen 1977a; Cherns 1976; Davis 1966).

Proponents of STS argue that jobs should:

1. Involve members in changing the technology and social system jointly to accomplish organizational missions.
2. Provide opportunities for continuous learning. Feedback to workers about their performance is necessary.
3. Encourage experimentation. Systems evolve; managers must continuously attend to adaptation.
4. Optimize communication for high performance and quality of work life.
5. Promote self-regulation of work groups through autonomy. Locate the decision making at the task requiring the decision.
6. Allow people to perceive and complete whole tasks that they consider meaningful.

7. Administer policies with flexibility and encourage experimentation.
8. Provide for upward mobility, and for reassignment if the individual does not interact well with the group.

The principles of STS are often emphasized differently by different researchers. There are three generally accepted principles, however: minimization of control, self-regulation, and experimentation.

The first of these three principles is the stimultaneous maximization of redesign and the minimization of control. For example, essential components of the system must be identified, but no more than those should be specified; in that way, alternatives can be developed about how to accomplish unit goals.

The second, related principle is the self-regulation of work groups. The work group must perform four major functions: attain organizational goals, adapt to the environment, integrate people's activities in order to resolve conflict, and maintain essential roles by means of recruitment and socialization (Cherns 1976). Attempts to achieve these four functions by external control (i.e., sanctions instead of socialization) will be less successful than by allowing the work group to regulate itself. Cummings (1978) notes that self-regulation is more appropriate in some conditions than others. These conditions include (a) when a task can be differentiated from other tasks, (b) when control of the task's boundary is possible (including rate and type of inputs and outputs, standards, and expertise), and (c) when workers have control over their own behavior (method of work, access to feedback on performance, and ability to adjust activities).

A third fundamental principle is the legitimacy of experimentation (Cummings and Srivastva 1977: ch. 7). The STS approach itself is often introduced to organizations by means of limited experiments in selected parts of the organization. From an innovation perspective, this approach increases observability but also improves compatibility, as the change slowly becomes congruent with organizational norms. Further, if the experiment works well in a typical unit headed by an organizational opinion leader, the approach will diffuse through interpersonal channels more quickly.[3]

POTENTIAL NEGATIVE OUTCOMES OF WP JOBS

To emphasize the argument that principles of job design and are an important component of successful system implementation, this section briefly reviews the kinds of negative outcomes possible with WP. The proposition is that basic assumptions about work and workers' motivations, approaches to job design, and attention to the fit between social and technological systems can have serious implications for acceptance and outcomes of WP jobs.

There is considerable evidence that WP jobs *can* be unsatisfactory, unhealthy, and noninnovative. The principal rationale for fragmenting jobs is to obtain increased control over performance. But with the added control comes decreased motivation. In reorganizing to secure control of clerical work, organizations can create the kind of coordination that Fred Emery (1982) calls "inherently error amplifying." In such systems people will behave in a preprogrammed way regardless of the evidence of their senses or common sense.

Much has been written in the popular and academic press about the impending dangers of WP removing the discretion and flexibility from work that secretaries often enjoy. The result would be not only poor jobs, when jobs weren't replaced by technology, and unhealthy work conditions, but limitations on what clerical workers could contribute to their organizations.

Some of the earliest scholarly writings about WP jobs concerned the impact of WP on clerical work.[4] Sociologists Glenn and Feldberg (1977) synthesized some literature on this history of clerical work and compared it with their own investigations of WP installations. They took as the "standard modernized office" one that conforms closely to that advocated by IBM and others in the early history of WP; that is, information work designed according to the industrial model. Glenn and Feldberg examined through informal interviews five WP installations; two fit the IBM model (called WP/AS "word processing/administrative support") closely, one had "all-around clerical and secretarial arrangements with finely graded steps for upward mobility," and two others were "somewhere in between." They found in the WP/AS organizations many personnel problems noted in other studies of fragmented jobs—alienation, lack of motivation, "work to rule" attitudes. Administrative support people complained about "loss of typing skills" because they were denied typewriters. The WP personnel complained of dull jobs with no advancement potential.

Buchanan and Boddy interviewed three managers, twelve authors and eleven WP operators before and after the implementation of WP in an engineering consulting company and found that although pay, promotion opportunities, and control over the quality of typing increased, there was "reduced task variety, meaning and contribution, control over work scheduling and boundary tasks, feedback of results, involvement in preparation and auxiliary tasks, and communication with authors" (1982:1).

One review of six prior studies of differences in job characteristics and job satisfaction between WP operators and traditional secretaries found some, but not consistent, evidence for lower job satisfaction and need for esteem in correspondence secretaries or WP operators (D'Onofrio 1983). The author's replication found no differences by job type.

Indeed, though some have argued that the advent of the typewriter was in many ways a liberating force for women, because it created a demand for a new labor pool and thus provided economic resources to otherwise dependent women (Aron 1981), others have argued that in most forms, office work simply maintained gender discrimination in a new work setting (Scott 1982). That is, the sweatshop mentality of "women's work," job rationalization, and specialization institutionalized in textile mills and sewing machine work was perpetuated in secretarial work, stenography pools, and WP centers (Kessler-Harris 1982; Taylor 1980). The dramatic rise of women in clerical work paralleled the diffusion of the typewriter and the expansion of office work. The 1880 census shows that only a tiny percentage of office clerical workers were female; by 1910, 83 percent were (Scott 1982:173). Thus, these issues are particularly salient for WP operators and supervisors, as 90 percent of most low-level information handling jobs are now held by women (Werneke 1985). An office automation study of 1,100 people in 110 corporations highlighted the prevalence of such major problems in women's jobs, including "impoverished jobs," close work monitoring, unequal pay, discrimination in pro-

motions, and health problems (Westin, Schweder, Baker, and Lehman 1985).
It is crucial, then, to understand how these negative outcomes can be avoided.

CONCLUSION

The essential argument of this chapter is that the successful implementation of information systems, and the management of those systems to foster organizational innovation, require an awareness of principles of job design. The technology of an information system cannot fruitfully be considered separate from the organization's structure, the makeup of work groups, and the ways in which work is designed.

From the basic principles of industrial work, principles of job design have evolved to include a consideration of individuals' psychological needs and motivations, work group communication, participation in management, the role of social cues and information on perceptions of work, and the proper fit between social and technological systems. Each of these approaches has something to offer in the management of the implementation process.

Chapter 2 listed some contingencies that prevent innovations from diffusing, or the implementation of information systems from succeeding. Similar contingencies apply to job design interventions. For example, the reviews of the literature on participation emphasize that, at the level of the work unit, the most important aspect of participation and job design is access by workers to relevant expertise and information.[5] When participation is relevant to the task, when information obtained through participation (of designers or workers) leads to real or meaningful outcomes, and when effective performance is within worker control, then participation is likely to lead to improved worker satisfaction and organizational productivity (Dachler and Wilpert 1978).

The general principles of successful job design that emerge from this brief review are self-regulation of the work group, wholeness and discretion of the tasks, flexible administration of policies, opportunities for upward mobility, participation in change, continuous learning, encouragement of experimentation, and optimization of communication.

The next three chapters argue that the relations between WP technology, organizational structure, workers' needs and attitudes, and the nature of WP work may be mediated by management assumptions, goals, and perceptions. Managers must make "strategic choices" in job and organizational design when implementing technology (Child 1972). These chapters apply the principles introduced in this chapter to the specific context of word processing as part of office information systems. Chapters 6 through 8 progress from a focus on the immediate tasks and career aspirations of WP operators to the relationship of WP work to organizational goals and structure, and finally to the interdependencies and competition among organizational units.

Chapter 6

The Design of Word Processing Jobs: Improving Tasks and Worker Satisfaction Through Self-Regulation, Wholeness and Discretion, Flexible Administration, Upward Mobility

This chapter looks at those job design principles concerned with improving the task itself and the development of work unit members: self-regulation, wholeness, flexibility, and upward mobility. The first section identifies managers' assumptions about evaluating and assigning jobs and about operators' motivations. Two representative cases follow that discussion. Then each of the four principles are used to explore why some organizations had more adaptive WP systems than others. The final section discusses the ergonomic issues of WP work from the perspective of job design. Managerial assumptions and job design as well as technology, furnishings, and space all influence operator satisfaction and comfort with WP work.

MANAGERIAL ASSUMPTIONS ABOUT TASKS AND MOTIVATION

Managerial Assumptions About Planning and Assigning WP Work

Assumptions that managers hold constrain the kinds of implementation strategies and job designs applied to WP.[1] Thus, the four principles considered in this chapter must be placed in the context of how WP managers felt about implementation and operator motivation.

In 1955 Davis, Canter, and Hoffman reported the results of a study that examined the planning and design criteria used by manufacturing production planners and designers. They undertook this study to test the existence of underlying principles for design production processes that would carry over to the design of jobs. Their results showed that the most important consideration in job design was the minimization of the time required to perform the operation (maximum throughput/time). They reported planners' preference for emphasizing highly specified, low-skill operations, and the lack of emphasis on job satisfaction. Some twenty years later these managerial assumptions were collected again from a sample of U.S. and European systems analysts (who plan and design computer-based systems for plants and offices) and industrial engineers (Taylor 1979). The results found that both engineers and the systems analysts valued maximum throughput, efficiency of machine use, simple jobs, better information, and reduced manpower as more important criteria for assigning work to people than the satisfaction people would derive from that work.

Questionnaire items from these studies were adapted to assess the criteria used by WP managers at the sixty sites for designing jobs and assigning work to people. WP managers and supervisors were asked to rate the following items as being "major considerations in deciding who does what work": minimizing turnaround time, making jobs as simple to perform as possible, using the machines efficiently, providing management with better information, providing more job satisfaction, maintaining or reducing the number of personnel, improving the overall quality of the product, and satisfying a broad range of author needs.

The common result found among the four levels of WP systems was that "quality of product" was rated highest. In these times of increased awareness of quality this uniform response should be no surprise, especially when WP is often purchased to produce high-quality text with minimum rekeying. The four levels differed on their ranking of the other criteria, however, and differed from the rankings by the systems analysts.

The managers of high-integration sites reported that turnaround time and operator job satisfaction ranked equally high, followed by service to authors and providing management information. The last three rankings were efficient use of equipment, work simplification, and reducing the number of employees. Note that this ranking is nearly the reverse of that found in the two earlier studies.

Expanding systems supervisors ranked author satisfaction highest, followed by efficient use of equipment, operator satisfaction, job simplification, and turnaround time. Supervisors in clockwork systems ranked efficiency of equipment first, followed by turnaround time, author satisfaction, operator satisfaction, information for WP management, job simplification, and reducing labor.

Managers in the low-integration sites reported that both efficiency and quick turnaround were as important criteria as product quality. These were followed by author satisfaction, job simplification, job satisfaction, management information, and reducing labor.

Managerial Assumptions About Operator Motivation

Managerial assumptions about employee motivations were also measured by questions adapted from the two earlier studies. Nine questions were asked about "how work should be assigned" to people using WP, and nine other questions were asked about the "average nonsupervisory employee" doing the work as assigned in the first items. The shape of the profile obtained over the eighteen items matched that obtained from U.S. systems analysts to a remarkable degree. For a number of items, however, in particular those dealing with employee characteristics, the WP managers described a significantly more responsible, skillful, and competent person than did systems analysts in both the U.S. and European samples. For items rating employee interest, ability to be self-starting or to work with little direction, both the WP managers and U.S. systems analysts rated employees similarly, and lower than the European systems analysts.

A factor analysis of these items produced three factors that together comprised 85 percent of the common variance. The first factor, employee capability, comprised items measuring employees' interest in being involved, their skill/knowledge, and their ability to take initiative on the job, do a variety of jobs, and choose good procedures. The second factor, job flexibility, included items about delegation of authority, reliance on employee self-discipline, degree of job definition, and job flexibility. The third factor, job direction, was represented most strongly by a question about targets being set by supervisors. It also included items about employee desire for job clarity, job definition, and financial reward.

For the first factor, there were no significant differences in the answers of WP supervisors who were describing full-time operators, and coordinators of distributed sites where WP is done by secretaries and professionals as well as operators. There were no significant differences among respondents in the four kinds of systems.

For the second factor, the managers of the high-integration and expanding systems were more likely to believe that good management should be flexible in administering rules and relying on employee self-discipline.

Results for the third factor reveal that most managers believed they must direct the efforts of people who operate WP equipment. This factor received the lowest scores, indicating a belief in managerial rather than work group direction. Respondents see goal setting as the supervisor's responsibility and believe almost as strongly that motivators should be financial. There were no significant differences among the four types of WP systems on this factor.

The joint results of the scores on the three factors present a picture of assumptions of managers in the high-integration and expanding systems in which good jobs involving WP should be varied, and flexibly administered, but the focus on mission is the responsibility of management. Work toward that mission should be motivated by financial reward as well as by intrinsic factors; people who operate WP are capable and demand autonomy, but they do not want (or are not capable of) the responsibility of goal setting and mission determination.

This picture of operator motivations is quite consistent with the perception gained from interviews with the supervisors. The answers to semistructured interview questions point to three assumptions that most managers make about people in WP jobs:

Though relationships with peers are important, they are independent in their work. For example, "I let them do their own little quirks. None does a job the same in terms of format, etc. They aren't good at sharing. They feel that others might be insulted if they told them how to do a job. I encourage them to share. If someone has a problem they help. I let them control their own little revisions. That is very important to them. I don't assign a person to help another person even if she is behind. They would get bent out of shape if I did."

They will leave for better jobs. For example, "One difficulty we have is that good word processor operators come in, see the opportunities to move into other, better jobs, and leave. We have a pretty high turnover of operators."

They want state-of-the-art equipment and sometimes are insulted if the organization won't provide it. For example, "I'd like to hire experienced operators, but that's tough because most operators don't want to move backward from more sophisticated equipment."

For the most part, then, managers (supervisors) tend to hold assumptions about human motivation and reliability generally in line with sociotechnical systems principles. They hold reasonably positive assumptions about self-regulation, discretion, flexibility, and career mobility. Yet they do not believe in or support much participation by operators, which, as the next chapter argues, characterizes an important difference between adopting and adapting systems.

REPRESENTATIVE CASES

Two cases illustrate that management assumptions about implementation and human motivation shape administrative practices and subsequent outcomes of WP. In the "Worst Case," motivations were minimal. Rigid rules were enforced to secure reliable output from the operators. They were required, for example, to put in a certain number of hours and produce a set number of lines. In the "Best Case," the supervisor had a well-articulated sociotechnical understanding of work; the administrative practices that resulted shaped operators' jobs to be personally satisfying and productive. This site illustrates motivation through intrinsic rewards—operators have more discretion and opportunities for career advancement. These cases were chosen because they provide stark contrasts in approaches to personnel management in WP centers and clearly demonstrate how management practices influence adaptation.

The Worst Case

The WP center at Private Consulting Inc. was formed in 1981. Secretaries in several departments have WP equipment. Because they complained that WP work kept them from required administrative duties, a small center of one experienced operator, one trainee, two temps, and a working supervisor was created. Molly, who volunteered to learn the equipment when it was first brought into the company, was appointed supervisor; she is the only supervisor in the firm without management status. Molly is enthusiastic about the potential for WP, but frustrated in her work. Their equipment is designed to be easy to use for occasional use by a part-time secretary; it is slow and cumbersome for their production work load. The center is located in the middle of a large room "with no privacy or status." Molly feels this communicates the company's view of WP.

Sharon, the experienced, full-time operator, complains of very high pressure in the center. She is continually placed in conflicts between authors. When requests for top priority jobs conflict, the authors are supposed to resolve the conflict between themselves. When no resolution is reached, Sharon does both jobs. She is paid for hands-on keyboarding only. She must sign off when interrupted for any reason. She doesn't get paid for the time spent discussing jobs with authors, bathroom breaks, etc. She has daily headaches and eye strain; she is looking for another job. She asked the interviewer for information about the safety of the equipment.

Although a "floating" terminal is for the use of any company secretary, it is housed in the center near Sharon. When a company secretary coming to the center to use this terminal asks Sharon questions (a frequent occurrence) Sharon must sign off, answer the questions, then sign back on. The off time must be made up from her lunch hour if she is to work the required 7½ hours that day. She said she typically loses fifteen to thirty miuntes of her lunch hour because she helped someone else. She often works after hours to put in the mandatory 7½ hours a day. When she searches for misplaced diskettes, she must log off again, losing more lunch time. She also loses time each morning as she gets coffee, cleans her desk, etc., getting ready for the day.

Sharon complained that getting in her 7½ hours is the unbearable pressure. She asked her supervisor if operators could have coffee breaks as part of their 7½ hours, but she has never gotten a response. Her supervisor told the interviewer that coffee breaks are taken, but was ambiguous about whether they are paid or not. Sharon has no time to find better work procedures, though she thinks that would be fun. She would like to learn graphics. She thinks she is paid less than the company secretaries. She wants some flexibility to be able to leave early occasionally when needed. She wants more work space and the right to rearrange the machines.

The log to which Sharon refers was instituted by the supervisor in response to a review by the finance department. All center expenses are charged back to the requesting department. The purpose of the log is to allow more careful accounting for jobs. Because the reasons for the log were never discussed with the operators, these people view the supervisor's way of providing for more accurate billing simply as a way of more closely controlling their work.

Molly told of several incidents in which she unsuccessfully attempted a positive change. She recommended that operators' jobs be upgraded, but the proposal was denied without comment. She also attempted to assist the company's marketing efforts by improving the print quality of presentations to clients. At the urging of the marketing manager, Molly prepared a memo on the use of proportional spacing with samples. The vice president rejected this since it violated the approved format for such presentations.

Molly's current aim is to "market" the WP center and promote operators' pride in it by creating an identity for the center. Operators would wear WP center pins; the center would have a slogan and letterhead stationery. Printed documents would give credit for center work. Essentially, however, because upper management does not view WP as important in dealing with the competitive environment of consulting, the supervisors's attempts to relate the contributions of the unit to the mission of the organization are ignored, leaving her to seek a mission for the unit by means of pins and slogans.

The result of a lack of mission focus and understanding of the interrelationship of technology and people hurt both jobs and the organization here. The logging system, instituted to increase operators' documented output, is having the opposite effect because it is demoralizing operators. A floating WP unit was put into the center so that secretaries could use it instead of sending work for operators to do, but it too is having the opposite effect.

No one here set out to demoralize operators, but their assumption that more control equals more production led to practices that have such an effect. Their failure to communicate the mission of the organization and the place of WP in it puts pressure on operators that will lead to high rates of turnover. Their failure to understand how a change in technology such as a floating unit can impact the social system leads to inequities and complicating conflicts. Their failure to manage conflicts among authors leads to unnecessary conflicts within the WP center.

The Best Case

The best WP jobs involve people in challenging work. Occupants of those jobs are reflective about WP; they are articulate about how word processors "think" and how information processing might be improved through the use of the technology. They are motivated to advance.

Hi-Tech is a growing company on the leading edge of its industry, chemical manufacturing. WP has grown with the company. The president's secretary started WP at Hi-Tech four years ago when the company had fifteen employees. Today they have 438. A center of seven terminals is being decentralized. The shared-logic word processor is being replaced by a WP program on a computer. The goal is to move toward a terminal on every desk, connecting everyone with a system providing electronic mail, calendaring, business graphics, and forms management. The supervisor, Evelyn, recognizes that the major uncertainty of these plans is the future of the operators: "Will I have a job when we decentralize?"

Kitty was the first operator to be "spun out" of the center to the finance department. She primarily does financial statements, proposals, and contracts. Kitty had done work for finance in the center since she came to Hi-Tech eighteen months ago.

"In the center there was a lot of turning around and talking, joking, teasing, and group activity. I miss that. New applications take time out of the regular workload. It takes time to figure out the equipment and the new applications. Takes concentration to learn new routines. Here we don't always have that time."

Is WP different from typewriters?

"At first I thought they were totally different, now I don't think so. They really are not so different in that they are both machines that operate within specific boundaries, and so you are basically learning to manipulate those boundaries. Now with [brand name] you have a glossary, and you can do a lot more with it than you can by moving the tabs on the typewriter. But basically the concepts are the same. When you get into real high tech you can start manipulating these boundaries in more complex ways, and get really innovative. That is where the opportunity is—and the money."

Like other operators who have moved from a center to a satellite location, Kitty finds the transition difficult. Kitty has a sophisticated understanding of the work and the social as well as technical relationships that comprise it. Kitty thinks of her work in high-level abstractions such as "boundary manipulation." She understands how working in a satellite affects her work and her relationships. Because Kitty understands this relationship of the social environment to the work process, she appears to work within her new setting better than others who had been "spun out" (to satellites).

A distinctive difference in management assumptions leads to this difference in appreciation of work. Here is how Evelyn, Kitty's supervisor, describes WP work:

"The center concept was carefully designed to: (a) assure interaction between operators and users, and (b) give operators a clear sense of responsibility not only for their own, but for certain groups of users.

"Working in a center is a high-pressure job where the users [clients] usually have no idea what it takes to do it. I look at it this way, if I have respect for an operator, that person will respect me as a person, too. Operators are not a bunch of kindergarteners and you don't manage them that way. They are given specific responsibilities for specific users [clients]. If there is no work from their department, they see if they can assist some of the others. This requires a working together as well as a sense of your own work.

"We use a kind of flextime, if you call it that. Three people work four-day weeks, one works from 6:00 to 3:00 instead of 8:00 to 5:00 because she has horses and likes to ride while there is still daylight. Another operator called in last week saying she had broken up with her boyfriend and felt she couldn't cope with work that day. We understood. I would rather know what problems we are really dealing with than to have people lie to cover up.

"There are almost no rules in the center itself. There is a lot of joking and teasing, but the work gets done and that is all that is important. The operators are always there, backing each other up. Money doesn't do all the motivation. Pay is never enough to keep people happy.

"The operators are a little bit uneasy about the phase-out of the center. They are concerned about whether they will have a job after we decentralize. The human issue is always the major problem. We will relocate people as specialized gurus in each area. For example, one operator has already been moved over to the satellite in the financial area. Another has indicated her interest in graphics. Another will become a specialist in software and technical systems, and another will do training." Will any become secretaries? "No."

Evelyn's attitude includes examples of four characteristics of job design that promote adaptation:

1. Promote self-regulation. Each operator works for a specific department. They identify with a mission-focused unit though they are housed in the word processing center.
2. Design jobs for wholeness and discretion. Operators see the job from beginning to end and therefore have a sense of how their

own work fits into a larger mission of the organization. People here have the discretion to do their job as their experience says it seems to need to be done.
3. Administer policies with flexibility. WP operators, like other employees, want policies to be administered with flexibility.
4. Provide opportunities for upward mobility. As the center is decentralizing, each operator will be given the opportunity to move on to a creative job.

APPLYING FOUR DESIGN PRINCIPLES TO WORD PROCESSING JOBS

Analysis turns again to the operator questionnaires collected at the sixty sites. The WP systems are compared on the basis of four design principles which focus on the task itself.

Promote Self-Regulation

Well-designed work units need little "supervision" because they provide coordination, control, and motivation through job design. A sociotechnical systems assumption is that employees want to do a good job and that information about how well they are doing is important to them. From this assumption come practices that include measures designed to provide feedback on job performance, so that employees can regulate their own performance, and a job structure that includes responsibility for large chunks of the work process, so that employees will be motivated by knowing that their work contributes to producing something of value. People in such a system motivate and regulate themselves.

Most of the organizations surveyed still grapple with performance measures that are relevant to organizational effectiveness and to employees' perceptions of their work. About a third count some output such as lines or pages; however, several respondents insisted that counting is an invalid performance measure. Some have abandoned line count because it is cumbersome and foolish. However, some approaches to evaluating performance are related to mission. About a third monitor turnaround time, and almost as many have some measure of author satisfaction.

There were statistically significant differences among the four systems on items referring to operator input into performance measures. The differences are between high-integration systems and all the others. This is not surprising given the findings from interviews that supervisors of expanding systems are the focus for adaptation and that operator involvement is not encouraged. Table 6.1 summarizes the percentages.

The extreme opposite of principles of self-regulation are principles of work measurement. There were only two organizations with formalized work measurement systems. In one the WP supervisor is allowed to enforce the measures with discretion and flexibility. In the other organization work measurement is enforced by management systems engineering, a powerful group that reports to a senior vice president. The work measurement engineers are described as "heavily into ergonomics." It is true that the WP center was one of the best designed we visited. It was large with scenic windows and specially designed workstations. Yet WP jobs were tightly controlled with little room for self-regulation by the operators. The supervisor describes her ambivalence about both work measurement and quality assurance.

"Of the two, I like quality assurance better. I don't know how I would work if I had work measurement. In word processing, there

TABLE 6.1

Operator Input in Performance Measures

Site	Personnel Performance	Unit Performance
High-integration	39% [a]	61%
Expanding	17	39
Clockwork	19	46
Low-integration	29	29
	$\chi^2 = 23$	$\chi^2 = 18$
	$p < .03$	$p < .11$
Total N	287	

[a] Percentage answering "some" or "much."

is always a better way. Volume is not usually what is important here, though that is what I have to evaluate on. Because of work measurement, there is never a reason to take that extra step to do things right or to find a better way. At low times I get to play with the system. Only the good operators do that. Most do not. I suppose maybe most operators have to be on work measurement just to make sure they work. I never thought I'd say that."

Interviews with operators at this site confirmed that, indeed, they found no reason to look for better ways of doing their work. In many of the site interviews, the operators couldn't think of much to say about their work. Most of them revealed that they were looking for other jobs. They felt demeaned by their positions, ill-paid for the work they can do, and ignored in advancement.

Another WP unit in the technical publications department of this same organization was also visited. The manager there had a higher ranking than the WP supervisor. He had managed to keep the management engineers from studying putting his operators on work measurement. In contrast to the operators in the WP center, the operators in technical publications talked at length about their jobs:

"We all try new things. The number one rule: you cannot be afraid to try something new. We hold little classes and seminars to keep each other informed of what's what with the system. The work is probably closer to basic data processing than to word processing. It involves a lot of symbol keying and programming. We have a different relationship to writers than they do in the center. We work more openly. We are not a production area. We are made to feel that we are in a professional area and treated as professionals by the writers and by our own administration. The attitude here is one of honor."

The manager pointed out the importance of management assumptions and how they lead to practices that encourage or discourage self-regulation, adaptation, and effectiveness:

"Management style is critical in the area of WP/DP. How are people addressed? Are they treated as professionals? This question is most clearly manifested in the area of work measurement and quality assurance. The assumptions of most management systems engineering seems to be: people are no good; people won't work; people need to be prodded to work. To manage people, you must establish measures that assure they are kept busy doing something—a measure of volume divided by time. . . . Here [in technical publications] we have so many people sitting on top of one another that we have a kind of built-in teamwork concept where professionals work with professionals and each one more or less regulates his/her own activities in relationship to the others in the group and the writers whom they work for or with."

Management that assumes that workers are not capable of achieving organizational goals or improving the nature of the task will design jobs that prevent people from being innovative. Thus, "efficiency" will crowd out adaptation.

Design Jobs with Wholeness and Discretion

The high turnover rates that characterized the early WP jobs were due in part to management assumptions that misunderstood the requirements of wordsmithing. Operators were assigned from the lowest ranks of the organization to units that resembled typing pools. The equipment was difficult to use, yet the popular notion was that electronic equipment would take all the problems out of typing. Eventually those organizations that tried to fragment work arbitrarily into WP administrative support have abandoned at least the extreme of that position. Those responsible for WP came to understand that the old maxim of data processing—garbage in, garbage out—also applied to them. The potential of WP is not met by mindless transcription.

There were some organizations in which threat and fragmentation characterized WP jobs, as the "Worst Case" exemplifies, and as the sociological literature on WP jobs emphasizes. However, this was not the general case in the present sample. Today, WP jobs are held by people who showed early aptitude. In general, they like their jobs. Only 12 percent of the responding operators would prefer a job that did not involve WP. But WP is more specialized than general secretarial work. Most operators regard themselves as specialized technicians. What kind of person becomes a word processor? The response in many sites was: "someone who does not like to get the coffee." Word processors like the sense of doing their own job, a technical job that involves secretarial skills, but is not a secretarial job.

Almost 88 percent of the respondents said that their job gives them the opportunity to do a job from start to finish. Further, this aspect of their job was important to them. Seventy-four percent of all respondents answered that their job has this characteristic and that it is very important to them. There were significant differences ($p < .05$) between workers in centers and in distributed units, but the direction was opposite from that predicted by early writers about WP. Ninety-two percent of workers in centers say they work with a job from start to finish; by contrast 83 percent of distributed users have responsibility for a whole job. There was no difference among operators' response to this variable among the four WP systems (although the variance in response was so low that a statistical difference is not likely).

Thus, managers who assume that workers do not want jobs that provide choice and challenge will design jobs that preclude achieving the potential of WP systems.

Administer Policies with Flexibility

The technology of WP improves efficiency by automating routine work, but routines can reduce flexibility. Flexibility is an essential characteristic of an adaptive system, yet the flexibility in roles and procedures must be consciously managed.

Over half of the respondents in the telephone interviews indicated that procedures had been changed, almost all in the direction of more formality and somewhat less flexibility. The most flexible sites were the expanding ones. Supervisors in these sites brought adaptability into their operations by being flexible. One supervisor in an expanding system, when asked "How do you compensate for the demanding nature of the work?" responded:

"We try not to talk about it outside, but we are more informal about breaks. We let them have a radio if they can agree on a station. We have nice physical surroundings. It is not a typing pool with grey steel desks. This causes problems for us elsewhere, however, because other secretaries don't get these things."

Discretion and flexibility have meaning only within a supportive context, however. In places where other messages tell operators they are unimportant, "flexible" procedures can be insulting. For example:

In a clockwork system where operators are paid on a strict production basis, the company-wide dress code is not enforced in the center. An operator complained: "They don't enforce the dress code here because management thinks we are invisible in here." She sees this sign of flexibility as an insult to her status within the company. "They don't think this is a professional career demanding respect and showing respect through proper dress."

Examples like the one above point to the important underlying attitude about operators' self-concept that flexibility and discretion should express: supervisors and managers sought to have personnel feel better about themselves and their abilities because they used word processors. Good management requires constant attention to the tradeoff of efficiency through discipline and inventiveness through flexibility. Organizations without discipline typically used word processors as typewriters; however, inflexible discipline discouraged new uses.

Provide Opportunities for Upward Mibility

WP provided many people with opportunities that they lacked in a secretarial career. The opportunity to advance in a technical career was the occasion for a change in self-concept for many. The phenomenon of ambition following from opportunity for promotion is described by Kanter in the example of a secretary who described herself as never wanting to be anything but a secretary (1977:135). Then she reluctantly accepted a promotion to assistant manager and found that she had changed her self-image:

"Now I'm ambitious, probably overly so. I will probably work twenty more years, and I expect to move at least six grade levels, maybe to vice president. Isn't that something for me? It's the climate for women now. . . . You learn you can, so you want to do more."

Table 6.2 shows how operators say they have changed their attitudes about work and their position in the organization. Contrary to early fears about WP clerical work, these responses indicated that WP has made people more career-oriented and innovative. WP work has meant increased salary and promotion for some people, though this is not always the case, particularly in government and low-integration sites.

In order to assess the motivations of WP operators, operators were asked if they had considered leaving for a job in another organization and what might be their reason for such a change. Table 6.3 shows the distribution of answers. Those in adapting organizations, especially those in expanding systems, are significantly less inclined to change jobs than are others. For those who are considering leaving, however, their reasons bear no particular relationship to the level of WP system. Table 6.4 summarizes those reasons. Figures on this table are divided into "centers" and "distributed" operations to show that there is also very little difference in motivations of people according to unit structure. Thus, the nature of the WP work unit is associated with *considering* to leave, but not with more general *rationales* for leaving. WP operators on the whole are eager to help the organization and get promoted. For a large majority of these

TABLE 6.2

Changes Attributed to Learning Word Processing

	No	*Little*	*Some*	*Much*
Works harder	25%	5%	27%	53%
More willing to try new things	13	5	28	56
More likely to meet new people	24	20	29	27
More likely to get more exercise	46	22	15	16
Demands higher salary	25	16	28	31
More eager for promotions	17	14	23	46
Total *N*	286			

people, as shown in the table, this motivation resulted from learning WP.

The basic conflict comes when WP operators want to advance, and most of them do want to advance, but find their career potential limited. An executive from an expanding system describes the career potential of WP:

"Promotion from WP is difficult. It is a cul de sac and will remain one until the time the organization goes to electronic mail and a lot more use of information technology, which won't happen any time soon. WP people are organizationally naive. They remind me of the security guard who once said, if they decided to have a VP for security, he wanted to apply for the job. WP is not important enough to have a VP. There is no career path for them here and they don't want to go into secretarial work. That is naive."

TABLE 6.3

Have You Considered Leaving for a Job in Another Organization?

	No Little	*Some Often*	*Total N*
High-integration	49%	51%	53
Expanding	72	38	102
Clockwork	38	72	84
Low-integration	36	64	56

$\chi^2 = 36$; p $<$ .001; $N = 295$

TABLE 6.4

Reasons for Considering Another Job

	Center	*Distributed*
More pay	88%	92%
More career potential	87	94
More diversity	74	75
More contact with people	54	53
More say in decisions	65	63
Total *N*	200	89

Career opportunities for WP operators expand when centers move to decentralize, as noted in the Best Case example in the beginning of the chapter. Site visits indicated that adaptive units were likely to be found in those organizations that systematically prepared WP operators for new responsibilities and put them into career ladders with growth potential. As an example:

In describing why her unit (an expanding one) performed better than a clockwork unit in the same company, one operator explained, "The pay scale is the same, but because this is the computer division, we can move into different positions, like technical writing and programming. In the center, they can't get a better job without leaving."

SKILLS AND ERGONOMICS

Much research about WP jobs, as well as popular accounts in the media, tends to concentrate on two issues: the fragmentation of WP work, and the physical stress and possible harm of working with video terminals. For example, Buchanan and Boddy (1982) found that operators became *less* skilled in some ways (less fear of error, less concern for spacing and format, less need to know technical terms related to layout, less understanding of authors' special needs) but *more* skilled in others (constant relearning of formatting and editing codes, greater concentration, handling lost or erased files). A sample of German operators was considerably more pessimistic, disagreeing with many positive specific statements about VDT use, but holding overall positive sentiments (Staehle 1982). This section briefly summarizes the findings from the telephone interviews and the operator questionnaires concerning these two issues.

Word Processing Skills

The evidence tends, if anything, to indicate that WP has raised skill requirements for clerical employees, not lowered them. While secretaries in Hicks' study (1984) reported that OA would improve aspects of work such as speed, accuracy, and productivity, over three-quarters also felt that OA would improve their job skills, and that OA was beneficial overall to secretaries. Indeed, WP jobs require more expertise than the work force in 1980–83 provided. Forty-four percent of the respondents in the telephone survey indicated that the availability of qualified WP operators was "poor"; 19 percent said it was marginally satisfactory; only 37 percent said it was "good." Because of the job requirements, 52 percent of respondents indicated that new hires had to have prior experience. Of respondents who answered the question (sixty-eight of the two hundred), 60 percent indicated that temporary help experienced in WP was used to fill in while searching for qualified personnel.

Reports of "poor" availability came mostly from government agencies in Washington, D.C. (64 percent reported "poor" availability), insurance companies (54 percent), and communication technology organizations (60 percent). Overall, public organizations reported having more difficulty in finding qualified personnel (59 percent) than private organizations (41 percent). One conclusion of a nationwide survey of five hundred companies by Kelly Services mirrors our results: "The supply of fully qualified employees will continue to lag behind demand, frustrating employers who attempt to staff automated offices solely by recruiting" (results reported in Hubbart 1983).

Low job classification and accompanying low pay appear to be a reason for the lack of qualified people. Low pay scales are particularly a problem in Washington, D.C., where law offices often pay twice as much as government agencies. A WP operator may be classified, in the government service job rankings, as GS-2 to GS-4; with such low pay grades, the federal ranks are filled with people who are there to get training and move on.

Agencies differ in their response to policies that keep them from paying operators more. One organization hired high school students part time. They were using equipment that was ten years old while new equipment, delivered a year before, sat untouched. The supervisor feared her staff would be unable to learn the equipment. In fact, the operators there were eagerly awaiting training because once trained, they would have marketable skills to go elsewhere.

As a contrast, another agency was acquiring word processors for use by professionals. The consensus here is that with electronics, most of the functions of clerical support can be replaced. An agency lawyer, for example, said that a support person would be useful to run errands, but that he and his professional staff (GS-10 and above) were handling all the information and document tasks done by clericals in other organizations. His uses were among the most adaptive and he could cite savings of several million dollars that might have been spent unprofitably had he not developed information uses for WP machines.

The most frequent way government agencies get around policy regulations is to use secretaries to do WP work on a part-time basis. Secretaries, according to long-standing government personnel policies, are paid on a higher scale. Most managers therefore abandoned WP centers because they could not provide incentives to keep good operators. The equipment is underutilized because no one encourages communication about system uses, no one provides rewards for adaptations, and no one standardizes codes, protocols, or priorities. This use of WP has consistently been criticized by investigations of the General Accounting Office (GAO 1979, 1982). There were few places where federal supervisors had succeeded in gaining the higher pay grades necessary to keep good people.

Personnel classification issues are a part of a larger issue of whether policies and procedures can keep up with technology. What happens when new technology creates new kinds of jobs and indeed new organizational boundaries? Figures from the Kelly survey noted above show that nearly half of the companies reported a belief that current job categories will be changed by office automation; further, 64 percent reported that technology changes will lead to upgrades in some categories. Classification personnel have traditionally been a bulwark for conservatism in organizations. Designing organizational policies to respond to the new demands, such as pay and reward schemes, career mobility, and job classification, will be a significant challenge for human resource departments.

Ergonomics: Health and Human Factors in WP Work

There has been a tremendous outpouring of literature dealing with empirical studies of office equipment design, use, and impacts; proposals for the establishment of standards for equipment use; and regulatory and union policies defining the contexts and limitations of office equipment (Grandjean 1983; Panel 1983; *VDT News* 1984; *9-to-5* 1984; Smith 1984).

The National Institute of Occupational Safety and Health studied clerical and professional workers at five California office facilities: 250 VDT users, and 150 nonusers. Table 6.5 summarizes some of its findings.

The NIOSH and some European studies have concluded that one-third of operators using VDTs for most of the day complain almost daily; more time spent using a VDT was associated with more fatigue; there were more eye-related complaints in situations of poor lighting and poor VDT quality and poor furniture; and the type of work as well as fear of automation, of unemployment, and of new technologies influenced negative attitudes toward VDTs. Overall, twenty-five health complaints were more frequent among clerical VDT users than among nonusers (Cohen 1983; Grandjean 1983).

Nine-to-Five magazine conducted a large-scale survey on work and stress, polling readers of four women's magazines, resulting in a sample size of 4,487 (*9-to-5* 1984). Nearly half used office automation

TABLE 6.5

Summary of Selected Results of NIOSH Study on Stress and Health Complaints of VDT Users and Non-Users

	VDT Users		
Complaints	*Clerical*	*Professional*	*Non-Users*
Stress			
Bored	48%	15%	23%
Have to work too hard	76	53	61
Worry about reprimands	24	3	8
Health Complaints			
Burning eyes	80		44
Blurred vision	71		35
Back pain	78		56
Hand cramps	49		16
Skin rashes	57		31
Fainting	36		17

equipment with video screens. Of those respondents, nearly two-thirds of clerical workers and three-quarters of both managerial and professional workers reported that using OA equipment made their job more interesting; half overall said that work was less stressful and easier. Although only about a fifth of each of the three categories of workers werre involved in work that was machine monitored, about 50 percent of those who were monitored felt their work was *very* stressful compared to 30 percent of all OA workers. If monitored, workers reported significantly more headaches, nausea, dizziness, exhaustion, fatigue, anxiety, anger, depression, and medical problems. The study noted that the work itself of these people may be more standardized and routine, so monitoring is confounded with these attributes.

Overall, in the *9-to-5* study, OA users reported slightly higher levels of health problems, but the differences were greater among occupational groups and job titles (i.e., more so for clericals than for managers) than between users and nonusers. The study concluded that

it appears that the conditions at work—how much control you do or do not have, how much interest or challenge there is in your job, whether or not you have the clout or authority to go with the pressures and responsibility, what your work relations are like—are the greatest sources of stress (1984:5–6).

Another large-scale survey interviewed over five hundred end users of office automation technology. Sixty to 70 percent of intensive VDT users reported bad effects; less than 10 percent of the 110 organizations had most of their VDTs in "satisfactory" condition—as classified by the responding managers (Westin et al. 1985). This study's conclusions also found that bad health effects were worse in jobs with higher control and pressure.

Reviewing most of the ergonomic studies of VDT work, Smith also concluded that "job demands, both physical and psychological, influence the type, severity and frequency of VDT operators' health complaints" (1984:209). The *amount* of VDT use was not nearly as strong a predictor as was the *type* of VDT work; jobs with insufficient participation, inadequate training, job insecurity, high stress, greater role ambiguity, performance monitoring, and close supervision were strongly associated with health problems.

The present study did not attempt to measure physical ailments or stress, but did ask operators a series of questions about their environment and its affect on their work. Table 6.6 is a summary of the machine use statistics of approximately three hundred operators who completed the questionnaire. Table 6.7 report operators' responses to a series of questions about how physical surroundings affect their work. Note that two-thirds to three-quarters of the respondents reported no, okay, or good effects of characteristics of the physical workplace or the equipment. However, a quarter to a third reported bad effects; this figure, even if a minority, still represents an unacceptable component of WP work. Other studies have reported that clerical workers complain about air quality, privacy, and lack of storage space, the major complaints here. Significant relationships between usage and bad effects are indicated in the first column. Infrequent users of VDTs tended to have more complaints about screen glare. Cross-tabulations of these physical effects with the four kinds of systems revealed a significant relationship only between air quality and clockwork systems—operators in clockwork systems complain more that poor air quality harmfully affects their work $\chi^2 = 16.6$; $p < .04$).

There is only anecdotal evidence that operators who are rigidly controlled complain more about their physical surroundings; the most explicit example is the "Worst Case" at the beginning of the chapter. However, the statistical analysis shows that perceived negative effects of the *physical* surroundings are *not* much associated with, or mitigated by, level of WP system. In one sense, this result emphasizes the importance of management policies in facilitating innovative work. Changing the physical surroundings is not sufficient. On the other hand, better-designed jobs do not much affect people's reports of the effects of their physical surroundings.

CONCLUSION

One common stereotype of WP operators is that they are resistant to technology and are forced to work in isolated centers without contact with authors; they know of or care little about the organization and its mission; their skills are degraded; and they suffer from eye

TABLE 6.6

Equipment Use Summary

	Center *(N = 200)*	Distributed *(N =89)*
Percentage of time at keyboard		
10–30	15%	37%
40–70	22	24
80+	63	39
Terminal for exclusive use?	80%	22%
Share with how many?	0	4
How many years on current machine?		
<1	8%	15%
1	44	27
2–3	38	47
4+	10	11
How long to be competent?		
0–2 mos.	67%	68%
3–4 mos.	16	15
5–6 mos.	12	12
7+ mos.	5	5

and back strain due to poorly designed equipment. In contrast, operators in this sample had positive attitudes about the technology, enjoyed their contact with others, and generally enjoyed their work except under situations of inflexible management, work measurement, and lack of career mobility.

The discussion has not been so concerned with how to make jobs better as with the relationship of jobs to productive organizations. There was systematic evidence across the cases that better jobs indeed produce more adaptations and more challenging work. In particular, productive jobs in WP:

1. Promote self-regulation.
2. Provide a sense of the whole job and discretion in doing work.
3. Have flexibility.
4. Provide opportunities for upward mobility.

WP operators do suffer from some physical conditions of their surroundings, but not in such large numbers as is reported in the popular press. The general measure of WP system level used in this

TABLE 6.7

Effects of Physical Surroundings

	Good effect	OK or none	Bad effect
Light conditions	34%	52%	14%
Level of noise	22	46	33
Amount of desktop	26	42	32
Height of keyboards	45	50	5
Chair support	33	47	20
Screen glare[a]	23	50	28
Air quality[b]	23	52	25
Heating[b]	20	53	27
Air conditioning	21	51	28
Attractiveness	29	50	21
Privacy	16	41	43
Storage space	18	48	34
Access to people[b]	44	47	9
Access to equipment	47	44	12
Access to supplies	45	47	8
Total N	289		

[a] = worse for infrequent users
[b] = worse for frequent users

research is not associated with different levels of health complaints. However, the level of WP system is not a direct measure of control, stress, pressure, or rigid procedures. Thus, management must consider two distinct goals: improve the nature of WP jobs, and improve the ergonomic aspects of WP jobs.

The reason why good jobs promote adaptation may be as simple as that people want to stay in good jobs, and longevity promotes expertise absolutely required in adapting WP. As one supervisor of an expanding system put it: "We want them to stay." It is likely that the reasons why good jobs promote good work go beyond longevity, however. Good jobs promote appreciation of the potential for WP, help operators to understand the mission of the organization, give them the discretion to promote change, and motivate them with the possibility of promotion.

Chapter 7

Adaptation in Word Processing Work: Achieving and Adapting Organizational Goals Through Participation, Continuous Learning, Experimentation and Communication

It is reasonable to hypothesize that the extent to which individuals understand the interrelationship of organizational mission, technical possibilities, and social aspects of their work influences the amount of adaptation that occurs. This understanding is created in the everyday conversations of work group members, and communicated by work design in which people see the relationship of their work to the overall mission of the organization. These principles need to become part of the overall culture and functioning of the operation. Managers and supervisors have a direct role in fostering good WP jobs. Unfortunately, this understanding is extremely difficult to measure directly. This chapter employs a number of measures related to the concept of adaptation, but none that exactly pins it down.

This chapter explores the relationship of four principles described in chapter 5—participation, learning, experimentation, and communication—to adaptation. First, two extreme cases from the legal profession are presented to show how these relations develop in one type of work. Then, each of the four principles is discussed by referring to data from the telephone interviews and the site visits. In the subsequent section, responses from operators are specifically analyzed to identify organizational practices and individual characteristics that are associated with individual adaptiveness. Finally, the forms of WP systems—centers and distributed units—are compared with respect to these principles.

REPRESENTATIVE CASES

Many respondents in law offices—both public and private—told us that "WP was invented for law offices." Because legal work is largely based on information retrieval and document manipulation—a prime example of information work—WP has an immediately recognizable benefit. Lawyers are "wordsmiths," as one respondent told us, and therefore the ability of word processors to facilitate basic revisions makes the introduction of even relatively unsophisticated text processing systems extremely valuable to legal work.

Yet most respondents clearly saw that the potential of WP is seldom realized. WP in most legal firms and legal departments is organized in the form of the roles, procedures, and uses characterized in chapter 4 as the most common version of WP. Centers are the common organizational form; text editing is virtually the only use, though telecommunications is a growing practice; boilerplating is uncommon. Secretaries type drafts and send them to WP centers for revisions. The major technological adaptation is the use of OCRs as an input device.

Thus legal offices form a subgroup that illustrates with particular clarity the dynamics of choices involved in the evolution of WP systems. Two such sites are described here.

Public Legal Work—A Low-Integration Site

This first legal office, though a low-integration system, actually performs better than several others in this classification because unlike them it does have a coordinator who oversees operations and has introduced some adaptations. WP equipment was brought in on a pilot basis because of an overload on secretaries, a lack of standardization, excessive reproduction of briefs, and generally poor-quality work. In the words of the coordinator: "We were getting killed!" (Many here use war metaphors to explain the work.)

Coordination of WP is fragmented and insufficient both for the needs of legal work and for the motivation of adaptations. Three reasons for this situation have to do with communication.

First, there is no clear direction from executives in the organization in support of coordinated WP delivery. Middle-level managers, in particular those with political clout, must trust the center to handle their documentation if a center is to succeed. One attorney who worked with a center in another office explains the problems that result from a lack of coordinated WP effort:

"You cannot give maximum support to an attorney on an important case unless that attorney can have behind him or her the same kind of support that a large law firm can provide. That means centralizing the services so that at any one time, sufficient staff can be allocated to a crucial task—even if it is for a day or two—which is about all that is ever required. But when personnel is needed, it cannot be had. It is distributed all over the place and everyone is working on their own thing. So the most support an attorney can ever get here is probably a secretary."

Second, the language of the attorneys in the office reinforced the value of secretaries over WP operators. A lawyer could say of a document: "I gave it to *my* secretary" instead of "I gave it to the WP unit." Symbolic rewards are important here and secretaries are one of the few status symbols available. In organizations where status differentials are particularly important, technological change threatens these relations. Across the sample, in those organizations where much of the communication was implicitly about status, little adaptation of the system occurred.

Third, poor communication with and administration by the central office in Washington prevented the development of effective centralization of WP services. Regulations by the U.S. Office of Personnel Management prohibit hiring a WP operator above the GS-4 grade. Public law offices have ways of getting around this policy so that they can hire more highly skilled people. The most common way is to distribute the equipment and call the operators "secretaries."

In this law office, since the legal secretaries (GS-6) do their own WP, they can be classified according to their legal knowledge rather than the tools they use.

Communication and participation problems impede productivity here. The coordinator's position is weak and therefore management varies from division to division. In one division an attorney uses the word processor to analyze the caseload of each attorney before assigning a new case. Another uses it to analyze information about recent court decisions. But managers in other divisions know little of the system. Secretaries in one area have organized their work and their work space so they can do both administrative work like handling phone calls and get their typing done. Others are frustrated by conflicts over who gets the equipment at critical times. In other places knowledge of machine operation is so concentrated in one person that when she is gone, the work stops.

The "Bloomingdale's" Law Office—A High-Integration Site

Martha started at a high-technology chemical firm six years ago when she was nineteen years old. She went to WP school to learn basic functions and then returned six months later to learn how to use programmable keys. Today she is in charge of a center of four operators supporting the patent department at the firm.

Her center is unique among legal offices in the sample: the two terminals allotted for use by attorneys (four hours at a time) in fact produce more lines than the terminals used by the WP operators themselves. Martha and the operators set out from the start to support attorneys doing their own work. The outcome shows what can result from such an exercise of creative vision.

"The secret to the work we do here is programmable keys. Once I learned about those, I could see the possibilities. Each attorney has his or her own programmed keys; we figured out how to get eighty-five combinations that take us all the way through some pretty complex decision processing. Most attorneys aren't technical enough to understand how to change programmable keys; most just don't want to, though some do. We make everything simple for them so that it is easier than using a pen. They get simple instructions on how to insert and delete. All the memo formats are set up. The date, the subject line, and their name is entered automatically. We maintain seven hundred archives. Usually, they can find information faster than we can. Everyone knows how to supercopy.

"The operators and I are learning to program in BASIC because many of the things we want to do require it. For example, we have outlined a file index system for tracking case dockets. It will require a calendar function. Because the file will be bigger than our system, we will tie into the main computer, so we have to use a database structure consistent with it."

Martha rotates supervisory responsibilities on a regular basis. Each of her operators relayed the same sentiments: they like their job; the site is an exciting place to work; they are encouraged to learn more and more and to do more and more to improve the operation. Each described her ambitions to be a WP supervisor.

When Martha was asked how her WP operation differs from others at her organization and elsewhere, the supervisor replied, "We're Bloomingdale's." She emphasizes style. She works hard. The result is an operation where operators and attorneys cooperate to get the work out. She maintains excellent communications with the executives who control the budget for her department. She asks for and gets the very best furnishings and equipment. Commenting on another legal office in the same corporation which does not receive such resources, Martha said, "They think text editing. We think computer!"

Why is it necessary to have leadership by a WP professional?

"You can't be strong enough if you don't know the technology. Mostly, you must be able to see the big picture so you can forecast five years ahead. You have to see your final product in advance. It's not as important to know what you want as it is to know what you *don't* want."

APPLICATIONS OF THE FOUR PRINCIPLES

The two cases give some flavor of the role of involvement, continuous learning, experimentation, and communication in fostering more satisfying and more adaptive WP jobs. The telephone survey and the sixty site visits provide information on the extent to which these principles are implemented, and their relation to WP adaptations. The results are summarized for each of the four principles.

Principle 1: Involve People in Changes

In less than half of the organizations surveyed by telephone were authors or operators involved in implementing decisions. Most organizations did not conduct assessments of employee attitudes. In general, planning focused more on equipment choices than on the relationship of the technology to organizational missions. Social and organizational arrangements tended to be seen as problems to be overcome, rather than opportunities for adaptation; solutions to such problems were left to chance in all but a few cases. Where people participated in changing their jobs and designing equipment uses, they often were able to invent uses that increased organizational capabilities, such as tracking loan authorizations and improving coordination methods. The capabilities in even relatively low-level staff to generate new ideas and applications of technology are usually underestimated by organizational planners.

Site visits reinforced this conclusion, but revealed differences according to WP system level. Clerical participation in initial decisions about the implementation of WP was usually limited. This was particularly the case in nonadaptive low-integration and clockwork sites. However, consider the process of an expanding site:

In an adaptive consulting firm, WP operator input was solicited during a needs assessment study, during the development of new procedures to guide WP, and during on-site demonstrations of potential equipment. The supervisor was allowed to critique the needs assessment report completed by the consultants. Operators and supervisors provided input for their own job descriptions.

Equipment change after initial installation more typically involved operators. In clockwork systems, however, this involvement was usually limited to technical questions about equipment choice. In expanding and high-integration sites, however, clerical employees often insisted on more widespread participation on both social and technical issues, and made their input felt to good effect. For example, at one site a group initiated by a secretary attempts to keep up on equipment, ensure appropriate training, provide insights into staffing, and improve communication between regions. They worked 1½ years building their credibility, forming subgroups for different tasks and concerns.

The participation items on the operators' questionnaire indicated that, indeed, participation in regular meetings about WP utilization took place more often in adaptive sites than in nonadaptive sites. Table 7.1 shows the frequencies. But regular meetings are not enough. Problems resulting from a lack of consideration of social or technical effects were mentioned frequently by respondents in many contexts.

For example, the WP supervisor in one organization described the office automation strategy of her corporation: the OA planners simply told her to choose among five systems they had identified. The result of this procedure was that the OA planners chose a system that will not meet her needs or offer her much advantage.

"I told them to get business people involved. OA people talk the whole picture, but they never sit down and say, 'OK, say what you need on a day-to-day basis.' They are not looking at things like vertical spacing, so we won't be able to use the system established."

Some organizations establish quality circles in order to get WP people participating in organizational decision making. Respondents

TABLE 7.1

Participation in Regular Meetings

	None	Work Group Only	In Org.	Outside Org.	Total N
High-integration	15.2%	15.9%	36.1%	27.3%	50
Expanding	28.0	40.9	44.4	27.3	92
Clockwork	29.5	29.5	8.3	36.4	72
Low-integration	27.3	13.6	11.1	9.1	53

$\chi^2 = 24.3$; $p < .005$; $N = 267$

were generally skeptical of this approach to participation. A typical remark was:

"Quality circles don't work—not enough time is allowed. The facilitator does not know the technical part of our work."

This intuitive response to quality circles echoes just one of the numerous inherent difficulties of quality circles identified by Lawler and Mohrman (1985). Quality circles can lay the initial groundwork for advisory groups, business teams or semiautonomous work groups, but those developments require skilled management of organizational design. Setting up mechanisms for participation in joint optimization requires understanding whose work will be changed and how they need to work with others. Those who try to facilitate such change have to be nearly as knowledgeable as those affected if these participative mechanisms are to operate effectively.

Principle 2: Provide Opportunities for Continuous Learning

Telephone interviews indicated that training, and maintaining professional awareness of WP practices and developments, are typically underemphasized.

Some operators received no formal WP training. Most operators reported, however, that it took them six to ten months to learn to use the machine. Almost all operators reported that they would have to learn more to use their equipment to greater potential. Training that does occur is usually limited to how to operate the keyboard. Except for occasional vendor-sponsored users' meetings, few operators received training on how the equipment might be used to increase capabilities.

Less than half found vendor training useful even for beginning to work on the system; very few found vendors helpful for ongoing training. The largest organizations usually have their own formal training programs, but most organizations do not. These findings are similar to those in Hicks' survey (1984), which reported that only 60 percent of the responding secretaries had training in their organization.

Only about one-fourth of the sample read WP-related publications regularly. Few operators are active in professional organizations;

about half (55 percent) of supervisors or managers belong to WP associations.

Results from a related study of 378 users of information system workstations in fifty-five offices in twenty-six firms ephasized some of the same points: there was a need for vendors to provide more training and support, organizations should provide ongoing training, self-instruction was insufficient, training should emphasize long-term objectives rather than initial use, and it should be broad in approach and keyed to the work unit's mission (Bikson and Gutek 1983).

Site visits reinforced these findings and provided examples of how training increases employees' choices about how to solve job-related problems. Given the seemingly obvious advantages of training, it was surprising to find how little of it organizations provide. For example:

Operators in a financial consulting firm receive no formal training; one operator quit for lack of training. The reason for no training? They are too rushed to train people. Whether training would increase productivity enough to counter their rush was apparently given little thought.

A user in a public service company was provided with her own terminal but received no formal training. This is characteristic of organizations where professionals key. Professionals tend to learn WP on their own.

Training and other means of increasing knowledge about how to use WP and possible applications receive high priority in organizations in adaptive WP sites. Usually, someone within WP is assigned responsibility for this training. Sometimes, someone is assigned responsibility for discovering new procedures and applications.

One of the goals of WP in a large hospital is "to train everybody." With the acquisition of new equipment, training will be offered to WP supervisors, center operators, satellite operators, and users. All managers who wish to be trained will be accommodated.

Over half of the scientists in a private company have received formal WP training. These professionals key their own material and ask operators to perform editing. Professionals reported that keying material themselves has improved their writing skills. Advanced WP training is now scheduled to begin.

Analysis of the operators' responses, as shown in tables 7.2 and 7.3, reveals that two training factors are closely related to the degree of work unit adaptation: (a) Conceptual training, not just routine keystroke instruction: "Training helped me understand how word processors think," and (b) A continuous learning environment: "Still learning new ways to use WP."

In each of the high integration sites, it was possible to identify a person assigned as a liaison trainer to work with employees. In some cases, a person who showed an early interest was reassigned to training responsibilities. In other cases, an outsider was hired whose job was to make sure that everyone in the work unit was a proficient user of the system. In some instances, these trainers were "temps," or people hired from agencies to temporarily staff a position. In addition to skills in how to use equipment, their experience with a

TABLE 7.2

Training Helps Me to Understand How Word Processors Think

	No	Little	Some	Much	Total N
High-integration	5%	5%	41%	48%	54
Expanding	4	11	42	44	101
Clockwork	1	6	53	40	90
Low-integration	5	30	38	27	56

$\chi^2 = 34.6$; p $< .00$; $N = 301$

TABLE 7.3

Still Learning New Ways to Use Word Processing

	No	Little	Some	Much	Total N
High-integration	2%	22%	61%	26%	60
Expanding	5	26	52	18	101
Clockwork	2	23	59	21	86
Low-integration	16	24	40	20	55

$\chi^2 = 22.6$; p $< .03$; $N = 301$

variety of organizations gave them better ideas about what to use the equipment for. About 10 percent of the telephone survey respondents said that their "training" had been done by temps, not by conscious design, but just because they had the ideas and the answers to questions when the regular workers were still struggling.

Principle 3: Encourage Experimentation

Few of the organizations in the telephone survey reported formal encouragement of experimentation. Only a handful of sites gave tangible rewards for adaptations; almost half the respondents complained that there is little or no time available to experiment with new methods.

Yet many respondents spoke of the need to experiment; as one put it, "In word processing, there is always a better way." Only one respondent said that the center was so well planned, no changes were (or presumably ever would be) necessary.

These results, although discouraging, are apparently typical according to other surveys about employee innovation. A Gallup poll involving 1,500 employees found that about 44 percent of the respondents spent a "lot of time" and 18 percent "some time" thinking about changes that could be made in the job or company to improve its performance. They even replied that the most common place (53 percent) to implement changes that would bring about performance improvements was their own attitudes and abilities, ahead of management's attitudes (37 percent), tools, rules, technology, etc. (Chamber of Commerce 1980). In a similar large survey, while 37 percent of the employees felt that having more say in decisions that affected them would contribute to overall productivity, only 16 percent of executives agreed. Conversely, while 67 percent of executives felt that the use of better equipment and tools would have such an effect, only 29 percent of employees agreed (Harris 1981). Another survey of 249 managers and technical professionals in R&D or planning departments found that the respondents valued innovation "more than they felt it was valued in their organizations" (Baran, Zandan, and Vanston 1986:24). When asked how often they were explicitly encouraged to be innovative in their work, about a third reported "frequently" or "always," and about a third said "rarely" or "never." In that study, implicit communication about innovation was more frequent and apparently important.

Site visits indicated that in organizations where people are finding new ways of extending their capability they (a) are encouraged to experiment (though seldom given time to do so), and (b) understand that their efforts to develop new methods and procedures are appreciated.

Adapters receive praise for turning ideas into new practices. The differences in terms of the experimentation and encouragement variables between adapting sites and others were striking, as shown in tables 7.4 and 7.5.

Results from questions about praise from coworkers and authors for adaptations are similar to those in table 7.5. In nonadapting organizations development of new uses and procedures is only sometimes assigned to operators. Often the work is shared on the basis of seniority, with only a few given the opportunity to experiment. In adaptive organizations, even when there is a career ladder that provides more "systems analysis" work for more advanced personnel, the new employees are encouraged to experiment.

Table 7.6 shows that talk about adaptation is strongly related to the development of new uses and procedures. Unit adaptiveness seems fostered by managerial encouragement of communication among coworkers. Thus, WP work and adaptations require training, time, and encouragement. However, most WP installations are viewed by outsiders as "magic rooms," where drafts are transformed into finished copy "with the wave of an electronic wand."

TABLE 7.4

Encouragement to Experiment

	None	*Little*	*Some*	*Much*	*Total N*
High-integration	9%	30%	41%	20%	54
Expanding	17	30	34	22	103
Clockwork	20	21	40	18	84
Low-integration	31	45	18	5	55
$\chi^3 = 27.7$; p $<$ .00; $N = 296$					

TABLE 7.5

Praise from Supervisor for Adapting

	None	Little	Some	Much	Total N
High-integration	7%	15%	43%	35%	46
Expanding	16	15	37	33	89
Clockwork	17	15	43	25	84
Low-integration	40	20	26	14	50

$\chi^2 = 30.1$; $p < .00$; $N = 269$

TABLE 7.6

Talk About Adaptation with Coworkers

	None	Seldom	Some	Often	Total N
High-integration	2%	15%	50%	33%	54
Expanding	10	17	48	28	103
Clockwork	8	15	38	38	86
Low-integration	19	11	43	26	53

$\chi^2 = 21.7$; $p < .04$; $N = 296$

Authors tend to view WP as an "event," rather than a continuing process, and they assign responsibility for missed deadlines to operators, ignoring factors under their own control (e.g., bad handwriting, frequent changes, looking over operators' shoulders, waiting until the last minute to rush something through, etc.). The reason? Authors see WP as a sort of public utility, a service they have a right to—as one said, "You don't thank a highway, you take for granted that it will be there." Where WP functions effectively, authors have been "educated" on the process, functions, and procedures of WP, and managers support a climate for adaptation. Where this does not happen, the mutual understanding necessary to make complex sociotechnical systems work is generally slow to evolve, if it ever does.

Principle 4: Design Work Units to Optimize Communication

As the tables above, and other data, indicate, communication among peers and between support personnel and others is a source of creativity and problem solving as well as increased quality of work life.

Indeed, two-thirds of the telephone survey respondents judged "relationships with coworkers" as a "great" or "very great" motivator of people operating WP equipment. Although informal contacts with others throughout the company are encouraged in about half of the sites, in some cases contacts are definitely discouraged. Thus many organizations are deliberately cutting themselves off from an important source of motivation and innovation.

While the literature on organizational communication's influence on satisfaction and performance is too broad to be reviewed here, the general conclusion from various reviews is that the more open, trusting, and participative the superior-subordinate relationship is perceived to be by the subordinate, the more satisfied the subordinate is likely to be with his or her job and organization (Pincus 1986). While the link between satisfaction and actual performance is not as convincing or pervasive, Pincus did find significant correlations of employees' performance with communication. In this and other reviewed studies, the forms of communication that had the most consistent relation with satisfaction and performance were supervisory communication, communication climate, and personal feedback to the worker.

In low-integration systems, communication is seldom encouraged. People operating WP equipment seldom meet to discuss common problems and share creative ideas. In adaptive work units—both centralized and decentralized—communication is encouraged informally, through informal meetings and people assigned as liaisons who spread ideas about applications and short cuts.

The stereotype that WP work is a low clerical function best done by sitting for hours undisturbed at a machine is prevalent especially among upper administrators with little or no direct contact with the actual nature of the work. Overcoming that stereotype takes a supervisor committed to keeping WP activities integrated with the rest of the organization.

Innovations diffuse via the process of communication. It is not surprising, therefore, that where communication is discouraged, there will be little innovation, and implementation tends to be mechanical rather than adaptive. Consider the following example from the site visits:

In a computer company, one professional holds responsibility for training clients who purchase the company's WP systems. She frequently learns new ways to operate and adapt the equipment to a variety of tasks. She is the resident expert trainer on this equipment. Company secretaries use the firm's WP equipment, but receive no formal training. The trainer writes a newsletter for clients which describes these tips and innovations, but does not provide copies to the company secretaries. Secretaries do not share their learning with each other. They just do not think to or do not have time to. For example, the trainer learned from a client how to underscore single words on this system. One of the secretaries discovered on her own how to do this. Three months later, another secretary asked her if she knew how to do it. So three months went by in ignorance for the second secretary and the first secretary struggled on her own to discover this method, while the trainer knew how all along.

Channels of communication are more open in sites that display adaptiveness:

In a large military systems consulting company, two liaisons connect four WP centers. New ideas and methods diffuse from center to center by this means. Most new methods are recorded in a binder, available to all centers. Additionally, the managers of information processing, each in a different building and heading four large WP centers, confer almost daily.

Communication in adaptive systems was not only (a) open and (b) topically related to adaptation; it was also (c) structured to involve appropriate people in the work process. Specifically, both authors and secretaries were seen as important in WP work, and communication was structured to include them. Consider the contrast in attitudes about the importance of communication with authors, first from a clockwork site, then from an expanding one:

"We try to discourage authors from talking to operators because operators are paid and evaluated on the basis of their production quotas."

"When operators have responsibilities for certain users, they get to know each other both as people and in work roles. It leads to things like candy and flowers from the users to the operators at Christmas, birthdays, special occasions, etc. That helps make work tolerable—even enjoyable."

There were few organizations where relationships between secretaries and WP personnel were particularly warm, but in adaptive systems, the supervisors understood the importance of communication with secretaries. Consider these examples, first from a clockwork system, then from an expanding one:

"There's quite a battle between the center personnel and secretaries in satellites. Center people don't want to be bothered by secretaries. Secretaries aren't part of the Quality Assurance Program. They are addicted to attention from their bosses. They refuse training, yet want to bother us with all their problems."

"Whenever we start a new project, we make the announcement to secretaries first. Their noses would be out of joint if they weren't in on it first."

OPERATORS AS ADAPTERS

Much of the discussion thus far has concerned adaptivity of the work unit. The fourfold distinction between levels of WP systems is based primarily on the judgments of the researchers. Individuals' perceptions of their own adaptiveness provides another perspective. Most operators at adaptive sites reported high self-esteem and a self-image of themselves as "innovative." WP operators in general see themselves as innovators and feel they could do much to improve the organization. In response to the question, "Do you enjoy seeking new ways to do things?" the overwhelming majority—70 percent—said "very much." Another 27 percent said "some." Only one of the three hundred respondents said no. To the question, "Do you find ways of solving a problem when there doesn't at first seem to be a way?" 41 percent said "often"; 48 percent said "sometimes." Table 7.7 summarizes the distribution of the individual-level version of the system-level rating: "Do you and your coworkers develop new procedures for using word processing?" This perception of the adaptiveness of oneself and one's coworkers was cross-tabulated with many of the variables representing the current four principles of job design.

Factors That Do Not Predict Operator Adaptation

The list of machine characteristics, personality variables, and participation items in table 7.8 represent much of the conventional wisdom about what makes a good WP operation. To find such features unrelated to adaptation is rather surprising. Self-perceived general innovativeness is not sufficient to lead to reported adaptive behaviors such as the development of WP procedures.

Surprisingly, communication, per se, did not predict adaptation. These results are admittedly perplexing given the important role of operator-author communication identified in the site visits and open-ended interviews. However, identifying the factors that *do* associate with adaptivity clears up this contradiction a bit.

Factors That Do Predict Operator Adaptation

The factors that do predict operator adaptations, as listed in table 7.9, closely parallel the principles that opened this discussion. Also unexpected was that the question on contacts in other parts of the

TABLE 7.7
Operator Development of New Procedures

	Do You Develop New Procedures for WP?
No	12%
Seldom	22
Some	48
Often	19
Total *N*	294

TABLE 7.8

Factors That Do Not Predict Operator Adaptation

Perceived technology attributes
    Reliability
    Ease of use
    Versatility

General innovativeness
    Play computer games
    Seek new ways to do things
    Seek ways to solve problems
    Enjoy being a leader

Communication
    Communicate directly with authors
    Prefer to communicate directly with authors
    Have friends elsewhere in the organization

Organizational orientation
    Talk about organization's product
    Talk about group product
    Think tasks could be done better with WP

Participation in decision making about
    Equipment choice
    Maintenance
    Personnel performance criteria

---

organizations was not associated with adaptation, because in the original survey of organizations the question, "How many of the staff have informal contacts around the organization that are sometimes useful to their work?" was the greatest predictor of creative changes in the work. It may be that this last question was too general to capture the specific communications related to adaptation; it may be that the level of communication perceived by an adaptive respondent may be scaled, psychologically, differently than that perceived by a less adaptive person. It is more plausible that relationships with friends in the organization are simply not specific or work-oriented enough to affect the development of new procedures. Further, as self-perceived innovativeness is not related to that variable, this common correlate of innovativeness (extent of interpersonal network, cosmopoliteness) would not be expected to be related either.

TABLE 7.9
Factors That Predict Operator Adaptation

Training
Helped me understand how word processors think
Still learning new ways to use WP
Experimentation encouraged by organization
Time available for experimentation
Organization encourages experimentation
Policies do not discourage experimentation
Communication
Talk about adaptation with coworkers, supervisor, authors
Participate in meetings where uses and procedures are discussed
Receive praise for adaptation from coworkers and supervisor
Participation in decision making about
Unit productivity
Formatting procedures
Training

It was expected that talk about the organization and the group's product, i.e., organizational mission, would be related to adaptation. Talk about product usually indicates an understanding of the wider significance of one's task. Yet, the questionnaire responses gave no reason to believe that an operator's concern for the mission of the organization and how best to improve performance toward that mission was useful in encouraging adaptation. It seems that concern for mission must be more complex than simply "talk about the organization's final product."

Most people in WP supervision spend a great deal of time in deciding on equipment choice. To the extent that they think that operators should be involved in decision making, it is decisions about equipment choice. There was no relationship between participation in *equipment* choice and operator adaptiveness. The lack of association emphasizes how the *form* of technology, even as influenced by users' involvement, does not necessarily determine its *use* or *role*.

Interesting to note, however, is that supervisor/managers and operators had very different perceptions of how much say operators have in these decisions. Table 7.10 shows just how wide this disagreement is. Supervisors report that operators have much more say in these decisions than operators report they have. While the supervisors may have a better understanding of the organization's constraints limiting any involvement—including their own—and thus may tend to perceive operators' involvement as considerable, operators nevertheless see a significant gap between the potential and the actual level of decision making they are allowed.

In a well-designed sociotechnical system, there is an emphasis on increasing the "response repertoire" of employees. The emphasis is on increasing the overall competence of people to achieve goals rather than on skills per se. The two training questions that relate to adaptation are not questions about "Did you learn how to operate the machine?" Rather, they ask whether training increased the ability of the respondents to make decisions. Operating a machine competently requires choosing the best approach for any particular task and that, in turn, requires some knowledge of machine logic that can be formally or informally acquired.

As many operators emphasized, training is an ongoing activity. Seventy-five percent of the responding operators said they became "competent" in three months or less; the interviews confirmed that operators understood the term "competent" to mean they had no

TABLE 7.10

Perceptions of Operator Input into Decision Making

	Operators' Report				Supervisors' Report			
Kind of Decision	*None*	*Little*	*Some*	*Much*	*None*	*Little*	*Some*	*Much*
Equipment choice	69.9%	16.1%	14.7%	4.2%	40.0%	35.0%	16.2%	8.7%
			($N = 85$)				($N = 80$)	
Maintenance	60.7	16.4	13.2		30.0	28.7	22.5	18.8
			($N = 280$)				($N = 80$)	
Appraisal criteria	57.5	18.5	16.4	7.7	27.8	34.2	24.1	13.9
			($N = 287$)				($N = 79$)	

NOTE: $\chi^2 > 23$ and $p < .005$ for all three comparisons more than limited skill at using the equipment. On the questionnaires, 72 percent said that they were still learning more than a little about new ways to use their word processors.

Finding the time to experiment with new uses and procedures is difficult. Commonly heard in nonadapting organizations was the frustrated, "We know we could save time by learning glossaries [or otherwise finding ways to automate frequently done tasks], but we just do not have the time." In adapting organizations more often heard was, "We cannot let the pressure to turn out work faster keep us from continually looking for ways to do our job better."

The participation that relates to adaptation is not about the equipment per se—its choice or maintenance—but about issues operators define as closer to their sphere of influence—decisions about formatting and training.

The interviews and survey results provide a beginning understanding of the complex relationship of communication to adaptation. More general communication does not necessarily lead to adaptation. Rather, communication about and praise for adaptation, and communication about adaptations that operators can actually influence tend to be associated with adaptation.

As noted in chapter 3 and the Appendix, the classification of the four kinds of systems was based on many factors. In order to check the validity of that classification, the system levels were cross-tabulated with the measure of individual operator adaptation: "Do you and your coworkers develop new methods and procedures?" The association was strong and significant, providing supportive evidence for the validity of the classification: table 7.11 shows that "adapting individuals" are *much* more likely to be found in adapting sites than in others.

A NOTE ON WORD PROCESSING STRUCTURE AND OPERATOR ADAPTATION

Opportunity for continuous training that helps one understand how word processors "think" appears to be one area where structuring WP as centers rather than in distributed units can be advantageous. Operators in centers have other full-time operators sitting near them so that asking questions and sharing ideas is potentially a rich source

TABLE 7.11

Operator Adaptiveness in Four Systems

	No	Seldom	Some	Often	Total N
High-integration	2%	10%	67%	21%	52
Expanding	13	18	40	30	101
Clockwork	6	28	53	13	96
Low-integration	28	31	35	6	54

$\chi^2 = 51.8$; p < .001; $N = 303$

TABLE 7.12

Strength and Significance of Differences Between Centers and Distributed WP

	Chi square
Centers show more:	
Ease of learning WP	12.0**
Training that helps explain how WP "thinks"	16.3****
Continual learning of new ways to use WP	19.7*
Encouragement to experiment	11.6**
Praise for adapting from	
supervisor	11.1**
co-workers	14.0***
Participation in regular meetings to discuss WP	
procedures and uses	9.3*
No Differences between Centers and Distributed WP	
Time available for experimenting	3.4
Policies discourage experimenting	3.5
Talk about new procedures with	
supervisor	4.9
co-workers	4.6
authors	4.9

NOTE: Sample sizes around 300 feet for each question.
* = p < .05; ** = < .01; *** = < .005; **** = p < .001

of information. Table 7.12 summarizes the statistical information for the following discussion.

The site interviews confirmed that in distributed settings, secretaries and others receive little systematic training or opportunities for ongoing interaction. For the most part, they are given the manual and told to learn for themselves. Operators in such distributed settings found their word processors more difficult to learn, and their training less often helped them to understand how WPs "think."

Unit structure was related to the encouragement to find new ways to perform tasks, but not to the time available or policies that discourage experimentation. In general, those respondents in centers are still learning more than those in distributed settings. In centers, the supervisor and the coworkers focus on the equipment and how to use it better becasue WP is their career. In distributed settings, WP is just another work tool; one's immediate colleagues pay less attention to continuous development through experimentation. The result is that those expectations to adapt may be absent in distributed settings—or are at least more affected by individual predilections than by organizational incentives.

But more global organizational practices related to how much time pressure there is on a job and how rigid the policies are seem not to relate to the centralization of WP. Some of the most rushed operators encountered in the interviews were in centers. Likewise, some centers adopt the policy that the development of new formats is exclusively the job of experienced operators. Operators in distributed settings without WP supervisors are more free to allocate their own time and energies to finding new uses and procedures. Without encouragement to experiment and adapt, however, few allocate much. Operators in distributed settings are just as likely to talk about new procedures with coworkers, supervisors, and authors. The pattern here is that talk about new procedures is most likely to happen with coworkers, second most often with supervisors, and only thirdly with authors. However, operators in centers are more likely to receive praise for adaptation from their supervisor and from coworkers than are operators in distributed settings. They are more likely to participate in regular meetings—such as user groups or staff meetings—to discuss procedures and uses for WP equipment.

Being together in a center does not necessarily lead to more discussion of new procedures. But praise for adaptation and organizational endorsement for adaptation in the form of holding regular meetings to discuss new uses and procedures is more likely to happen in centralized operations.

CONCLUSION

This chapter presents evidence of a consistent relationship between adaptive use of work processing and sociotechnical principles such as joint attention to social and technical factors, training, encouragement for experimentation, and structural encouragement for communication. These principles are associated with adaptation both at the level of the individual operator and at the work unit level.

Participation, training, encouragement for experimentation, and designing jobs to encourage communication are not just "nice to have" factors in office design. Across the sample, they were consistently related to more innovative uses of WP. However, communication, support, and participation were associated with adaptation when they were related to specific adaptational practices, and to activities that the operators could actually control. In this respect, these findings fit well in the context of the job design studies and concepts discussed in chapter 5.

Chapter 8

Managing Word Processing Boundaries: Gaining Resources, Interpreting Environments, and Focusing Attention

Entrepreneurs—and entrepreneurial organizations—always operate at the edge of their competence, focusing more of their resources and attention on what they do not yet know (e.g., investment in R&D) than on controlling what they already know. They measure themselves not by the standards of the past (how far they have come) but by visions of the future (how far they have yet to go). And they do not allow the past to serve as a restraint on the future; the mere fact that something has not worked in the past does not mean that it cannot be made to work in the future. And the mere fact that something has worked in the past does not mean that it should remain. (Kanter 1983)

Earlier chapters have examined the importance of assumptions about communication, motivation, and flexibility in shaping the administration and ultimately the adaptation of WP. This chapter examines how assumptions about boundaries and environments shaped managers' actions in adapting their units to the environments of those units. In this context, environments are largely "enacted" rather than preexisting. As Weick argues, "The human creates the environment to which the system then adapts. The human actor does not react to an environment, [but] enacts it" (1969:64). Here, managers often used symbols quite deliberately to effect change; they implemented systems by changing a microculture they defined.

The *boundary* of an organization is "where the discretion of the organization to control an activity is less than the discretion of another organization or individual to control that activity" (Pfeffer and Salancik 1978:29–32). The boundary of a subunit is the point at which the manager of that subunit has less control over the unit's activities than others do.[1] Typical means for managing boundaries include, from most to least effective: (a) buffering (converting and regulating input and output flows at the boundary), (b) leveling (reducing the number and amount of changes in input and output conversion by changing suppliers or markets), (c) anticipating (understanding cycles, changing demands), and (d) rationing (prioritizing task assignments) (Thompson 1967). These kinds of regulation are not possible, however, unless the boundary and internal task system are protected in the first place. Lynton reinforces this point: "linkage mechanisms" must be institutionalized "so that they function as permanent parts of a system; that is, continuously and flexibly engaged in change" (1969:74).

The ability to manage and protect a unit's boundary may interact with the nature of work within that boundary. For example, if there is little task differentiation, it may be difficult to control the boundary because relationships with the environment are diffuse, and inputs and outputs may be ambiguous; on the other hand, highly differentiated tasks may require strong interdependencies with external subsystems, also leading to difficult boundary management (Cummings 1978). It is the manager's task then to maintain role boundaries and to dynamically redefine those boundaries as clients' inputs and preferences become unpredictable. Paradoxically, it is the very expansion of the boundaries of a self-managed work unit and the rejection of routinized/programmed tasks that create greater unpredictability, and consequent interdependencies, from external clients. Thus, self-managing work units in some ways require more management and attention, but in less direct ways. Rather than monitoring workers, managers must monitor environments (Mills 1983; Mills and Posner 1982).

Managers of high-integration systems did not set out to influence large numbers of people. They confined their efforts to making *recognizable changes* within the defined boundaries of their departments and used their *observable accomplishments* to ask for more resources. While protecting their system from external forces of criticism and control, they promoted the value of their products and services to outsiders.

With a defined set of organizational activities over which they could exercise considerable discretion, WP supervisors and operators were able to develop expertise and authority. In turn this authority and expertise allowed them to make claims on organizational resources that typing pool supervisors were never able to make.

To the eight principles of sociotechnical systems discussed in the previous two chapters, then, two additional principles that influence the adaptation of office systems are added:

9. Establish boundaries.
10. Attend to the environment outside the boundary.

Innovative managers who successfully implemented adaptive WP systems established and managed their boundaries by:

1. Focusing their efforts on a microculture.
2. Recruiting respected members of the established culture as change agents.
3. Focusing on the core activity or mission of the culture.
4. Changing the meaning of significant symbols in ways that promoted innovation.
5. Keeping everyone informed in language they understood.

REPRESENTATIVE CASES

Four cases illustrate different approaches to boundary management.

In the first case, an agency in the federal government, WP was decentralized with no one to promote good management of the technology. The result was no "system" at all. WP activities were whipsawed by the organizational environment; uses never developed beyond the remedial level except for a few "pockets of brilliance." In the second case, the supervisor of a WP center concentrated on efficiently producing documents while the organizational needs changed dramatically. The center was dissolved because it misread environmental cues and failed to adapt to them in a productive way. The third case is a center in an organization that, like the one above, had declining revenue. The supervisor here, however, astutely recognized the importance of adapting to changing organizational needs. In the final case a technical manager in a regional government office accurately read the changing technological environment. He argued persuasively for resources for a pilot to use word processors for improving the productivity of auditors. He enlisted the support of key people in his office to change the mission of his technical assistance group to one of assisting auditors as end users of computing technology. At the same time, he helped auditors change their own self-images so that they accepted using computers themselves.

Government Contracting Agency

Contract Agency is a classic matrix organization. Ten regions and six topical areas make the agency highly diverse. People in one area have little in common with people in other areas. Database packages suitable for one are not suitable for another. Each region uses a unique information system built around applications on a minicomputer. Commonly cited reasons for differences in data administration are (a) the mainframe computer had limited capacity, (b) mainframe applications for upper levels in Washington are not very useful for operational information, (c) the minicomputers were available and readily adapted, and (d) the central information services group was weak and could not overcome problems of moving comparable information to the central office. In branch offices, office automation developed in an unstandardized way; one official observed that a vendor "made a fortune selling at the branch level."

In 1982 the agency procured a large number of word processors from a single vendor on the basis of competitive bidding. As the result of the procurement, the agency standardized its equipment by authorizing only one brand, and a department could justify WP equipment simply by showing that the application would be efficient. Through a provision in the contract for new equipment, the agency provided WP training for the first time. The vendor put thirteen machines in the basement of the agency for thirty days and gave two days of training to two people per machine. Procurement officials had no plans for any training after that.

Here are some comments by different people in the agency about the adaptation of WP technology, with a specific reference to training:

"Because clerks don't (can't) know how to use equipment, and the vendor is generally unhelpful, there's no way an office can do anything without a programmer. The vendor will set up a couple hours of programming."

"Something is missing in training or something. Not much cross-fertilization. I know there are a lot of capabilities that poorly trained people will never know."

There are pockets of cleverness, but little sharing. For example, a lawyer for the agency talks about his adaptations:

"I never thought of why we invented uses for word processing. We tend to move from day to day, doing our work with whatever we have. We track cases of debarment, give out lots of notices. We needed a way of moving from case to case. A day can't go by or we may lose money or unjustly deny an applicant. We don't need a secretary to type. Much of it is easier to do ourselves. I took eighteen major actions last month without clerical help. Without that machine, I'd be on my first case instead of my twentieth. We had to use it. I was forced because of scarce resources. I would have not developed these schemes if I didn't key. When I worked in a law office, I just was concerned about getting my typing done. I type faster now."

There were several individuals in the organization who were getting fantastic payback from their equipment. But the diffusion of their ideas was left entirely to chance.

"This office does not recognize a need to communicate among users. We have pockets of capability, but no way of communicating. I don't see any movement toward systems thinking."

For the first time, procurement was being coordinated, but those responsible for procurement were not responsible for ongoing management. Their charter for office automation was so broad, they had no meaningful boundaries within which to demonstrate accomplishment and thus to accrue resources for training and coordination to manage adaptation. When asked how WP could be coordinated if no management system was in place for continuous support and systems adaptation, the office automation manager replied:

"My job is procurement and audit. [WP is] not my job. I hope to start a user's group when I get the time. The problem here is no support for people to do implementation. There are WP program coordinators in the regional offices, picked by program officers. We've pleaded with them to take an active role, but they haven't. This is a writing organization; all we can do is provide them the tools to support themselves. What they do with them is up to them."

It is obvious that in such sites there is no basis for coordination; innovation is stifled because of a lack of cooperation on uses for the equipment. No one has the authority to lead. Those with coordination responsibilities do not appreciate the importance of deliberately changing the culture. A history of "do your own thing" continues.

Protecting the Boundaries at Hard Metals, Inc.

When Sue was promoted from operator four years ago, she had problems faced by many early supervisors—she inherited a center that "didn't work." Sue made the place efficient by establishing procedures, instituting policies that encouraged boilerplating, and giving her operators discretion instead of "watching them constantly" as her predecessor had done. She turned the center into one the vendor pointed to as a model of how a WP center should operate. The center is typical of the best of clockwork systems. The operators do not think of themselves as adapters. They only adaptation the best operator could think of was "doing several documents as one to save set-up time."

Like many good supervisors, Sue protected the operators within her center. For example, when an engineer complained to upper management that an operator "was not proud of her work" because the forty-page document had twenty errors, Sue investigated and discovered that it had been proofed by the engineer's department. Sue said that "he was trying to blame the center for the mistakes of his own department. If an operator were to hear that complaint, she would feel very bad." Much of Sue's talk is about authors as enemies to be fought rather than allies to be courted.

The center was under threat of being dissolved. In 1982 it went from seven to five operators. Sue attempted to manage symbols to protect it. She told the operators to look busy all the time, turning their desks around so that they can see when people are observing them. Her major effort was directed to keeping the equipment they have used for six years because it is difficult to use and thus it justifies having dedicated operators in a center. She sees opportunities in business outside the company and has proposed to do WP on contract with people outside the company, though she has not figured out how to recruit such business.

Sue's manager from data processing had been pushing for two years to get new equipment since their old equipment was no longer supported by the vendor. Sue brought her staff into discussions of what their requirements were. They generated a list of functions they used frequently like block moves and column manipulation. All the criteria concerned efficiently doing the kind of work they were currently doing, not versatility in allowing different kinds of work or accessing host data. In general Sue was skeptical of the need or use of "communicating with the host."

Sue won the first round of negotiations with her manager by having him try to type mathematical formulas using the equipment he preferred. When he saw the difficulty, he agreed to stall the decision. Eventually, however, the equipment was acquired for secretaries; no training was provided.

WP at Hard Metals works on a straight chargeback for hours of operator time. The controller pushed Sue to "cost documents at the counter" just as the rest of the company ran on a contract basis. Sue resisted. Her claim that she couldn't know how much a job would cost ("If Mary does the work, it costs less") was not seen as businesslike.

Her biggest problems as a manager were in mispreceiving the changing technological trends of her organization—that is, attending to the environment. Although there were engineers in the organization who were busily doing their own work at terminals, when asked whether engineers wanted to do some of their own document keying, Sue was adamant that they would never undertake the complicated work that was the fare of the center. If she could have "communicated with the host" she could have saved engineers keystrokes and provided a valuable service by finishing the documents as the boundary manager in the next case illustrates.

In 1983 the center was reduced to two operators and Sue, who became an operator-supervisor.

Financial WP vs. OA

Betty is the WP supervisor in the financial department of a Fortune 500 corporation. Because the business has been losing money, it has laid off a substantial number of personnel at all levels. The center seems to be flourishing, however, in service if not in numbers. Much of the reason is due to the astuteness of the supervisor in managing boundaries.

Although Betty values efficiency, her speech is full of references to service and what others think about the center. Managers were particularly concerned about highly confidential reports. According to Betty:

"No one thought they should be sent to WP. Real egos around here. Everyone likes to think his work is most important. I called those with the biggest egos and explained my idea about something new I want to do. I told each one I wanted to talk to them first because if it won't work for him, it won't work for others. Now when those same analysts have to go out to the districts to work, they cry because all they have are old typewriters."

Betty provides good service. This is measured not only by the number of people her center supports (more than twice the number as when it started), but also with the way it supports accounts in the work they consider the most important. She has been "communicating with the host" (mainframe computer) for several years, beginning with providing documentation service to a growing financial database management system. They have added graphics.

There is a high level of computer literacy among the financial managers she supports. Every accountant has a terminal. They do their own analysis on line. People can have their own PCs if they ask. Betty makes sure that her WP activities promote the core activity or mission of the financial department for which she works.

"When they travel to districts, instead of dictating to us, the auditor keys into a timeshare system; the supervisor checks the auditor's work and corrects on line. When ready, they print a copy on a high-speed printer. The general manager looks at it in that form and approves. The supervisor fills out forms; we pull it from the time-sharing facility, clean it up and print it. Everyone has access to the information. Before it took an operator 1½ hours just to input. Now it takes a half-hour to clean and print. A supervisor is in closer contact with people all over. All auditors aren't on it, though. I tell them to get with it."

Betty believes that standardization is the route to effectiveness in office automation, but getting commitment to standards requires changing the work habits and attitudes of people outside the center, who often have much more organizational status than she has. It takes changing some significant symbols in ways that promote innovation. She compares her success to that of the WP supervisor in the legal department:

"In acquisition and divestiture, the law department starts from square one every time. Lawyers believe all things are special since they think they are a special breed. Their WP people have given up. When I started in Finance, I got the same story from the analysts. I went out and got the mundane, ordinary work they hated to do. Once you get started with them, then they come to you with suggestions and problems."

She understands the importance of enlisting the support of respected members of the established culture and establishing credibility by keeping everyone informed in language they understand. These symbolic activities promote both short-term operational autonomy and long-term survival:

"To get things done, you need to enlist support. For example, we wanted to standardize type style. We were spending too much time just changing the wheel. I asked them, suggesting a more professional-looking style. Always give perks. We are a service function. Always call the top guy in the group first. Tell each one you called him first.

"We have few incentives to add functions. I still do it because in the long term they'll say we helped them by freeing up professional time. It builds credibility. We won't get cut back; we'll get new equipment when we need it.

"Word of mouth is the best way to build credibility for word processing. When one fellow tells another at lunch that you are great, it helps a lot."

Despite her successful efforts in building an expanding WP center, Betty's long-term success in the organization is in doubt because office automation planners in the organization are pushing for decentralization of information resources. Her frustrations mirror those of almost every successful expanding supervisor. Success in building WP does not mean that you have won a seat at the office automation table. WP still symbolizes "clerical" and therefore low-status activity to most decision makers in organizations. Betty's struggle illustrates the difficulty of even the most astute manager of WP boundaries in a time when office automation symbolizes professional activity:

"WP has not come into its own. I still can't convince people that I know what I'm doing. People don't think word processing is important. OA people look down on us. The OA people organized a communication meeting for us to explain baud rates, protocols, line speeds, modems, blackboxes. I felt insulted. They keep telling WP people we don't know anything. When I explain how we work here, they respond, 'Well you'll just have to change the way you are doing things'—like we can't print more than 128 columns. Are they planning on changing the government regulations for financial accounting?"

Betty is typical of successful WP supervisors. Through their understanding of both WP technology and the human relations in which it must work, they have built expanding centers. Ultimately, they still have to prove that their knowledge is worthwhile in the changing climate of emphasis on decentralized, integrated systems.

Government Analysis Agency

Like the personnel of Contract Agency, personnel in Analysis Agency do paper-intensive work. A single project may produce ten boxes of written material. Until 1983 this agency did almost all of its work with pad and pencil. Though time-sharing on a Washington computer provided some technical assistance, an MIS group, not the analysts, did the computer work.

Sam, a senior MIS manager in a regional office, provided an alternative when he suggested to a deputy commissioner visiting the region that word processors could substantially improve the productivity of professional auditors. This case is typical of many of the innovative sites: a single individual was responsible for "making it happen." Sam was careful to maintain boundaries on his work, to manage the change within the boundaries of his authority, and to attend to the symbols of outside activities. Although he assisted with implementation throughout the agency, he insisted that he could be most useful by providing a model for others to follow.

Sam recruited a senior analyst to assist him in the implementation. Joe was typical of most analysts: he was skeptical about the benefit of using computers, he could not type and had no desire to learn, and he was not particularly enthusiastic about change. However, after Sam showed him how the equipment could help analysts spend more time analyzing and less time just writing and calculating, Joe became an enthusiastic member of the implementation team. Recruiting Joe was important to cultural change, for Joe was a key player in the culture. From a diffusion perspective, Joe was an opinion leader whose evaluation would affect the perceived compatibility of the innovation. If Joe thought the system had merit, the others believed they should at least give it a try.

A significant difference between this case and the prior one is that the implementation effort here was directed at improving the productivity of the core activity or *mission* of the agency—analysis—

not just providing WP equipment to anyone who could write a justification. Professionals in Contract Agency were using the equipment to *do* their work, but no one talked about a coordinated effort to *change* work. In Analysis Agency, Sam and his fellow implementers consistently talked about how the equipment would support this mission. One of them put it this way:

"EWS (electronic work stations) are a way of reducing the tasks of data entry and giving analysts better ability to analyze. Under the present system any analysis requires going through people in MIS. The new system strives to remove that middleman."

The implementers acted to insure that the office system was seen as the tool for accomplishing the core mission by making sure that the key people, the analysts, actually used the equipment themselves when they were analyzing. In order to assure that the analysts—not MIS personnel or clerks—used the system, the implementers had to change several key meanings within the culture. They set about changing four cultural meanings quite deliberately.

Typing: What Is the Appropriate Status of People Who Type? In order to make the best use of the equipment, the analysts had to keyboard, not depend on a clerk—at least during the data analysis part of the project. Historically the agency had employed analysts from two different backgrounds: economics and journalism. Journalists, often called "green eyeshaders," were generally low-status and eventually became rare. The journalists typically used typewriters to draft their reports. Thus, in 1982 if an analyst was observed on a typewriter, a coworker might say, "So you've turned into an eyeshader today!" Sam started a program to change the *symbolic meaning* of typing before the first WP equipment was ordered. He sent out a letter asking who could use a typewriter; several senior auditors replied that they would use a typewriter if they could have one. Sam made sure that the typewriters were put in places where everyone could see these senior people using them. That is, he increased the compatibility and observability of the potential innovation. Soon typing was accepted as legitimate activity for professionals.

Territory: Who Owns the System? The meaning of *territory* or who *owns* the system had to be established. The equipment chosen was typically sold to do WP functions associated with administrative activities. It would be easy for senior managers to stake a claim on it as an administrative tool. In fact the same brand of equipment was ordered both for analysts and administrative personnel; to assure that a distinction was made between "administrative tools" and "professional analyst tools" the analysts' tools were ordered with more memory and were given a different name than those ordered for use by secretaries.

Even with these deliberate symbolic distinctions, about a month after the equipment was installed the regional administrator claimed one of the machines to use to maintain inventory of office supplies. Sam had to "fight him off" by explaining that inventory requires no analysis and that the machines were justified on the basis of their analytic capability. In the Washington pilot, executives claimed the machines for their secretaries; analysts could not use them. In another regional office the MIS group claimed them. In both of these groups, the implementation of the office system was delayed until an appropriate definition of *ownership* could be established.

MIS Support: What Is Their Role Relative to That of the Analysts? Traditionally MIS had done all the hands-on computer work. This role was comfortable for them and for analysts. MIS personnel liked being the high priests of computers and analysts liked not having to do the technical work themselves. In order to make the office systems implementation work, therefore, Sam and his colleagues had to help the MIS group redefine its role. Through team building sessions, MIS redefined their mission as teaching and developing the technical competence of analysts. They understood that they would still do the "leading edge stuff," but that simple statistical procedures were more productively done by the analysts who knew what they wanted. Thus, a "decade of antagonism" between analysts and MIS began to end even before the new equipment arrived.

Self-Concept: How Do People Feel About Themselves as System Users? A fourth kind of symbol that Sam and his associates set out to change was the *self-concept* of various kinds of personnel vis-à-vis systems use. "Professional work" in the agency was closely tied to knowing what kinds of data to collect in an organization being analyzed. The professional analysts collected the information themselves, writing it on yellow tablets and then turning it over to MIS for data entry and statistical analysis. The implementation team sought to establish a system in which clerical employees with instruction from analysts would key in the data directly from organizational records and then professionals would do the statistical analysis themselves.

This idea ran directly contrary to the culture as well as the personnel practices of the organization. Clerks were not allowed to key in data directly, because they were not seen as qualified to make decisions about what to input. Analysts were resistant both to having clerks collect the data (it demeaned their "key activity") and to having to do the computer analysis themselves, a job they felt was beneath their professional stature and should be appropriately done by the "computer jockeys" in MIS. Senior clerks chosen to do the input at first resisted because they considered the "data entry" aspects of it beneath them.

The implementation team worked with both analysts and clerks to help them redefine for themselves the meaning of "appropriate work." The implementation team helped clerks develop an enhanced sense of themselves as "information specialists" while they helped analysts understand how much more effectively they could do professional work with direct access to the equipment. The result was that members of both groups developed self-concepts that promoted the innovative use of the office system.

An important key to cultural change is keeping everyone informed in language they understand. Members of the MIS group learned how to communicate with analysts and executives in appropriate ways, as one explains:

"Some people in the agency once used us to try to sell the idea of a centralized computer to be used by analysts to top management. We went into that meeting fully prepared—we thought—with all the technical specs. We talked a mile a minute, totally unaware of the political reality. Later when we realized how we'd blown it, we developed the idea of 'shared experience.' We have to help others experience successes with technology for themselves. Here there is a policy that we in MIS can't play with the machines. It is too bad for us because we could use them, but it is a good decision because we taint them."

The implementation group reported to top management the productivity gains of the new system, concentrating on its effects on core mission: analysts saved 27 percent of the usual time spent in analyzing data, 17 percent in writing reports, and 26 percent in gathering data.

Managers here used their successes to get more resources for more systems and more learning. They taught seventy people to use the system in three months. They have an ongoing program of educating people to more productive uses and have subsequently changed from WP equipment to personal computers. By successfully managing boudaries, they have also successfully managed the evolution from WP to office information systems.

PROBLEMS IN BOUNDARY MANAGEMENT

Three general types of problems in the management of boundaries occurred in the sites visited. These are (a) establishing boundaries in order to gain resources, (b) understanding and responding to the boundary's environment, and (c) defining the managerial focus with respect to the boundary.[2] Each is discussed below.

Establishing Boundaries to Gain Resources

The Hard Metal, Inc. and Government Analysis Agency cases above illustrate the first principle about how boundary management supports adaptation. By establishing boundaries around WP activities, supervisors were able to build authority, expertise, and other resources that coordinators of low-integration systems never had. Conversely, by designing self-regulating systems, managers were more able to attend to their boundaries instead of controlling and monitoring members' activities.[3]

As evidence of the meager level of resources in low-integration systems, consider the high number of marginal activities they reported and the amount of time they spent justifying their existence. They identified considerable attention wasted on tasks that more advanced managers touch on lightly, if at all. Two examples illustrate this problem:

"There are too many rules. You have to use a yellow procurement for smudgeless ribbons. You can't use bond paper (it works best in the machines). People don't like the rules, so they don't use the equipment. It's not worth the bother for most people here."

"The problem is stability of the work force. You have to invest time to develop a good operation with good operators. When you are paying grade 3 or 4 wages, operators don't stay long enough. Secretaries who answer the phone are paid more. We can't hire qualified typists because of [Equal Employment Opportunity Commission] requirements which state they can't give a typing test."

The confusion shown in these examples demonstrates what happens when a complex technology such as WP is introduced without a management system that has a power base. Low-integration systems rarely moved beyond the basics of using WP equipment as typewriters because its members had difficulty collecting expertise. As a result, the units could not successfully compete with others for organizational resources.

Clockwork systems are somewhat less vulnerable because they have an operation under their control and are able to vie for a piece of the work. By scavenging for work, WP supervisors took on immediate tasks, reduced their substitutability and positioned themselves to take on a large share of tasks. In a center, when its work is getting out and the unit is satisfying customers, the supervisor can gain leverage based on performance. Individuals and units that become difficult to replace, because of their service and resources, will gain greater power in the organization (as argued by Mechanic 1964). Low-integration systems could not achieve that state, while clockwork systems could create some dependencies, but at some cost to their own management.

Creating boundaries around WP activities gave managers of WP power to compete for organizational resources because they gained expertise in an activity that was increasingly seen as important. However, expanding system supervisors were aware of the limits of expertise they had gained through establishing boundaries around WP activities. Their intuitions told them what Crozier states clearly:

The expert's success is constantly self-defeating. The rationalization process gives him power, but the end result of rationalization curtails his power. As soon as the field is well covered, as soon as the first intuitions and innovations can be translated into rules and programs, the expert's power disappears. (1964:165)

Thus, there is a purely political benefit from developing adaptations: by legitimizing the search for and creation of variety, the expanding and high-integration systems avoided the susceptibility of work units to replaceability due to routinization (Crozier 1964; Pondy and Mitroff 1979). While information work exists in a realm of potential adaptations which lead to increased productivity through accomnplishing organizational goals, the successful development of variety also serves to prevent restrictions on work unit autonomy and autonomy in gaining resources.

Understanding and Interpreting the Boundary's Environment

The second principle concerning boundaries has to do with the need for organizational units to understand and respond to their organizational environments. Adaptive systems appeared more able to attend to those environments. Clockwork systems tended to misread cues that could have led them to increased responsiveness to the wider organization, and to increased adaptiveness. Pfeffer and Salancik describe reasons why organizations—as systems in general—fail to adapt:

Although organizational decisions and actions are determined by the enacted environment—that set of definitions of the environment constructed by the organization's attention process—organizational outcomes can be affected by parts of the environment not noticed or heeded. . . . Problems may arise because the organization misreads its situation of interdependence, or it misreads the demands being made on it. Organizations also face problems arising from a commitment to the past and from the necessity to balance conflicting demands. (1978:78–79)

The first problem, misreading interdependencies, occurs when an organization, or in this case, the WP unit, fails to recognize the existence of external groups or their importance to the organization. In 1980, WP supervisors tended to misread the importance of data processing managers. As the Hard Metals case illustrates, WP supervisors often underestimated the importance of decisions to integrate word processors with mainframe computers. They judged efficiency by keystrokes, not by possibilities for distribution and manipulation òf information.

Supervisors also underestimated the potential demand by authors for access to their own WP equipment. In interviews, supervisors and operators in clockwork systems often expressed negative attitudes toward the use of WP equipment by secretaries and authors:

"There is quite a battle between the center personnel and secretaries in satellites [decentralized portions of centers]. Center people do not want to be bothered by secretaries."

"A couple of years ago we pushed decentralization. Operators and leaders were very resistant. They had this nice little business. They were afraid of losing their jobs."

At places like Hard Metals, supervisors of WP centers who misread their interdependence with data processing and with authors who wanted their own terminals were eventually put out of business. They failed to appreciate and adapt to real changes in their environment which represented issues of interdependence.

A second kind of misunderstanding the environment is misreading demands. According to Pfeffer and Salancik:

This misunderstanding frequently involves a response stressing efficiency and missing the point that the output itself is being questioned. . . . Most formal organizations generally have very good internal reporting systems, while they are relatively weak in attending to changes in the environment. It is, therefore, not surprising that the first reaction to organizational problems typically involves solutions focusing on efficiency dimensions, for frequently, that is about the only thing the organization can measure. (1978:81)

This observation about organizations in general is certainly valid for WP units. Supervisors of shrinking centers often responded to demands for new services with charts of how many lines of text they keyed each month without seeing that the demand was for a different kind of service, not just more of the same.

The third problem stems from a commitment to past ways of working. According to Pfeffer and Salancik:

A further limitation on organizational adaptation derives from a commitment to doing things a certain way. Organizations differ in their commitments to the past. Most build up traditions, mythologies, and rituals. More than mere psychological recalcitrance is involved in commitment. In many instances, the beliefs and successes of the past become entrenched in physical and managerial structures. When they do, they are nearly impossible to change. (1978:82)

WP supervisors had to overcome the history of typing as symbolic of secretarial activity in order to establish effective systems. They complained about the recalcitrance of managers who were unwilling to use a different approach to providing typing services. As WP work evolved from typing to information processing, some supervisors were unable to make that transition. They clung to traditions, though new ones, that had been effective in establishing WP centers. For clockwork systems, most of these traditions focused on efficient internal operations. In contrast, supervisors and managers of expanding systems focused their attention outward to promote the center and raise its position among peer and client units.

Because there was no body of experience about how to manage WP, it was difficult to stake a claim based on the "right way of doing things" without being trapped in past norms and standards. Therefore, supervisors needed to develop informal networks. After they established working units that could produce the work they recruited, the expanding supervisors spent time building networks of support. Through these networks they got involved in the early definition of problems and thereby had more leverage because influence was applied early. Recall how Betty, the supervisor in the financial WP case at the beginning of the chapter, was involved in early decisions about how to improve the work of auditors by having them do their audit reports on line and how aggravated she was to be called late into the discussions of the office automation team after the agenda had been set. Supervisors' involvement in a network gave WP the definition of professional activity in which discretion replaced the strict production themes of clockwork systems.

There were a small number of sites, mostly high-integration sites, that displayed a conscious awareness of boundary management and avoided most of the problems discussed above. Indeed, they did away with the most obvious boundary of a discrete WP center— WP was integrated from the first into the regular procedures of a work group, by means of decentralized equipment and service. Thus, their approaches and characteristics are particularly relevant to managing the wider range of office systems today because the low cost of WP on microcomputers is making distributed WP a possibility in almost every organization.

In order to understand and interpret the boundary's environment, then, managers must successfully identify interdependencies, focus on organizational goals, and avoid inappropriate criteria for performance.

Defining the Managerial Focus

There were three distinguishing characteristics of managers of such systems with respect to their relationship with the wider organizational environment: their tenure in the organization, their focus on business results, and their insistence on focusing their efforts within manageable boundaries.

First, their tenure in the organization was longer than that of many other managers. For example, one was a senior auditor, another a senior engineer and project manager, another the head of corporate communication. The discrepancy between their level and those from whom they requested resources was smaller than for the supervisors in the other systems. They were able to contact directly the commissioners of their agencies and the presidents of their firms. Their tenure and knowledge showed in the confidence and mission orientation they expressed in talking about how implementation is accomplished.

The second characteristic was that WP was seen as only a means to an organizational objective. Managers of such units were insistent that they had not set out to "implement WP," but rather to do their jobs better. Although both expanding system supervisors and managers of high-integration systems focused on the core activities or mission of the organization in their interviews, the managers obviously had more experience with the central concerns of their organizations because in each case they had a significant role in organizational leadership. Where other managers would claim, "I don't know what this could do for me," these managers had the vision to know it would help and the determination to do what was necessary to see that it did. They could be unstructured about global issues of accomplishment. They were flexible in matching rules to job needs. The manager of a corporate communication department summed up what he felt was important in implementing an office information system: "Being curious; thinking the idea is interesting; having vision."

The third characteristic had to do with knowing the limits of a manageable boundary, and focusing on the bounded subsystem. Each of the high-integration systems in the sample was a specific installation in a specific, relatively small (less than seventy people) organizational unit. There were no cases of very large-scale high-integration systems in organizations. Managers of high-integration systems, like WP supervisors, attended to the boundaries of their influence. None tried to change a whole organization.

CONCLUSION

This chapter has examined how WP supervisors and managers managed the boundaries of WP systems. This process consists of (a) establishing the points where relations with the wider organization were more interdependent than were relations within the work unit and (b) attending to the environment outside that dividing line. Successful boundary managers used their words and actions to protect a set of activities, promote the services they offer, and gather organizational resources. They understood that they were engaged in a process of cultural change that required changing the meaning of work procedures.

Problems that had to be overcome in order to successfully manage a work unit's boundary included: (a) establishing that boundary to gain subsequent resources, (b) understanding and interpreting the demands and needs of the environment outside that boundary, and (c) defining the managerial focus clearly and narrowly enough. (A fourth problem, coping with boundaries imposed by technological change and incompatibility, is mentioned in note 2.)

Specific activities used to overcome these problems include:

1. Focus on a microculture: Identify a specific group to work with. While recognizing that there may be a need for technological innovation beyond the group, stress that the best approach is to succeed *within* the group as a model for others.
2. Recruit respected members of the established culture as change agents: Talk often about the people issues in implementation. Be realistic about the benefits that each and every person must experience if he or she is to be motivated to use it. Talk about how support was enlisted from key cultural members.
3. Change the meaning of significant symbols in ways that promote innovation: Talk knowledgeably about the technology. You learn from others that the manager is the primary trainer. Help others define technology use as worthwhile.
4. Focus on the core activity or mission of the culture: While you are obviously skilled, do not dwell on technical aspects of the system. Stress the benefits and promises of use of the system to do the mission of your unit.
5. Keep everyone informed in language they understand: Talk about opinion leaders outside your microculture—usually executives—and about the importance of keeping in touch with them. Emphasize the importance of talking in ways people understand instead of using technical jargon. Choose your language and actions to help others see the benefits of what they are doing.

Chapter 9

Transforming Word Processing Into Office Information Systems

This final chapter first describes the application of some of the implementation principles from the preceding chapters to the diffusion of microcomputing at a major corporation. The chapter ends by summarizing ten major principles for fostering the evolution of word processing to office information systems.

APPLYING IMPLEMENTATION TECHNIQUES TO MICROCOMPUTING

It has been argued throughout this book that understanding the technology, use, organizational structuring, implementation, and job design of word processing systems has applicability to the development of office information systems in general. The reasons for this argument include: (a) the processing and management of textual information is a fundamental, and expanding, aspect of office work; (b) lessons about job design and about implementation from the first form of end-user computing are useful for later forms, such as microcomputing; (c) work unit and organizational structures of word processing systems, such as centralization or information centers, can serve as lessons for structuring other user-oriented information systems; and (d) the needs of word processing users and clients which can identify and integrate related activities can be used to foster a greater awareness of the complexity of organizational task dependencies that come about from office automation.

As an example of the relevance of the results from the study of organizations adopting word processing, the following section describes how some of the principles were applied in diffusing microcomputing at a West Coast, Fortune 500, high-tech corporation.

Paradoxically, although firms in this area of the country are associated with leading-edge technology, most divisions outside of engineering are somewhat behind in the day-to-day use of information technology. Indeed, here the only word processing equipment was an antiquated system with seven terminals shared by both secretaries and applications engineers. Only one secretary was responsible for maintenance and training, and she was overworked, so there was little time for teaching or for encouraging experimentation. However, the division had a high stake in promoting productivity with computer-based technology as much of the profitability of the division came from microcomputer sales.

Between February and July of 1984, sixty-five microcomputers were installed in the microprocessor division of the corporation. Activities in implementing micros focused on three efforts:

- The Continuous Learning Center (CLC).
- The Office Systems Center (OSC).
- Implementation Meetings held twice a month for all division secretaries.

Continuous Learning Centers

Based upon the lessons from the word processing study, the CLCs were set up as locations where learning about *how* to use the micros as well as *what* applications would be possible, and where *new* developments could be diffused.

The technical compatibility problems discussed in chapter 8, footnote 2, are intensified when micros are considered. Instead of just one vendor for a particular system, several vendors are often involved in providing consoles, graphics boards, memory chips, printers, and monitors. Since the equipment was delivered from two different sources, and because the company produced their own, without boards or memory chips, there was even greater need for personnel to configure these systems. So, the initial CLC decided to teach the first secretaries to install the boards and chips themselves. They left with smiles, saying they would never again be afraid of the machines. In later weeks, when the other secretaries received their equipment, engineers put in their boards and chips. These secretaries were not as confident as were those who did their own installation.

Office Systems Center

One of the most valuable services of the OSC was system help designed to solve immediate software and hardware problems—both through a "hot line" and "house calls." When new problems come up and are solved, a memo is sent out to users alerting them to this possibility and what the solution may be. In this way, local disasters do not discourage nearby users, but rather generate knowledge and lessons for all users.

At first, there was a considerable overload of business. Secretaries liked being able to send their documents to the OSC as they were learning to use their micros. Because they were spending most of their days doing word processing on the micros, the two OSC secretaries became experts in using the software; therefore, they became valued and adept instructors for other secretaries.

Soon, the OSC did less and less word processing work, as others became proficient. Instead, the OSC's primary activities are training, developing software applications, and system evaluation. They have targeted four secretarial stations for in-depth analysis and are developing new uses for the micro to improve the productivity of those stations as a prototype for what can be done throughout the division.

Implementation Meetings

The first few regular, bimonthly meetings were designed to introduce secretaries to the idea of adopting micros. Their attitudes initially ranged from indifferent, to critical about why they could not have word processors, to hostile because they were going to be required to do more work without receiving monetary reward. After a couple of months, the general attitude changed to one of enthusiasm; their biggest complaint was that it took so long to get their equipment.

During the early phases of implementation, the meetings provided an important arena for airing the many frustrations about equipment and job uncertainties. Later, the topics of the meetings reflected the interconnection and routinization stages of implementation. Micros are no longer a mystery or threat, or even a promise. They are just a tool for accomplishing work tasks. The meetings are devoted to sharing ideas about new uses and procedures. They work best when they are entirely managed by the secretaries themselves; that is, self-regulation of and participation in the diffusion of ideas, rather than control and measurement of activities from supervisors, are the managerial practices applied.

Evaluation of the Implementation Strategy

Indicators of the success of this strategy are based on twenty questionnaires collected in July and October of 1984 in the division as well as nine questionnaires administered in a comparable division where micros had been implemented in a more conventional way—that is, distribution of equipment followed by training classes and documentation. Questions focused on perceived productivity increases and the development of new uses and procedures. Table 9.1 shows these results. The comments from secretaries in the two groups are also instructive about the differences good implementation makes. The control group received eight hours of training from some of the division's best word processing instructors. But their comments are typical of secretaries who are uninvolved in the implementation of office information systems:

"My micro is a dust catcher."

"I'm not convinced it will increase my productivity."

"I will always need a typewriter."

In the division, comments from secretaries reflect a more sophisticated and involved understanding of the technology:

"It has been tough to get up and going on the micro, but once over that initial period, it has been great."

"My micro was very slow unless I used the RAM-drive."

TABLE 9.1

Reported Changes in Productivity and Innovation from Implementation and Nonimplementation Groups of Microcomputer Users

Change	Division with Planned Implementation	Division without Planned Implementation
Productivity	50%[a]	11%
New procedures developed	80	11
New uses in place	70	22
Total N	20	9

[a] Indicates percent responding "yes" to question. Results from survey conducted in July 1984.

The secretaries were again interviewed in October to determine (a) how much time they were actually saving, (b) what they were doing with that time, and (c) whether their managers were now expecting more from them.

They reported an average of over two hours a day saved due to avoiding typing revisions. They reported using this time to:

1. Support more people.
2. Provide better support for their managers.
3. Eliminate the need for temporary workers.
4. Develop more microcomputer skills.

The head count in the CLCs has been offset by the reduced need for temporary workers, and secretaries have more time to spend in the CLCs and Implementation Meetings. Their managers generally were expecting them to become information specialists. The more new applications they found, the more their managers looked to them as a source of creativity and rewarded them for their new applications. Managers said that secretaries working in this division were more respected than those in other divisions because they were making good use of information tools.

It should be noted that congruent with the findings of chapters 4 and 7, the CLCs, OSCs, and Implementation Meetings have not obviated the need for managerial direction of office systems innovation. The division has a specific managerial position that develops as well as seeks out problems and directions for use of the microcomputers. The CLCs, OSCs, and meetings provide material for consideration, but division-wide applications are revised and distributed from this position, thus facilitating the appropriateness, formal diffusion, and routinization of adaptations.

APPLYING IMPLEMENTATION TECHNIQUES TO INFORMATION CENTERS

Earlier discussion has pointed out that WP *centers,* when managed in ways that foster high-quality jobs, provide opportunities for the development and sharing of new and better ways of using the technology. Additionally, *distributed* and *decentralized* approaches are putting word processing capabilities under the direct control of users, and are providing organizational mobility for WP operators. Two forces are apparent here: the control of locally relevant *computing by users,* and the *managed* diffusion of expertise and personnel.

In light of the developing trends in WP mentioned in chapter 1, the interaction of WP with other information-based organizational activities mentioned in chapter 4, and the dangers of too widely or too narrowly defining the unit's boundaries mentioned in chapter 8, this section applies some of the lessons from the word processing study to current issues in information centers.

The concept of an information center was developed by a Canadian division of IBM in 1973, and was reported on formally as early as 1977 (Lugsdin). The notion of an information center at that time was a place to help users develop their own database applications, as a way to reduce some of the more accessible mainframe backlog that DP departments were experiencing. If the simpler, more diverse, and more ad hoc requests for data could be handled by the users themselves, both they and DP would be happier, there would be fewer transfer points which lead to misunderstood needs and goals, and the valuable information could lead to improved performance rather than to long waits for unreadable reports. Demand processing involves the generation and analysis of local reports and the accessing of business information. Nearly a decade later, information centers are becoming a crucial force in the diffusion of end-user computing, the success of office automation, and the widening of the concept of computer processing to include text management. An information center can be viewed as a facility dedicated to technology transfer

(Head 1985). End-user computing—direct access to computing power by the users of the output—has been growing from 50 percent to 90 percent in some major corporations (Rockart and Flannery 1983). The growing uncertainty in organizations' environments is one of the factors driving corporations to adopt end-user computing and to apply it to market analysis and decision making.

Of course, the purview of information centers is much wider than that of word processing, strictly defined. In general, they attempt to satisfy needs for end-user education, nontechnical access to corporate data, individual use of automated spreadsheets, ad hoc reporting, generation of one-time graphics for presentations and reports, training on microcomputers, and occasionally high-level computer programming. Table 9.2 lists the ranking of operating modes in a survey of information centers. In addition to the concerns these centers reported, as listed in table 9.3, other sources indicate that creating organizational awareness and countering resistance from DP and management are realities to be overcome (Karten 1985).

Comparing WP and Information Centers

Information centers often must compete with other priorities (including microcomputer budgets), the drifting of managerial attentions

TABLE 9.2

Information Center Hardware and Operating Modes

Mode	Percentage of Information Centers
Standalone microcomputers	82%
Micros downloading from mainframes	76
Dumb terminals for mainframe use	71
Graphics	70
Micros uploading to mainframes	53
Intelligent terminals	50
Local mainframe reducing central mainframe load	19
Networked microcomputers	17
Total *N*	70

NOTE: From Hallady 1985. Sample represents 50 percent rate from first year's subscription list of *Information Center* magazine.

TABLE 9.3

Information Center Management Concerns

Concerns	Percentage of Information Centers
Marketing services to increase use	61%
Developing a career path	57
Establishing work priority criteria	44
Recruiting appropriate personnel	39
Establishing chargeback criteria	34
Maintain stability of staff	23
Developing controls to limit IC use	21
Total N	70

NOTE: See table 9.2 for source.

after the center is established, and the traditional view that information technology means data processing. Michtom (1985) makes an argument about the difficulty of measuring the productivity benefits of information centers that is similar to the discussion in chapter 1: simple usage measures, efficiency, effectiveness, impact and adaptivity constitute approaches to measure the output of information work. And another survey of the status of information centers in over one thousand companies (CRWTH 1985) found that more "mature" information centers (in place for over three years) reported increases in end-user productivity and better decision making than did "pilot" centers (86 percent compared to 50 percent).

The point of this quick overview of information centers is that, as mentioned in the first chapter, many lessons learned from the management of WP have relevance to the development of office information systems. Note the concerns: lagging interconnection with other systems, organizational awareness, DP resistance, career paths, staff mobility, the development of new uses and procedures, breaking away from the DP model of computing, managing boundaries, the fleeting focus of upper management, the differential results from more and less evolved systems, and the difficulty of precisely defining productivity. Principles of information work, the diffusion of information technology, job design, and boundary management are useful in managing the evolution of information centers in particular and integrated office systems in general.

PRINCIPLES FOR IMPLEMENTING OFFICE INFORMATION SYSTEMS

The preceding chapters have examined the concepts and history of word processing, with particular reference to nearly two hundred organizations that had adopted WP from the mid-70s to 1983, for lessons in how to manage the implementation of an information technology and how to foster adaptations in information work. The discussion emphasized the following question: What did some organizations *do* that led the people who used word processing to be more innovative than people in other organizations? Innovation in the form of adaptations technology and tasks was largely the result of management practices. Managers who were successful in implementing word processing so as to foster adaptations operated in congruence with a set of sociotechnical systems principles, though, of course, few people labeled them as such.

As note 5 in chapter 5 briefly discussed, there are, of course, many approaches that organizations may take to improve productivity, performance, innovation, and creativity. Some of those include the development of team-building and group problem-solving skills, improving the flow of work between departments, ongoing productivity measurement, quality control, the development of human resources, developing employee survey/feedback programs, improving environmental conditions such as furniture and lighting, implementing explicit reward programs such as the Scanlon plan, quality circles, and the like. However, we focus on the following ten principles both because they were clear influences in our questionnaire and site visit data, and because they are more generic than many of these specific approaches. Clearly, all approaches should be considered and compared.

The rest of this chapter summarizes the management principles that typically separate innovative from noninnovative word processing users and systems. Because of the pervasive nature of information work, the experience gained from word processing as an initial form of end-user computing, the continuing developments in and integration of text manipulation technology, the prior development of these principles in other forms of organizational work, and the wide range of organizations that provided the examples and evidence in this book, these principles will be useful not only in managing word processing systems, but in office information systems in general.

1. Involve Members in Changing the Technology and Social System Jointly to Accomplish Organizational Mission. Resistance to new technology is widely discussed. There was little resistance to technology per se, but widespread resistance to poor implementations. Social researchers since the 1930s have argued that participation fosters commitment to, involvement in, and acceptance of change. In implementing word processing, users wanted to be involved.

Two practices stood out as important in distinguishing innovative from noninnovative sites. First, user involvement was part of the routine structure of the organization. In the innovative sites, users participated in regular meetings where word processing was discussed. Second, the participation was not limited to discussions of the technology itself. Users are as concerned about the human issues as the hardware and software issues. They needed to be involved in joint changes of technology and work roles.

Three participative activities in particular were associated with innovative WP use: involvement in decision making about unit productivity, formatting procedures, and training. These findings are evidence that it is productive to involve users in decisions about how their activities will contribute to the overall mission of their unit (unit productivity), decisions about the most relevant and controllable procedural questions (in this case formatting procedures, because they are what word processors do to produce documents), and their own learning and development (training). That is, users should be involved in decisions about instrumental and relevant activities or policies.

2. Provide Experiences for Continuous Learning. Although most people acknowledge that training is the key to effective use, "training" per se is not the issue. After the initial period, center operators had little need for training courses since they were constantly learning new methods and teaching them to each other. In well-run centers there was a natural "hothouse" effect of *learning*. With encouragement from the management, operators had the expertise to assist each other and had incentives to learn to make their jobs easier. Work in innovative word processing centers was consciously focused on constant problem solving activity—learning how to do jobs more easily, faster, with higher quality, and often in very different ways. To label an activity as "training" led implementers to think of a few hours or perhaps days of formal instruction given when the system is first installed.

Two processes separated the "training" of users in innovative and noninnovative centers. First, in innovative centers users were taught the logic of the software: their training helped them to understand "how word processors think" rather than simply what buttons to push to accomplish what tasks. Second, the emphasis was on continuous problem solving. "In word processing there is *always* a better way," as one supervisor put it. Word processing operators said that they were "still learning new ways to use word processing."

3. Encourage Experimentation; Systems Evolve, and Managers Must Continuously Attend to Adaptation. The best word processing supervisors and managers understood that they were not just changing how typing got done. They were inventing new ways of doing the organization's work. They gave priority to providing *time to experiment* whereas their noninnovative counterparts were more focused on the efficient production of typed output.

Implementation in most WP sites began with more faith, hope, and charity than rational planning. Once installed, however, innovative managers gave careful attention in word and deed to encouraging experimentation to develop new uses and procedures. Their operators reported that the organization "encouraged them to experiment." They reported more praise for adapting from their supervisor, coworkers, and authors. Most significantly, they reported more *talk about new uses and procedures* than operators in noninnovative sites.

4. Design Work Units to Promote Communication. Innovations must be diffused among people to result in productive applications. It is not surprising that communication is essential for creativity in organizations. Operators in innovative word processing systems reported more talk about new uses and procedures. Open communication was also essential; regular meetings and information sharing were policies that distinguished innovative from noninnovative units.

To promote innovation, communication must not only be topically related to ways to achieve innovation, it must be structured to involve the appropriate people in the process. When word processing is done in centers, policies and practices should encourage frank and friendly communication between operators and secretaries or authors. In all cases, special considerations were made to make sure that authors, secretaries, and high-level managers had sufficient understanding of the technology and the procedures to insure cooperative working relationships—this understanding must be developed and established by the unit's manager.

The management of communication is more difficult without centers, for professionals and secretaries spread over large work groups will not have the focused talk about new uses and procedures that occurs in centers. Therefore, managers must attend to task forces, steering committees, and other means for insuring that people talk about how to continuously improve work performance. The present research shows that these special occasions, while useful, do not substitute for talking about new uses and procedures in regularly held organizational meetings.

5. Promote Self-Regulation of Work Groups Through Autonomy; Locate the Decision Making at the Task Requiring the Decision. Among the least innovative organizations were those in which word processing jobs were heavily influenced by "work measurement." Where work measurement systems were in place, operators reported that they simply had no interest in developing new methods because they could not see how such methods would help them achieve the established levels and forms of productivity.

In innovative organizations, operators were more autonomous. They participated in deciding criteria for evaluating their performance. They were provided independence in deciding how the work was to be done. Innovative supervisors, for example, would not even assign a person to assist an operator with a job unless the operator who "owned" the job specifically asked for help. Their philosophy was that the operator made the decision about how to do each job.

Word processing centers and distributed installations worked best when they operated as work groups rather than collections of individual operators/users. To date, end-user computing has largely been a collection of tools for individual workers; the real productivity gain will be realized when tools are used to enhance group productivity. In implementing office systems, managers have much to learn from the experiences of those who implemented word processing in ways that promoted *both* creativity and cooperation.

6. Design Jobs so that People Can Perceive and Complete a Whole Task. Many social critics feared that the division of secretarial work into "word processing" versus "administrative support" would fragment the work, denying the secretary a sense of doing a "whole job." Word processing centers in particular were described as places where work was fragmented and the workers "de-skilled." Although we found some organizations where word processing work was divided into minute specialties so that less skilled workers could be hired and paid lower wages, these were relatively rare and disappeared after a few years because they were unsuccessful.

Word processing jobs have the potential to become jobs for specialists in "wordsmithing." Eighty-eight percent of all respondents said they have the opportunity to do a job from start to finish. Seventy-four percent of all respondents said they have this opportunity and that it is *very* important to them. This figure was the same for operators whether in innovative or noninnovative sites. Quite in contrast to early stereotypes, operators in centers were slightly more likely to report the opportunity to do jobs from start to finish (92 percent) than operators in distributed settings (83 percent).

Supervisors found creative ways of making sure that operators had a sense of doing a whole job. Operators were made responsible for finishing any job they started; they did their own revisions. At more innovative organizations, operators, though in centers, frequently worked for certain departments. Supervisors took responsibility for making sure that loads were equally distributed while helping each operator develop a feeling of ownership for the work of specified departments.

End-user computing tools permit individuals and groups to do a much wider range of job activities. Writers can be involved in the typesetting of their work. Analysts can do their own statistical analysis. Implementing office systems should be the occasion to examine the work flow of coworkers and to determine how much more effectively they could work if they had more autonomy and a broader range of responsibilities. After the initial implementation, there will be more opportunities for enlarging jobs as people become more proficient at using and adapting the technology. Alert managers will attend to the possibilities for ongoing work enrichment.

7. Administer Policies with Flexibility. Managing innovation is a balancing act. In word processing this shows up as a continuous tradeoff of efficiency through automated routine and flexibility. In the telephone survey, over half of the organizations said that their units had evolved in the direction of more formality in communications and more procedures. Innovative supervisors were savvy in the flexibility with which they administered these procedures. They told how they bent the rules to make life in centers pleasant, even fun. The findings are in agreement with those of the National Institute for Occupational Safety and Health that rigidly enforced procedures lead to stress. In addition, the development of innovative changes was stifled when workers were managed rigidly.

Supervisors of expanding systems in particular talked in ways that convinced us they were good listeners. They did not talk about their operators as a "group," but called attention to the differences among them in style. It was clear that they managed each one according to the special needs of that person.

Supervisors of innovative sites understood that the technology could be used to rigidify the work process, for example by counting lines or clocking how many minutes a day an operator was keying. They realized, however, that such attempts at tight control could be met by operators becoming creative at beating the system rather than being productive.

End-user computing and other office systems can be used to make jobs more flexible or more rigid. It was not the technology per se that predicted the impact of word processing on people or performance; rather, it was the assumptions and attention of the managers who helped implement the system. Managers should be alert to their basic assumptions about human motivation and communication. There is clear evidence in the history of word processing that rigid procedures do not work. Managers who set out to implement office systems that are flexible will develop more innovative, productive, and satisfying systems.

8. Design Jobs for Upward Mobility. One of the most startling results of the present research is the impact of learning word processing on operators' career aspirations. Eighty percent of operators said they were harder workers since learning word processing. Eighty-four percent said they were more likely to try new things. Fifty-nine percent said they now demand high salaries. Sixty-nine percent said they were more eager for promotion.

Unfortunately, while word processing jobs raised operators' (and supervisors') expectations, they did not as often fulfill them. One executive described word processing in his organization as a "cul de sac." Operators in noninnovative organizations are more likely than others to be looking for a job in another organization.

Innovative supervisors who were disbanding their centers to decentralize word processing services placed their operators in jobs that advanced their careers as trainers and graphics specialists.

Word processing and newer forms of end-user computing are now maturing in their impact on organizations. People are developing new skills and demanding more rewards for their contributions. Those organizations that rewarded enhanced skills kept their people longer. It is essential to keep people, for high turnover means that valuable learning about how to use the equipment and what to use it for is walking out the door.

Organizations need to begin looking very carefully at how they are managing human resources in light of the special skills now required to be productive in offices. To keep these people, human resource departments must begin to develop appropriate career ladders. It is also clear that much of the innovation work as well as the use of end-user tools will be done by people who are not dedicated systems personnel. It is time to investigate how best to reward these individuals for their work.

9. Establish Boundaries so that Recognizable Successes Can Lead to Claims of Expertise and Authority. The major way that managers in this study developed expertise and authority was by establishing word processing centers. However, with no clear boundaries over what constitutes word processing work, and who has expertise to speak for improved capabilities (and the equipment needed to produce them), work in low-integration sites stayed at marginal levels. Coordinators were always justifying the basic necessities. "Reinventing the wheel" was prevalent.

Innovative word processing supervisors, unlike less innovative ones, used the success of their units to promote the expansion of the centers. In other words, they used internal success as a means to more powerful external communications to get resources to become even more successful. They got new equipment; they spent less time just justifying their existence.

Managers of successful distributed sites in our sample were already successful in their organization before they implemented word processing. They used their prior successes as grounds of credibility to get the "faith, hope, and charity" necessary to start an office automation system. They understood, however, that to implement such a system successfully, they had to draw boundaries around it. Their attentions were focused on implementation with a particular group of people and directed toward accomplishing a particular mission with those people. They focused their scarce attention resources on the people problems of support and ongoing learning more than on the technical questions of what equipment to get. In contrast, coordinators of low-integration systems were typically providing equipment for hundreds of people with little attention to support. Their efforts were diffused. They did not gain enough resources for the system to become successful and so they continued to operate at marginal levels.

10. Attend to the Environment Outside the Boundaries. Innovative managers established boundaries around their work, but their attentions were not constrained within them. The managers of noninnovative centers concentrated their efforts on internal efficiencies to the extent that they misread the changing environment of word processing. They failed to understand the extent to which powerful authors were demanding access to word processing equipment and so were unprepared for disbanding centers as authors began to do their own keying. They misread their interdependence on data processing organizations and authors. Much of their talk concerned how much data processing managers failed to understand word processing operations, but they had few resources for helping data processing managers understand it better and so they were unprepared for their centers being taken over by data processing.

CONCLUSION

The future of office systems in organizations will be shaped by how well managers can attend to the changing culture that accompanies the best implementations. For example, personal computers began replacing dedicated word processing systems and increasing in importance as individual productivity tools in 1983, but by 1985 users began to realize the limitations of standalone systems. In word processing the same people who were adamant resisters at one time were adamant enthusiasts six months later.

Managers must be alert to changing demands as well as to changing technologies. One of the primary ways to do this is to manage the system of technologies, people, tasks, and work unit structures to generate adaptation and re-invention as one of the results of information work. That is, a sign of potential productivity is the ongoing exploration of alternative ways of accomplishing the goals of the unit and of the organization. Particularly in information work, increases in efficiency and even effectiveness may not be sufficient, and, if emphasized at the expense of responses to changing environmental conditions, may even be harmful to organizational performance. Thus, innovation, adaptation, and appropriate job designs must be a significant focus of managerial assumptions and practices.

Appendix
The Research Process

The research was conducted in two phases. A telephone survey of 194 organizations assessed the general state of uses and procedures of word processing. From information gathered in these initial interviews, 54 initial sites were selected for on-site visits (a few particularly interesting sites recommended to the research team were added as well). During these visits, personal interviews and observations were conducted to provide the basis for qualitative case write-ups, and for unit-level evaluations. Also, questionnaires were distributed to managers, operators, and authors.

Phase One: The Telephone Interview

In previous innovation studies, researchers had developed the concept of a "main-line" or standard form of an innovation, and the possibility that such an innovation could be "reinvented" or adapted from its original form or purpose. Chapter 2 discusses these developments in greater detail. For phase one of the research process, a telephone survey was designed to provide descriptive data from which inferences could be drawn about standard usage and from which cases for follow-up visits during the second phase could be selected.

From December, 1981 to February, 1982, the research team was ooccupied with:

1. Selecting sub-project leaders to organize the collection of data around Washington, D. C., San Francisco, and Oklahoma City.

2. Contacting local word processing associations for lists of their members as possible respondents.
3. Revising a draft of the questionnaire for the telephone survey.

The revised questionnaire included 239 questions in the following categories:

• Identification of installation and respondent's expertise.
• Description of the installation.
• History of initial adoption phases.
• Training and development.
• Products and/or services.
• Changes in methods and procedures.
• Client (author) relationships.
• Characteristics of personnel.
• Evaluation (of unit effectiveness).
• Strengths and weaknesses of the unit and word processing.

In February, 1981, five members of the research team visited a large installation in the San Francisco Bay area that had one hundred different WP work units (over twelve hundred keyboards). Twelve word processing managers (some supervisors of WP centers, others managers of work groups that use word processors to do work such as editing) were interviewed. Critiques and suggestions from the respondents were obtained in order to refine the questionnaire into its final form. (The questionnaire is available from the authors upon request.)

Phase One Sample. The initial sample (55 percent of the total) was drawn from lists of members of local word processing associations in each area. A second source of organizations was provided by evening course students in the Masters of Public Administration program at the University of Maryland and the Masters of Business Administration programs at Golden Gate University in San Francisco and at San Jose State University. Students were asked to fill out a brief form asking if they knew of organizations with word processing and to give the name of a person we might contact there.

After 150 organizations had been interviewed, the distribution of organizational types in the sample were compared with that in a study published by the Internatinal Association of Information and Word Processing. Organizations in the field of finance (banking and insurance) and petroleum were added to bring the sample into approximately the same distribution as that one.

Thus, it should be made clear that the present sample of organizations is in no way random. It is essentially a combination snowball/convenience sample, with cluster sampling in three primary geographical areas, and approximate proportional adjustments. Thus, the present research cannot make claims for representatives per se.

In each case, the interviewers attempted to qualify the respondent as one with first-line supervisory responsibility for a unit where word processing was used. In some cases, such as where WP services were distributed, this person was the organizational planner or coordinator. In order to qualify as a site, the organizational unit had to have: (a) four or more word processing keyboards or terminals (or computer terminals used for text editing); and (b) initial installation of word processing capability prior to January 1980 (approximately two years before).

About 10 percent of the organizations contacted failed to qualify for one of these reasons. A summary of organizations by type, industrial classification, site and respondent title is presented in table A.1.

Data Collection. Telephone data were collected by ten people. Each person who was not a member of the instrument design team received three hours of training that included instruction in the purpose of the overall project and an opportunity to practice. Interviews varied in length from one to three hours. The longer interviews were conducted in two or more sessions. The open-ended format invited respondents to tell their story in their own words; in general, respondents were eager to talk about their installations.

Data Analysis. After the first 150 interviews were completed a group of four from the interview team met to determine codings for the semistructured items. Codes were constructed from actual answers; the result was a list of possible codes for each answer. After the interviews were completed and coded, frequencies were run for each

TABLE A.1

Sample Characteristics

	Organization Type		
Private, Profit	58%	Private, Nonprofit	15%
Public	27%		

	Industrial Category		
Manufacturing	13%	Local Govt.	4
Consulting	12	Medical	4
Legal	12	Retail	4
Nat'l. Govt. Bureau	7	Associations	4
Education	8	Petroleum	2
Insurance	6	Military	2
Nat'l. Govt. Agency	6	Service	1
Banking	5	State Govt.	1
System Tech. Manf.	5	Transportation	1

	Site Location		
Washington, D.C.	49%	Oklahoma	5
San Francisco	39	Michigan	1
Kansas	6	Wisconsin	1

	Respondent Title		
WP Supervisor	34%	WP Mgr.	12
Other	20	Info. Systems Mgr.	12
Admin. Mgr.	16	Communication Mgr.	5

questionnaire, and infrequent responses were combined. The telephone survey data were analyzed mostly using the Statistical Package for the Social Sciences running on Stanford University and the University of Southern California's IBM 3081 computers.

Phase Two: Case Studies

Instruments.   In May 1982 the research team met to select initial organizations for on-site follow-up visits, design the interview protocol, and refine the questionnaires. The team visited two sites, conducting interviews, administering the questionnaires, and asking respondents about the interpretations of the questions. The protocol and questionnaires were refined based on these pretests and follow-up visits began in late June. The items for the questionnaires came from several sources. Some were taken from a parallel study directed by Rand researcher Tora Bikson and colleagues (1984). Others were taken from instruments developed by Hedberg and Mumford (1979) to assess the design assumptions of systems analysts. Many standardized items on supervisory and peer communication, managerial assumptions, and support for innovation, were taken from Taylor and Bowers (1972). The remainder were written for this study using data from the telephone questionnaire and the objective of the study to investigate assumptions, administrative practices, and adaptations.

Phase Two Sample. Initial sites were chosen that seemed on the basis of the telephone interview experience to be most typical. Also, the first sites seemed to be the simplest kinds of sites—for example, centers where the researchers could easily talk to a half-dozen operators and a defined management structure—rather than large organizations with distributed use. Ten were identified to start; the rest were chosen, usually in groups of three to six, according to a developing set of criteria. The following is a chronology of criteria:

1. Small, well-established installations (usually word processing centers) with no particular signs of adaptiveness.
2. Small sites where respondents indicated unusual uses or procedures.
3. Large organizations with multiple centers to compare, at least one of which indicated unusual uses or procedures.
4. Large organizations with distributed uses (particularly, large Washington agencies planning telecommunications.)

After forty organizations had been visited, both questionnaire and interview data were analyzed and interpreted. Fifteen more sites were then selected in order to refine the interpretations. In selecting the last sites, sites where word processing was done on personal computers with word processing programs were sought. Four sites that were not in the original telephone questionnaire were also added.

Data Collection. Each site was visited for a day by one to three researchers. The telephone survey respondent was usually the host for the visit. By phone and letter prior to the visit, the host was informed that the following respondents were requested:

1. The phone respondent once more for details of some issues.
2. An executive responsible for implementation.
3. Several operators.
4. Others knowledgeable about the history and decision making.

During the visit, questionnaires were administered to one to three decision makers and all the operators or as many as possible (in decentralized sites, hundreds of people operate WP equipment). Fifteen questionnaires were left with the host to distribute to authors along with envelopes for return directly to the researchers. Selection of the authors was left to the discretion of the host. Thus, again, at the individual level, there was no systematic sampling, due to the large, diverse, and unknown potential target respondents.

At two sites, it was not possible to administer questionnaires, once because of security clearance problems and another time because of an organizational policy preventing data collection at corporate headquarters. The return rate for author questionnaires was 47 percent. The operator and manager questionnaires were presented in person to assure a 100 percent rate of return.

Interviews focused on adaptations and the respondent's systems perspective. Questions were asked to gain information about the level of uncertainty faced by the overall organization and to assess (a) whether WP has any role in coping with that uncertainty and (b) how much this role is explicitly understood by WP personnel, both managers and operators.

Interviews were also designed to elicit respondents' understanding of the mission of the overall organization and the place of WP within it. Notes recorded the respondents' own words so that the vagueness or certainty in their understanding of mission and system could be assessed. A solid systems perspective was indicated by clear statements about environmental demands on the organizatin and examples of how personnel use word processing technology to assist the organization in adapting to those demands.

Some questions probed communication and the diffusion of ideas about adaptive use, such as the extent to which the technology is a topic of conversation in the work group, and how adaptation spreads among coworkers, other WP users in the larger organizations, and members of professional associations.

Responses from individuals about their motivations associated with word processing work were stimulated by questions such as: "Is it pleasant work?"; "How does it compare with other work done previously?"; "How has the respondent changed since learning word processing?" Why the respondent likes (or occasionally does not like) word processing was asked in order to gauge how much simply "playing with the machine" is a motivator or source of job satisfaction.

Some questions explored the "variances" or key factors that retard the unit's ability to accomplish its mission. For example, in some units it was the poor quality of input; in other cases it was the policies of the organization that restricted what word processing is permitted to do.

Data Analysis. As mentioned above, for the quantitative analyses, the Statistical Package for the Social Sciences (SPSS, version six) was used. The bulk of the analyses involved cross-tabulations and measures of association. Significance levels are reported, but because the sample was not randomly selected, such inferential statistics are helpful more as a relative guide than as a precise measure of deviation from chance occurrence.

The researchers recorded the qualitative data from the interviews using word processing programs on microcomputers; each comment or incident was then put into a separate paragraph with an identification number specifying the site, interviewer, respondent, and approximately how far into the interview the comment occurred. Approximately four hundred pages of data resulted. The comments were sorted into twenty four categories that were generated by the data:

Adaptation	Applications
Communication	Early history
Equipment	Future directions
Job classification	Job design

Justification

Morale
Organizational culture
Politics
Rationale for structure
Resistance
Success examples
Training

Management support
   philosophy
Motivation
Personnel
Procedures
Reference groups
Secretaries
Supervisor's career
Understanding of sociotechnical
   systems

DERIVATION OF FOUR LEVELS OF WP SYSTEMS

Comments in each section were then sorted according to the fourfold system typology which had been developed as follows.

Four researchers read all the interview data (without examining the questionnaire results) to classify the sites into one of four categories. The original names were "super adapters," "supervisory adapters." "static, efficient," and "nonfunctioning." The categories were defined in the following way:

1. Super adapters: the whole system seeks and institutes adaptations in word processing to use it effectively. "Effective use of word processing" is an increase in capability directed toward organizational mission. Look to see whether people are adapting word processing technology to do tasks that are impossible or impractical without it. After establishing whether word processing is used to do these kinds of tasks, ask to what extent the work done pursues organizational and unit mission.
2. Supervisory adapters: systems where the supervisor or one person seems to be adapting the system and finding ways of using word processing to increase capacity, but the adaptations do not appear to be organization-wide. These places may be highly efficient.
3. Static, efficient: places where word processing is fast typing. Evidence of some increases in efficiency because of the system, but not a sense of word processing as a resource.
4. Nonfunctioning: inefficient use of word processing. Minimum competence, even at efficiency of typing.

In ten of sixty classifications one researcher disagreed with the others about the classification. To test the validity of the classifications, the relationship of the system level categorization to the measure of individual adaptation (the survey question, "Do you develop new uses and procedures?") was assessed. The relationship was strong and significant (χ^2 = 51.8, ρ < .001), indicating that researchers' and unit members' perceptions of the innovative level of the unit were relatively congruent.

Conclusions about differences were then combined into analyses according to the principles of sociotechnical systems design mentioned in chapter 5. The research process at this point was data synthesis rather than analysis: the research team produced five iterations of interpretations of the information. After consistent patterns were found in the qualitative data from phases one and two, the quantitative data from phase two was analyzed to test, extend, and supplement the various interpretations.

The concept of this four-level typology of adaptation developed out of the interviews and site visits, rather than from a prior, mutually exclusive coding scheme generated by a theoretical framework. Thus, it has unknown reliability, but considerable face validity. Its construct validity lies in the theoretical strength of the relationship between the nature of information work and the necessity for adaptation in organizations operating in the complex environment of an information economy. There is some threat of a tautology between how the levels and indicators were derived and the measures of job design compared throughout chapters 6, 7, and 8 with those levels. However, as noted, the levels were derived after much discussion and several iterations by the researchers, while the data were produced by operators and managers, and analyzed separately after the levels were developed. So, there is some confidence that there are separate sources of data and separate conceptualizations of the nature of the work groups.

Notes

1. Word Processing: A Foundation for Office Systems

1. See Beniger 1986; Markus and Yates 1982; Whalen 1983; and Yates 1982, on which parts of this discussion are based.

2. The mainframe computer of course transformed the way organizations handled transactions, and personal computers promise to continue the trend, but those topics are outside the scope of this immediate discussion. The topic of office automation is widely covered elsewhere: see Chorafas 1982; Doswell 1983; Edwards 1982; Forester 1985; Hiltz 1983; Hirschhiem 1985; Keen and Scott Morton 1978; Lieberman, Selig, and Walsh 1982; Otway and Peltu 1983; Pava 1983; Perlin 1985; Rice and Associates 1984; Tapscott 1982; Tapscott, Henderson, and Greenberg 1985; Uhlig, Farber, and Bair 1979; Westin, Schweder, Baker, and Lehman 1985.

3. See chapter 2 for a discussion of shadow costs, media transformations, and other information-based obstacles to increased office performance.

2. Foundations: Information Work and Innovation

1. In a study of five-hundred people in four organizations, improvements in productivity were linked to eighteen needs, and twelve of those were communication-related (Culnan and Bair 1983). Also see Bair 1979; Giuliano 1982; Johnson et al. 1983; Paisley 1980; Rice 1980; Strassman 1980.

2. Strassman's book (1985) is an excellent source for detailed and practical analyses of the ratios of the costs and benefits of technology, clerical and managerial workers, and office work. Chapters 6 through 9 provide more challenging thought and figures on office productivity than any other source known to the authors. See also Rice and Bair (1984) for a discussion of how different stakeholders can define performance differently.

3. In one case of WP work monitoring in an Oregon state unemployment benefits division, one workstation had been calling up others' documents and deleting a few pages, thereby bringing down the page count. Then the document was deleted, removing the evidence. Further, on the workstation itself blank documents were created, followed by several "end-of-page" commands; these documents were also then deleted (Miller 1985).

4. See Ackoff 1967; Christie 1981; Feldman and March 1981; Galbraith 1977; Rogers and Kincaid 1981; Weick 1979. Paradoxically, both because use and control of information systems is often symbolic and political, and because such systems allow multiple outputs from the same information, the flow of information may well *increase* rather than *decrease* with the implementation of information systems.

5. See also Bikson, Gutek, and Mankin 1984; Curley and Gremillion 1983; Elizur and Guttman 1976; Hanser and Muchinsky 1978; Lucas 1981; McCosh 1984; O'Reilly 1977; Pfeffer and Salancik 1978; Tornatsky et al. 1980.

6. See, for example, Harvey 1974; Keen 1981; Bronsema, and Zuboff 1982; Kole 1983; Kraemer 1981; Lucas 1981; Markus 1981; Meyer 1982; Pierce and Delbecq 1977; Pirow 1983; Robey and Zeller 1978; Sheposh, Hulton, and Knudsen 1982; Wetherbe, Davis, and Dykman 1981.

7. Kotter and Schlesinger (1979) have suggested a contingency model for implementation that allocates strategies (from straightforward education through persuasion up to explicit coercion) according to the causes for resistance (self-interest, misunderstanding and lack of trust, differences in assessments of the benefits and costs, and low tolerance for change). The literature on how to use media to influence adoption of innovations is summarized by Rice and Paisley (1981).

8. Daft (1984) suggests the first four of these models, and evaluates the empirical evidence for each.

9. Zaltman and Lin (1971) listed twenty dimensions upon which innovations are evaluated. Rogers' (1983) fivefold typology is most commonly used. Sources of research for the following points include: symbolic value of a system: Bariff and Galbraith 1978; Dutton 1981; Feldman and March 1981; Keen 1981; Kole 1983; Kraemer 1981; Markus 1981; Zuboff 1982; perceived accessibility of information source: Culnan 1983; Hardy 1982; Kerr and Hiltz 1982; perceived organizational need for the innovation: Ackoff 1967; Coe and Barnhill 1967; Hopelain 1982; unmet expectations after the innovation has been adopted: Coe and Barnhill 1967; technical performance: Lucas 1981; phased versus "turnkey" implementation: Alavi and Wetherbe 1982; Ginzberg 1981; Hopelain 1982; Klaeysen 1983; Keen 1981; Keen, Bronsema, and Zuboff 1982; Sheposh, Hulton, and Knudsen 1982.

10. Nolan (1973) described four stages in the diffusion of computer systems through an organization, based upon budgetary allocations and control mechanisms: (a) initiation (acquisition), (b) contagion (intense system development), (c) control (proliferation of controls), (d) integration (orientation toward users and service). That is, this phasic model says nothing about the total number of users or adopters, and does not necessarily imply any particular level of technological sophistication. It emphasizes organizational responses and behaviors, and is a rough measure of the *organizational forms* of growth of an information system.

11. For other research on this link between attitudes and system success, see Coe and Barnhill 1967; Danzinger, Dutton, Kling, and Kraemer 1981; Ein-dor and Segev 1978; Hiltz and Turoff 1981; Keen 1981; Kling 1980; Rice 1984; Rice and Associates 1984.

12. The concept of "mutual adaptation"—the iterative process of adapting innovations from their initial form—was developed by Berman and McLaughlin (1975) in their study of educational programs. Hall and Loucks (1977, 1978) discussed "innovation configurations," or the different combination of innovation components, in explaining variations in educational innovations. The term "reinvention" was first

used by Agarwala-Rogers, Rogers, and Wills (1977) in explaining how innovations were adapted by professors.

13. See, for example, Emshoff 1982; Fawcett, Mathews, and Fletcher 1980; Mankin, Bikson, and Gutek 1983; Rice and Rogers 1980; Roitman and Mayer 1982.

3. Implementing Word Processing

1. The details of this analysis are reported in Johnson and Rice 1984: 170–175.
2. Correlational analyses cannot prove a causal relationship among these variables. WP units that provide more services may attract greater interest by authors (which is a useful implication itself). Moreover, the variance explained is too small to be useful for practical management concerns.

4. Four Word Processing Systems

1. The main arguments concerning open systems, environmental variability and organizational design are presented by Ashby 1956; Burns and Stalker 1961; Emery and Trist 1965; Hannan and Freeman 1977; Galbraith 1977; Lawrence and Lorsch 1969. Specific reviews and concepts of contingency theory are presented by Ford and Slocum 1977; Fry 1982; Hage, Aiken, and Marrett 1971; Miner 1980; Perrow 1970; Reimann 1980; Reimann and Inzerilli 1979; Thompson 1967; and Woodward 1965.
2. However, Reimann (1980) and Reimann and Inzerilli (1979) provide considerable evidence for the predominant influence of size and interdependencies. Fry (1982) also analyzes why the Aston studies arrived at their erroneous conclusions, focusing mostly on definitional limitations.
3. For similar conclusions, see Bostrom and Heinen 1977a, b; Elden et al. 1982; Kraemer, Dutton, and Northrop 1981; Kling 1980; Kling and Scacchi 1980; Markus 1981; Reimann and Inzerilli 1979; Tenne and Mannheim 1977.
4. A generally unstated assumption behind the managerial approach to contingency theory is that managers can perceive and identify environmental characteristics and trends in order to match them to technology and structure. However, in the few studies that have attempted to test this assumption, managers' perceptions of environmental uncertainty were more strongly associated with managers' cognitive complexity than with objective measures of the environment (Ford and Slocum 1977). One implication of this result is that managers must become more aware of and informed about their wider organizational environment. Another is that managers' personality types and assumptions have a strong influence on implementation success.
5. There are at least two conditions in which limited organizational adaptation may be a wise strategy (Hannan and Freeman 1977). The first is if environmental changes are frequent and random and the organization successfully competes over a wide range of resources (is a "generalist" as opposed to a "specialist"). In that case, change is simply wasted energy and not conducive to survival. The second is if environmental forces favor inertia. Such forces include barriers to entry and exit, the need to maintain legitimacy, exchange relations, institutional support, and narrow bounds in which organizational accountability operates.

5. Principles of Job Design and Sociotechnical Systems

1. See, for example, Alavi and Wetherbe 1982; Coch and French 1948; Collins and Moores 1983; Edstrom 1977; Ginzberg 1981; Klaeysen 1983; Kole 1983; Lucas 1981; Markus 1982; Mumford, Bancroft, and Sontag 1983; Pirow 1983; Sontag 1983; Taylor 1982. Of course, there are many other ways in which organizations can influence workers' performance, including pay schedules, goal setting, consideration, benefit packages, recruitment, selection, socialization, job descriptions, allocation, termination and the like (Kerr and Slocum 1981; Kimberly 1984; McCann and Galbraith 1981). The discussions in this book do not intend to imply that these mechanisms are not useful and effective, just that they typically are not linked to actual job design or the encouragement of innovation.

2. See, for example, Cherns 1976; Davis 1966; Emery and Trist 1969; Holland, Kretlow, and Ligon 1974; Mumford and Weir 1979.

3. Precise methods and instruments for conducting these STS phases are provided by Bostrom and Heinen 1977b; Cherns 1976; Cummings and Srivastva 1977; Herbst 1974; Mumford 1981; and Pava 1983. There are typically three operational phases in the STS approach. The *strategic design* phase identifies the goals and responsibilities for the project, and early on emphasizes user participation and responsibility as guides to system design. The *sociotechnical design* phase analyzes the problem (identifying sources of negative expectations and attitudes, unsatisfactory social conditions, inter-relationships of tasks and interactions which magnify variations in the system), and proposes alternate, experimental designs. Finally, the *ongoing management* phase is based upon the concept that changes create further changes, so evaluation and evolution of systems must be encouraged and supported. Pava (1983) updates these procedures to handle the nonroutine aspects of information work. While his approach is complex and detailed, the fundamental difference is a concentration on *deliberations*. That is, most nonroutine information work consists of deliberations that involve coalitions of people that operate in a variety of forums which may involve print, electronic, or face-to-face interaction. STS analyses such work to identify the responsibilities of the coalitions, the human resource policies that support effective deliberations, the technical enhancements that assist coalitions in their deliberations, and the structural changes that facilitate the purposes of deliberations.

4. See, for example, Bird 1980; Downing 1980; Gordon 1976; Gregory and Nuss-baum 1982; Harkness 1978; Machung 1983; Smith 1984; and Zimmerman 1982. The social outcomes of implementing computer systems in general have been widely reviewed elsewhere (see Kling 1980; Rice 1980; Rice and Associates 1984).

5. There have been several comprehensive reviews and comparisons of the approaches discussed in this chapter. Cummings, Molloy, and Glen (1975), Nicholas (1982), and Pasmore (1980) looked at job design approaches in general. Locke and Schweiger (1979) took on the whole of the participative decision making literature. Miller and Monge (1986) used statistical methods to compare forty-four studies. Hirschheim (1983) and Ives and Olson (1984) specifically considered the involvement of users in the design and implementation of information systems.

Cummings, Molloy, and Glen (1975), analyzing fifty seven studies, found that participative management (as opposed to autonomous work groups, job restructuring, or organizational restructuring) was the most effective in improving employees' attitudes, although job autonomy was sufficient to improve attitudes. However, participative management was least effective at improving productivity; providing information and feedback was the most successful. The outcomes of different interventions are subject to nearly a score of contingencies identified in the review. For example, participative management was more successful when worker groups' skills were high, or when direct supervision was otherwise difficult. Interventions were also more successful when at least the immediate supervisor was involved in the change process, and when the organization was sincere in accepting the outcomes of worker participation. Fitting technology to the social systems was more successful when tasks were interdependent and they formed identifiable wholes.

Nicholas (1982) concluded from a review of sixty five studies that job enrichment with worker participation, as well as a more general sociotechnical systems approach, both had greater impacts on reduction in work force turnover and absenteeism, and on increases in productivity, than any other approach. However, they had the lowest impact on production costs and product quality. The general category of technostructural approaches was most effective at the group level, and particularly for workers and supervisors. Human process approaches, which focused only on group processes but not on job redesign, were better for improving monetary outcomes (costs, sales) and product quality, had more impact at the organization-wide level than at the group level, and were more beneficial for management, staff, and supervisors than for lower-level workers.

Pasmore (1980) did not find great differences among STS, job redesign, and survey feedback interventions in influencing outcomes in a field experiment involving around 350 workers. All approaches improved employees' attitudes. The STS intervention led to higher productivity and cost savings.

Locke and Schweiger's (1979) review of participation research first emphasized that productivity, not satisfaction, should be the proper goal of a for-profit organization, and then proceeded to show that, in general, satisfaction is not much linked to productivity. (Macarov states the extreme position on this relationship: "no generalizable, functional, replicable relationship between workers' satisfaction and their productivity has been found" [1982: 118]). One factor that *does* improve this relationship is when subordinates in participatory situations have knowledge about (a) their specific tasks and (b) the process of participation. In general, however, the authors found that participation was more associated with satisfaction than with productivity. Of the forty-six studies testing the productivity association, 22 percent found participation a positive influence, 56 percent found no difference, and 22 percent found participation a negative influence. Of the forty-three studies testing the satisfaction influence, the figures were 60 percent, 30 percent, and 9 percent. Case studies and multivariate field experiments were excluded from this summary because the authors claimed there was no way to unravel the separate effects of all the variables.

Miller and Monge (1986) arranged their meta-evaluation along the lines summarized in the section on participation. They found, overall, no support for the third model, that individual differences in needs and the extent to which the job provides challenge affect the relationship between participation and productivity. The second model, that participation facilitated cognitive processes whereby information leads to better understanding of the job and new ideas, received moderate support. Relationships were stronger for productivity than satisfaction, and stronger for decisions about which workers have specific knowledge. The first model, that attitudes and values are the path through which participation affects outcomes, received the greatest support. The relationship was stronger for its effect on satisfaction than on productivity, stronger for lower-level employees, and stronger in climates that supported participation in general. While Miller and Monge's study reinforces the primary conclusion of Locke and Schweiger (1979) that participation is most influential when workers have, and gain, information directly relevant to the target work processes, they also argue (on the basis of an overall correlation of .46) that a participative climate in the organization is the most significant factor.

Hirschheim (1983) is quite pessimistic about the effect of user participation on the design of systems. His review of prior studies and his own study of sixty information system users in twenty organizations concluded that user involvement shows (a) few associations with system use, (b) contradictory associations with positive attitudes toward the system, and (c) contradictory associations, when they exist, with system quality. He suggests that participatory design is much more complicated than usually described; it tends not to be formally evaluated; it is praised by participants; and it is not normally used a second time.

The most comprehensive and analytic review of involvement in the development and implementation of management information systems to date is by Ives and Olson (1984). In general, only about one of three studies showed positive effects of participation on these outcomes: system quality, system usage, user behavior and attitudes, and information satisfaction. One of the contingencies influencing the relationship between participation and implementation success was the life cycle of the information system. For example, involvement may improve acceptance, but have no effect on the actual design of the system. Problem definition and installation are likely to profit more by participation than system design and actual construction. Edstrom's study (1977) of four key actors in each of sixteen companies suggested that the stage of system development would interact with user participation in affecting system success. User involvement in the determination of project scope phase, and the system analysis phase, were significantly and positively related with success (r = .58, .57).

There seems to be an exceptional number of factors affecting, and affected by, involvement. Studies do not involve comparable organizations, systems, or measures, and are seldom explicit about whether system usage is required or voluntary. The ideological arguments are often confounded with practical evidence, different researchers use different models, and methodological designs may not be conclusive. Methodological problems in the early participation and human relations studies have largely discredited their findings (see Bartlem and Locke 1981; Franke and Kaul 1978). For example, the substantial productivity differences found in participative vs. nonparticipative groups in the Coch and French study (1948) could as well have been due to the way job changes were explained, the way the time studies were conducted, the amount of additional training the experimental groups received, differences in group size, the perceived fairness of pay rates, and organizational trust. Bartlem and Locke (1981) conclude that the perceived fairness of the new pay rates was likely the main factor, though participation was one way to convince the workers of such fair pay.

6. The Design of Word Processing Jobs

1. This section is based upon analyses and interpretation by Dr. Jim Taylor, currently principal of Socio-Technical Design Consultants, Inc. of New York.

8. Managing Word Processing Boundaries

1. Another typology identifies boundaries according to technology, time, and territory (see Miller 1959) but information flow is not completely described by these obstacles.

2. A fourth problem in boundary management concerns technical issues of standardization, compatibility, and integration.

As installations became more sophisticated in the use of WP they began to expand into an integrated environment. For example, respondents at forty sites specifically mentioned the recent addition of telecommunication services. Thirty-three percent regularly communicated using WP at the time of the survey. In most cases, this involved transfer of information between WP machines or units; only seven percent were communicating with mainframes at that time. Communication, networking, and integration of WP with mainframes, microcomputers, and external information sources will heighten the need for technical boundary management.

Nearly a quarter (23 percent) of the organizations reported serious problems with system compatibility, while fifteen percent said they had some problems, but compatibility was not a major problem. Sixty-three percent reported no problems. The trend was for problems to occur initially as organizations got their first equipment with little understanding of potential compatibility problems; they solved these initial problems by standardizing on one vendor who provided all the equipment they needed to do production word processing work. But compatibility problems may likely rise again with the increasing need to communicate with mainframes and to use personal computers with peripherals from many different vendors.

Therefore, technical boundary management must not only concentrate on the identified vendor of a particular machine, but must also foresee the needs and consequences of integration and expansion plans with respect to other equipment by the preferred vendor as well as secondary or competing vendors. The integrated systems environment produces a new situation, one almost without precedent in consumer history: which vendor is responsible for potential or actual interconnectivity solutions? Alert buyers can get legal documents guaranteeing that promised compatibility will be realized. Enforcing such guarantees, however, is expensive and unpredictable.

This topic is discussed in greater detail by Johnson and Rice (1985).

3. See Cherns (1976) for a discussion of the conceptual foundations of this outcome.

References

Ackoff, R. 1967. "Management Misinformation Systems." *Management Science* 2(4):147–156.

Agarwala-Rogers, R., E. M. Rogers, and R. Wills. 1977. *Diffusion of Impact Innovations from 1973–1976: Interpersonal Networks Among University Professors.* Stanford, Calif.: Applied Communication Research.

Akiba, E., S. Ehrlich, and V. Munson. 1982. "Automated Proofreaders: What Do People Want?" Lowell, Mass.: Wang Laboratories.

Alavi, M. and J. Wetherbe. 1982. "Reducing Complexity in Information Requirements Planning." *Systems, Objectives, Solutions* 2:143–157.

Aldrich, H. 1972. "Technology and Organizational Structure: A Reexamination of the Findings of the Aston Group." *Administrative Science Quarterly* 17:26–43.

Aldrich, H., B. McKelvey, and D. Ulrich. 1984. "Design Strategy from the Population Perspective." *Journal of Management* 10(1):67–86.

Arnett, T. 1981. "Intelligent Copiers-Printers Can Save You Time and Labor." *The Office* (November), pp.155, 158.

Aron, C. 1981. "To Barter Their Souls for Gold: Female Clerks in Federal Government Office, 1862–1890." *Journal of American History* 67(4):835–853. (Cited in Whalen 1983).

Aschner, K. 1982. *The Word Processing Handbook: A Step-by-Step Guide to Automating Your Office.* White Plains, New York: Knowledge Industries Publications.

Ashby, W. R. 1956. "Self-Regulation and Requisite Variety." In *Introduction to Cybernetics* pp.202–218. New York: Wiley.

Astley, W. 1984. "Toward an Appreciation of Collective Strategy." *Academy of Management Review* 9(3):526–535.

Austin, S. 1986. "Image Makers." *Business Computer Systems* 5(6):69–76.

Bair, J. 1979. "Communication in the Office of the Future: Where the Real Payoff May Be." *Business Communications Review* 9(1):1–11.

Baran, S., P. Zandan and J. Vanston. "How Effectively Are We Managing Innovation?" *Research Management* 29(1):23–25.

Barcomb, D. 1981. *Office Automation: A Survey of Tools and Techniques.* Bedford, Mass.: Digital Press.

Bariff, M. and J. Galbraith. 1978. "Intraorganizational Power Considerations for Designing Information Systems." *Accounting Organizations and Society* 3:15–27.

Bartlem, C. and E. Locke. 1981. "The Coch and French Study: A Critique and Reinterpretation." *Human Relations* 34(7):555–566.

Beniger, J. 1986. *The Control Revolution.* Cambridge: Harvard University Press.

Bennett, R., D. Durand, and S. Betty. 1986. "Managerial Evaluation of End-User Generated Communications: An Empirical Investigation." Denver: University of Colorado.

Berman, P. and N. McLaughlin. 1975. *Federal Programs Supporting Educational Change.* Vol. 4: *The Findings in Review.* Santa Monica, Calif.: Rand.

Bernstein, A. 1985. "Fit to Print." *Business Computer Systems* (January), pp.48–55.

Bigelow, C. and D. Day. 1983. "Digital Typography." *Scientific American* 249–2:106–119.

Bikson, T. and B. Gutek. 1983. "Training in Automated Offices: An Empirical Study of Design and Methods." In *Training for Tomorrow Proceedings.* Leiden, The Netherlands.

Bikson, T., B. Gutek, and D. Mankin. 1984. "Implementation of Information Technology in Office Settings." Santa Monica, Calif.: Rand.

Bird, E. 1980. *Information Technology in the Office: The Impact on Women's Jobs.* Manchester, England: Equal Opportunities Commission.

Bliven, B., Jr. 1954. *The Wonderful Writing Machine.* New York: Random House.

Bostrom, R. and J. Heinen. 1977a "MIS Problems and Failures: A Socio-Technical Perspective. Part I: The Causes." *MIS Quarterly* (September), pp. 17–32.

Bostrom, R. and J. Heinen. 1977b. "MIS Problems and Failures: A Socio-Technical Perspective. Part II: The Application of Socio-Technical Theory." *MIS Quarterly* (December), pp. 11–28.

Brenner, D. and R. Logan. 1980. "Some Considerations in the Diffusion of Medical Technologies: Medical Information Systems." In D. Nimmo, ed., *Communication Yearbook 4,* pp. 609–624. New Brunswick, New Jersey: Transaction Books.

Bridges, L. 1986. "Steady Growth Seen for Scanner Market." *PC Week* May 20, 1986 3(20):5.

Buchanan, D. and D. Boddy. 1982. "Advanced Technology and the Quality of Working Life: The Effects of Word Processing on Video Typists." *Journal of Occupational Psychology* 55:1–11

Buell, B., G. Bock and G. Lewis. 1986. "Now the Print Shop Is Just a Few Keystrokes Away." *Business Week* Industrial/Technology Edition, March 17, 1986, pp. 106–108.

Burns, T. and W. Stalker. 1961. *The Management of Innovations.* London: Tavistock.

Campbell, J. 1977. "On the Nature of Organizational Effectiveness." In P. Goodman and J. Pennings, eds., *New Perspectives on Organizational Effectiveness.* San Francisco: Jossey-Bass.

Chamber of Commerce. 1980. "Workers' Attitudes toward Productivity: A New Survey." Washington, D.C.: Chamber of Congress.

Chandler, A. 1977. *The Visible Hand.* Cambridge: Belknap Press of Harvard University Press.

Chartock, D. 1985. "Desktop Publishing Bandwagon Gaining Momentum with Dealers." *Computer and Software News* 3(37):1 ff.

Cherns, A. 1976. "The Principles of Socio-Technical Design." *Human Relations* 29(8):783–792.

Cherry, L., M. Fox, L. Frase, P. Gingrich, S. Keennan, and N. Macdonald. 1983. "Computer Aids for Text Analysis." *Bell Laboratories Record* 61(5):10–16.

Child, J. 1972. "Organization Structure, Environment and Performance: The Role of Strategic Choice." *Sociology* 6:1–22.

Chorafas, D. 1982. *Office Automation: The Productivity Challenge*. Englewood Cliffs, N.J.: Prentice-Hall.

Christie, B. 1981. *Face to File Communication: A Psychological Approach to Information Systems*. New York: Wiley.

Coch, L. and J. French, Jr. 1948. "Overcoming Resistance to Change." *Human Relations* 1(4):512–532.

Coe, R. and E. Barnhill. 1967. "Social Dimensions of Failure in Innovation." *Organizations* 26(3):149–156.

Cohen, B. 1983. "An Overview of NIOSH Research on Clerical Workers." In D. Marschall and J. Gregory, eds., *Office Automation: Jekyll or Hyde?* Cleveland: Working Women Educational Fund.

Cohen, M, J. March, and J. Olsen. 1972. "A Garbage Can Model of Organizational Choice." *Administrative Science Quarterly* 17:1–25.

Coleman, J., E. Katz, and H. Menzel. 1966. *Medical Innovation: A Diffusion Study*. New York: Bobbs and Merrill.

Collins, F. and T. Moores. 1983. "Microprocessors in the Office: A Study of Resistance to Change." *Journal of Systems Management* (November), pp. 17–21.

Comptroller General. 1984. "Strong Central Management of Office Atuomation will Boost Productivity." *Systems, Objectives, Solutions* 4:35–50.

Cordell, R. 1984. "Rock-Solid Office Architecture." *Computerworld on Communications* October 3, 1984, pp. 21–23.

Crozier, M. 1964. *The Bureaucratic Phenomenon*. Chicago: University of Chicago Press.

CRWTH. 1985. "The Second CRWTH Information Center Survey." Santa Monica, Calif.: CRWTH Computer Courseware.

Culnan, M. 1983. "Environmental Scanning: The Effects of Task Complexity and Source Accessibility on Information Gathering Behavior." *Decision Sciences* 14(2):192–206.

Culnan, M. and J. Bair. 1983. "Human Communication Needs and Organizational Productivity: The Potential Impact of Office Automation." *Journal of the American Society for Information Science* 34(3):218–224.

Cummings, T. 1981. "Designing Affective Work Groups." In P. Nystrom and W. Starbuck, eds., *Handbook of Organizational Design* 2:250–271. New York: Oxford University Press.

Cummings, T. 1978. "Self-Regulating Work Groups: A Socio-technical Synthesis." *Academy of Management Review* 3(3):625–634.

Cummings, T. and S. Srivastva. 1977. *Management of Work: A Socio-Technical Systems Approach*. Kent, Ohio: Kent State University Press.

Cummings, T., E. Molloy, and R. Glen. 1975. "Intervention Strategies for Improving Productivity and the Quality of Work Life." *Organizational Dynamics* (Summer), pp. 53–68.

Curley, K. 1981. *Word Processing: First Step to the Office of the Future? An Examination of an Evolving Technology and Its Use in Organizations*. Unpublished Ph.D. dissertation. Cambridge, Mass.: Harvard Graduate School of Business Administration.

Curley, K. and L. Gremillion. 1983. "The Role of the Champion in DSS Implementation." *Information and Management* 6(4):203–209.

Curley, K. and P. Pyburn. 1982. "Intellectual Technologies: The Key to Improving White-Collar Productivity." *Sloan Management Review* (Fall), pp. 31–39.

Dachler, H. and B. Wilpert, 1978. "Conceptual Dimensions and Boundaries of Participation in Organizations: A Critical Evaluation." *Administrative Science Quarterly* 23:1–39.

Daft, R. 1982. "Bureaucratic Versus Non-Bureaucratic Structure and the Process of Innovation and Change." *Research in the Sociology of Organizations* 1:129–166.

Daft, R. and R. Lengel. 1984. "Information Richness: A New Approach to Managerial Behavior and Organization Design." *Research in Organizational Behavior* 6:191–233.

Daft, R. and N. Macintosh. 1981. "A Tentative Exploration into the Amount and Equivocality of Information Processing in Organizational Work Units." *Administrative Science Quarterly* 26:207–224.

Danzinger, J., W. Dutton, R. Kling, and K. Kraemer. 1982. *Computers and Politics: High Technology in American Local Government.* New York: Columbia University Press.

Datapro. 1984. "All About Word Processing Systems, Including User Ratings." Delran, N.J.: Datapro.

Dataquest. 1985. *SWIS Markets Report.* New York:Dataquest.

Davis, J. 1969. *Group Performance.* Reading, Mass.: Addison-Wesley.

Davis, L. 1966. "The Design of Jobs." *Industrial Relations* 6(1):21–45.

Davis, L. and J. Taylor, eds. 1979. *Design of Jobs.* 2d edition. Santa Monica, Calif.: Goodyear.

Davis, L., R. Canter, and J. Hoffman. 1955. "Current Job Design Criteria." *The Journal of Industrial Engineering* 16:1–7.

Delgado, E. 1979. *The Enormous File.* Norwich, Great Britain: Fletcher and Son.

DeSousa, M. 1981. "Electronic Information Interchange in an Office Environment." *IBM Systems Journal* 20(1):4–22.

Dewhirst, H. 1971. "Influence of Perceived Information-Sharing Norms on Communication Channel Utilization." *Academy of Management Journal* (September), pp. 305–315.

Dickson, G., R. Leitheser, J. Wetherbe, and M. Nechis. 1984. "Key Information Systems Issues for the 1980s." *MIS Quarterly* 8(3):135–159.

D'Onofrio, M. 1983. "Investigation of the Relationship Between Task Design and Job Satisfaction of Traditional Secretaries and Word Processing Operators." *Office Systems Research Journal* 2(1):1–10.

Dordick, H. and R. E. Rice. 1984. "Transmission Systems." In C. Meadow and A. Tedesco, eds., *Telecommunications for Management,* pp. 55–90. New York: McGraw-Hill.

Doswell, A. 1983. *Office Automation.* New York: Wiley.

Downing, H. 1980. "Word Processors and the Oppression of Women." In E. Forester, ed. *The Microelectronics Revolution,* pp. 275–287. Cambridge, Mass.: MIT Press.

Drucker, P. 1979. "Work and Tools." In *Technology, Management, and Society.* New York: Harper.

Duncan, R. 1976. "The Ambidextrous Organization: Design Dual Structures for Innovation." In R. Killmann, L. Pondy, and D. Slevin, eds., *The Management of Organizational Design,* pp. 167–188 New York: North-Holland.

Dunlop, J., ed. 1962. *Automation and Technological Change.* Englewood Cliffs, N.J.: Prentice-Hall.

Dutton, W. 1981. "The Rejection of an Innovation: The Political Environment of a Computer-Based Model." *Systems, Objectives, and Solutions* 1:179–201.

Edelman, F. 1981. "Managers, Systems and Productivity." *MIS Quarterly* 5(3):1–20.

Edstrom, A. 1977. "User Influence and the Success of MIS Projects: A Contingency Approach." *Human Relations* 30(7):589–607.

Edwards, N. ed. 1982. *Office Automation: A Glossary and Guide.* White Plains, New York: Knowledge Industries Publications.

Ein-dor, P. and E. Segev. 1978. "Organizational Context and the Success of Management Information Systems." *Management Science* 24(10):1064–1077.

Elden, M., V. Havn, N. Levin, T. Nilssen, B. Rasmussen, and K. Velum. 1982. *Good Technology Is Not Enough: Automation and Work Design in Norway.* Norway: Institute for Social Research in Industry.

Elizur, D. and L. Guttman. 1976. "The Structure of Attitudes Toward Work and Technological Change within an Organization." *Administrative Science Quarterly* 21:611–622.

Emery, F. 1982. "New Perspectives on the World of Work." *Human Relations* 35(12):1095–1122.

Emery, F. and E. Trist. 1965. "The Causal Texture of Organizational Environments." *Human Relations,* 18:21–31.

Emery, F. and E. Trist. 1969. "Socio-Technical Systems." In F. Emery, ed., *Systems Thinking,* pp. 281–296. Harmondsworth, England: Penguin.

Emshoff, J. 1982. "Innovational Processes: The Issues and the Research" In C. Blakely, *Adoption, Implementation and Routinization of Organizational Innovations.* Washington, D.C.: Symposium at the American Psychological Association.

Englebart, D. 1962. *Augmenting Human Intellect: A Conceptual Framework.* Summary Report. Menlo Park, Calif.: Stanford Research Institute.

Eveland, J., E. Rogers, and C. Klepper. 1977. *The Innovation Process in Publication Organizations: Some Elements of a Preliminary Model.* Ann Arbor, Mich.: Dept. of Journalism, University of Michigan.

Fawcett, S., R. Mathews, and R. Fletcher. 1980. "Some Promising Dimensions for Behavioral Community Technology." *Journal of Applied Behavior Analysis* 13:505–518.

Feldman, M. and J. March. 1981. "Information in Organizations as Signal and Symbol." *Administrative Science Quuarterly,* 26:171–186.

Ford, J. and J. Slocum. 1977. "Size, Technology, Environment and the Structure of Organizations." *Academy of Management Journal* (October), pp. 561–575.

Forester, T. ed. 1985. *The Information Technology Revolution.* Cambridge, Mass.: MIT Press.

Fortune. 1985. "Office Systems for the Eighties: The Productivity Challenge." *Fortune* (October 14), advertisement section.

Franke, R. and J. Kaul. 1978. "The Hawthorne Experiments: First Statistical Interpretation." *American Sociological Review* 43:623–643.

Fry, L. 1982. "Technology-Structure Research: Three Critical Issues." *Academy of Management Journal* 25(3):532–552.

Galbraith, J. 1977. *Organization Design.* Reading, Mass.: Addison-Wesley.

GAO. 1979. "Federal Productivity Suffers Because Word Processing Is Not Well Managed." Government Accounting Office/FGMSD–79–17. Gaithersburg, Md.: Document Handling and Information Services Facility.

GAO. 1981. "Office Automation in the Federal Government: A Special Report." Government Accounting Office. Washington, D.C.: National Archives and Record Service.

GAO. 1982. "Strong Central Management of Office Automation Will Boost Productivity." Washington, D.C.:Government Accounting Office/AFMO-82-54.

Gilheany, S. 1985. "Quarto Documents in Digital Engineering Document Management." Paper presented at the Conference on Engineering Data Management, Automation Technology Institute, Pebble Beach, Calif., (February).

Ginzberg, M. 1978. "Redesign of Managerial Tasks: A Requisite for Successful Decision Support Systems." *MIS Quarterly* (March), pp. 39–52.

Ginzberg, M. 1981a. "A Prescriptive Model for System Implementation." *Systems, Objectives, Solutions,* 1:33–46.

Ginzberg, M. 1981b. "Key Recurrent Issues in the MIS Implementation Process." *MIS Quarterly* 5(2):47–59.

Giuliano, V. 1980. "The Hidden Productivity Factor." *Telephony Magazine* (July 21).

Giuliano, V. 1982. "The Mechanization of Office Work." *Scientific American* 274(4):148–165.

Glenn, E. and R. Feldberg. 1977. "Degraded and Deskilled: The Proletarianization of Clerical Work." *American Journal of Sociology* 25:52–64.

Gordon, F. 1976. "Telecommunications: Implications for Women." *Telecommunications Policy* 1(1):68–74.

Grandjean, E. 1983. "Ergonomics and the Information Technologies." *Information Resource Management* 1(1):38–39.

Gray, R. and G. Evans. "Document Interchange Format (DIF)." In J. Goldthwaite ed., *OAC '85 Conference Digest,* pp. 35–40. Washington, D.C.: American Federation of Information Processing Societies.

Gregerman, I. 1981. *Knowledge Worker Productivity.* New York: Amacom.

Gregory, J. and K. Nussbaum. "Race Against Time: Automation of the Office. An Analysis of the Trends in Office Automation and the Impact on the Office Workplace." *Office: Technology and People* 1:197–236.

Grove, A. 1983. *Hi-Output Management.* New York: Random House.

Hackman, J. and E. Lawler. 1971. "Employee Reactions to Job Characteristics." *Journal of Applied Psychology Monograph* 55:259–286.

Hackman, J. and G. Oldham. 1976. "Motivation Through the Design of Work." *Organizational Behavior and Human Performance* 16:250–279.

Hage, J., M. Aiken, and C. Marrett. 1971. "Organization Structure and Communications." *American Sociological Review* 36:860–871.

Hall, K. 1981. "The Economic Nature of Information." *The Information Society* 1(2):143–166.

Hall, G. and S. Loucks. 1977. "A Developmental Model for Determining Whether the Treatment is Actually Implemented." *American Educational Research Journal* 14(3):263–276.

Hall, G. and S. Loucks. 1978. "Innovation Configurations: Analyzing the Adaptations of Innovations." Austin, Tex.: Research and Development Center for Teacher Education.

Halladay, M. 1985. "More Alike Than Different." *Information Center* 1(8):60–66.

Hannan, M. and J. Freeman. 1977. "The Population Ecology of Organizations." *American Journal of Sociology* 82:929–64.

Hannan, M. and J. Freeman. 1984. "Structural Inertia and Organizational Change." *American Sociological Review* 49:149–164.

Hanser, L. and P. Muchinsky. 1978. "Work as an Information Environment." *Organizational Behavior and Human Performance* 21:47–60.

Hardy, A. 1982. "The Selection of Channels When Seeking Information: Cost/Benefit vs. Least-Effort." *Information Processing and Management* 18(6):289–293.

Harkness, R. 1978. "Office Information Systems: An Overview and Agenda for Public Policy Research." *Telecommunications Policy* (June), pp. 91–104.

Harris, L. 1981. "Perspectives on Productivity: A Global View." Stevens Point, Wis.:Sentry Insurance Company.

Harvey, A. 1974. "Factors Making for Implementation Success and Failure." *Management Science* 16(6):312–321.

Head, R. 1985. "Information Resource Center: A New Force in End-User Computing." *Journal of Systems Management* (February), pp. 24–29.

Hedberg, B. and E. Mumford. 1975. "The Design of Computer Systems." In E. Mumford and H. Sackman, eds., *Human Choice and Computers*, pp. 31–59. Amsterdam: North Holland.

Hedberg, B. and E. Mumford. 1979. "Design of Computer Systems." In L. Davis and J. Taylor, eds., *Design of Jobs.* 2d edition. Santa Monica, Calif.: Goodyear.

Herbst, P. 1974. *Sociotechnical Design.* London:Tavistock.

Hicks, L. 1984. "Secretaries' Beliefs and Attitudes Toward Office Automation: A Summary of the Major Findings." Ithaca, N.Y.: Cornell University Dept. of Communication Arts.

Hiltz, S. R.1983. *On-line Research Communities: A Case Study in the Office of the Future.* Norwood, N.J.: Ablex.

Hiltz, S. R. and M. Turoff. 1978. *The Network Nation: Human Communication Via Computer.* Reading, Mass.: Addison-Wesley Advanced Book Program.

Hiltz, S. R. and M. Turoff. 1981. "The Evolution of User Behavior in a Computerized Conferencing System." *Communications of the ACM* 24(11):739–751.

Hiltz, S. R. and M. Turoff. 1985. "Structuring Computer-Mediated Communication Systems to Avoid Information Overload." *Communications of the ACM* 28(7):680–689.

Hirschheim, R. 1983. "Assessing Participative Systems Design: Some Conclusions from an Exploratory Study." *Systems, Objectives, Solutions* 6:317–327.

Hirschheim, R. 1985. *Office Automation: A Social and Organizational Perspective.* New York: Wiley.

Holland, W., W. Kretlow, and J. Ligon. 1974. "Socio-Technical Aspects of MIS." *Journal of Systems Management* 25(2):14–16.

Hopelain, D. 1982. "Assessing the Climate for Change: A Method for Managing Change in a System Implementation." *Systems, Objectives, Solutions* 2:55–65.

Hubbart, W. 1983. "A Personnel Policies Primer." *Office Administration and Automation.* 44(1):40 ff.

Huber, G. 1984. "The Nature and Design of Post-Industrial Organizations." *Management Science* 30(8):928–951.

IBM. 1983. "Introducing the Professional Office System." International Business Machines document GH20–5601-3.

Information Today. 1985. "ISIS Dishes Up Silver Platter CD Rom Service." *Information Today* 2(3):1,17.

Infoworld February 6, 1984.

Ives, B. and M. Olson. 1984. "User Involvement and MIS Success: A Review of Research." *Management Science* 30(5):586–603.

Johnson, B. and R. E. Rice. 1984. "Reinvention in the Innovation Process: The Case of Word Processing." In R. E. Rice and Associates, *The New Media: Communication, Research and Technology*, pp. 157–184. Beverly Hills, Calif.: Sage.

Johnson, B. and R. E. Rice. 1985. "Policy Implications in Implementing Office Systems Technology." In V. Mosco, ed., *Policy Research in Telecommunications*, pp. 278–285. Norwood, N.J.: Ablex.

Johnson, B., J. Taylor, D. Smith, and T. Cline. 1983. *Innovation in Word Processing: Report of a Maturing Technology*. Stanford, Calif.: Institute for Communication Research.

Judson, A. 1982. "The Awkward Truth About Productivity." *Harvard Business Review* 60(5):93–97.

Kanter, R. 1977. *Men and Women of the Corporation*. New York: Basic Books.

Kanter, R. 1983. *The Change Masters: Innovation and Entrepreneurship in the American Corporation*. New York: Simon and Schuster.

Karten, N. 1985. "When the Honeymoon Is Over." *Information Center* 1(8):50–54.

Katz, D. and R. Kahn. 1978. *The Social Psychology of Organizations*. New York: Wiley.

Keen, P. 1981. "Information Systems and Organizational Change." *Communications of the ACM* 24(1):24–33.

Keen, P. and M. Scott Morton. 1978. *Decision Support Systems*. Menlo Park, Calif.: Addison-Wesley.

Keen, P., G. Bronsema, and S. Zuboff. 1982. "Implementing Common Systems: One Organization's Experience." *Systems, Objectives, Solutions* 2:125–142.

Kelly, P. and M. Kranzberg. 1978. *Technological Innovation*. San Francisco: San Francisco Press.

Kerr, E. and S. R. Hiltz. 1982. *Computer-Mediated Communication Systems*. New York: Academic Press.

Kerr, S. and J. Slocum, Jr. 1981. "Controlling the Performances of People in Organizations." In P. Nystrom and W. Starbuck, eds., *Handbook of Organizational Design*, 2:116–134. New York: Oxford University Press.

Kessler-Harris, A. 1982. *Out to Work: A History of Wage-Earning Women in the United States*. New York: Oxford University Press.

Kimberly, J. 1984. "The Anatomy of Organizational Design." *Journal of Management* 10(1):109–126.

Klaeysen, A. 1981. "Case Study of Two Information System Implementation Efforts Using the Kolb-Frohman Model of Consultation." *Systems, Objectives, Solutions*, pp. 227–235.

Klauss, R. and B. Bass. 1982. *Interpersonal Communication in Organizations*. New York: Academic Press.

Kling, R. 1980. "Social Analyses of Computing: Theoretical Perspectives in Recent Empirical Research." *Computing Surveys* 12(1):61–110.

Kling, R. and W. Scacchi. 1980. "Computing as Social Action: The Social Dynamics of Computing in Complex Organizations." *Advances in Computers* 19:249–327.

Knuth, D. 1979. *TEX and Metafont*. Bedford, Mass.: Digital Press.

Kolb, D. and A. Frohman. 1970. "An Organizational Development Approach to Consulting." *Sloan Management Reveiw* 12(1):51–65.

Kole, M. 1983. "A Non-Developmental MIS Strategy for Small Organizations." *Systems, Objectives, Solutions* 3:31–39.

Kotter, J. and L. Schlesinger. 1979. "Choosing Strategies for Change." *Harvard Business Review* (March) pp. 106–114.

Kraemer, K. 1981. "The Politics of Model Implementation." *Systems, Objectives, Solutions* 1(4):161–178.

Kraemer, K., W. Dutton, and A. Northrop. 1981. *The Management of Information Systems.* New York: Columbia University Press.

Krois, P. and P. Benson. 1980. "Word Processing and Personnel." *Personnel Journal* 59(1):992–995,1008.

Labuz, R. 1984. *How to Typeset from a Word Processor: An Interfacing Guide.* New York: Bowker.

Lawler, E. and S. Mohrman. 1985. "Quality Circles after the Fad." *Harvard Business Review,* 65–71.

Lawrence, P. and J. Lorsch. 1969. *Organization and Environment.* Homewood, Ill.: Irwin.

Leddy, M. 1986. "Desktop Publishing Systems Growth Anticipated." *PC Week* January 21, 1986.

Leffingwill, W. 1926. *The Office Appliance Manual.* Office Equipment Catalogue, Inc. (Cited in Whalen 1983.)

Lehman, J., D. Vogel and G. Dickson. 1984. "Business Graphics Trends." *Datamation,* November 15, 1984, pp. 119–122.

Lerner, R., T. Metaxas, J. Scott, P. Adams, and R. Judd. "Primary Publication Systems and Scientific Data Processing." In M. Williams ed. *Annual Review of Information Science and Technology,* 18:127–150. New York: Knowledge Industry.

Lieberman, M., G. Selig, and J. Walsh. 1982. *Office Automation: A Manager's Guide for Improved Productivity.* New York: Wiley.

Link Resources. 1984. *The New Database Delivery Channels.* Report no. 93. New York: Link Resources.

Locke, E. and D. Schweiger. 1979. "Participation in Decision-Making: One More Look." *Research in Organizational Behavior,* 1:265–339.

Lubaz, R. 1984. *How to Typeset from a Word Processor: An Introductory Guide.* New York: Bowker.

Lucas, H. C., Jr. 1981. *Implementation: The Key to Successful Information Systems.* New York: Columbia University Press.

Lugsdin, J. 1977. "Computing Power on Demand to the End User." IBM Canada, Ltd. Information Systems Division Information Center. Presented to GUIDE, London.

Lum, V., D. Choy, and N. Shu. 1982. "OPAS: An Office Procedure Automation System." *IBM Systems Journal* 21(3):327–350.

Lynton, R. 1969. "Linking an Innovative Subsystem into the System." *Administrative Science Quarterly* 14(3):398–414.

Macarov, D. 1982. *Worker Productivity: Myths and Reality.* Beverly Hills, Calif.: Sage Library of Social Research.

McCann, J. and J. Galbraith. 1981. "Interdepartmental Relations." In P. Nystrom and W. Starbuck, eds., *Handbook of Organizational Design,* 2:60–84. New York: Oxford University Press.

McCartney, L. 1985. "Image Processing: Gearing up for Office and Factory Use." *Dun's Business Month* 126(1)81–82.

McCosh, A. 1984. "Factors Common to the Successful Implementation of Twelve Decision Support Systems and How They Differ from Three Failures." *Systems, Objectives, Solutions* 4:17–28.

McFarlan, F. and J. McKenney. 1983. "The Information Archipelago—Governing the New World." *Harvard Business Review* (July/August), pp. 91–99.

McGregor, D. 1960. *The Human Side of Enterprise*. New York: McGraw-Hill.

Machung, A. 1983. "Turning Secretaries into Word Processors: Some Fiction and a Fact or Two." In D. Marschall and J. Gregory, eds., *Office Automation: Jekyll or Hyde?* Cleveland: Working Women Education Fund.

McLeod, R., Jr. and D. Bender. 1982. "The Integration of Word Processing into a Management Information System." *MIS Quarterly* December: 11–29.

McNeill, D. 1985. "Image Processing." *Popular Computing* 4(10):4–66, 124–125.

Mankin, D., T. Bikson, and B. Gutek. 1983. "Factors in Successful Implementation of Computer-Based Office Information Systems: A Review of the Literature with Suggestions for Organizational Behavior Management Research." Santa Monica, Calif.: Rand.

Manross, G. and R. E. Rice. 1986. "Don't Hang Up! Organizational Diffusion of the Intelligent Telephone." *Information and Management* 10:161–175.

March, J. 1978. "Bounded Rationality, Ambiguity, and the Engineering of Choice." *Bell Journal of Economics* 9:587–608.

March, J. 1981. "Footnotes to Organizational Change." *Administrative Science Quarterly* 26:563–577.

March, J. and H. Simon. 1958. *Organizations*. New York: Wiley.

Markus, M. L. 1981. "Implementation Politics: Top Management Support and User Involvement." *Systems, Objectives, Solutions* 1(4):203–216.

Markus, M. L. and J. Yates. 1982. "Historical Lessons for the Automated Office." *Computer Decisions* (June), pp. 116 ff.

Marshall, H., E. Popham, and R. Tilton. 1978. *Secretarial Procedures and Administration*. Cincinatti: Southwestern.

Martin, J. 1976. *Principles of Data-Base Management*. Englewood Cliffs, N.J.: Prentice-Hall.

Maslow, A. 1943. "A Theory of Human Motivation." *Psychological Review* 50:370–396.

Mechanic, D. 1964. "Sources of Power of Low Participants in Complex Organizations." In W. Cooper, H. Leavitt, and M. Shelly, eds., *New Perspectives in Organizational Research*, pp.136–149. New York: Wiley.

Melin, N. 1983. "Optical Disks in Libraries." *Information Today* (September), pp. 7, 33.

Meyer, N. D. 1983. "Office Automation Cookbook: Management Strategies for Getting Office Automation Moving." *Sloan Management Review* (Winter), pp. 51–59.

Meyer, N. D. 1982. *"Organizing an OA Support Staff." Computer Decisions* (October), pp. 74, 78.

Michtom, J. 1985. "Does Your IC Measure Up?" *Information Center* 1(8):42–47.

Miller, E. 1959. "Technology, Territory, and Time: The Internal Differentiation of Complex Production Systems." *Human Relations* 12:243–272.

Miller, K. and P. Monge. 1986. "Participation, Satisfaction and Productivity: A Meta-Analytic Review." *Academy of Management Journal* 29(4):727–753.

Miller, M. 1985. "Productivity Spies: Computers Keep Eye on Workers and See If They Perform Well." *Wall Street Journal,* June 3, 1985.

Mills, P. 1983. "Self-Management: Its Control and Relationship to Other Organizational Properties." *Academy of Management Review* 8(3):445–453.

Mills, P. and B. Posner. 1982. "The Relationships Among Self-Supervision, Structure and Technology in Professional Service Organizations." *Academy of Management Journal* 25(2):437–443.

Miner, J. 1980. *Theories of Organizational Behavior.* Hinsdale, Ill.: Dryden.

Moreno, J. 1960. *The Sociometry Reader.* Glencoe, Ill.: Free Press.

Mumford, E. 1981. "Participative Systems Design: Structure and Method." *Systems, Objectives, Solutions,* 1:5–19.

Mumford, E., N. Bancroft, and B. Sontag. 1983. "Participative Design—Successes and Failures." *Systems, Objectives, Solutions* 3:133–141.

Mumford, E. and M. Weir. 1979. *Computer Systems in Work Design.* New York: Wiley.

NBS (National Bureau of Standards). 1980. "Guidance on Requirements Analysis for Office Automation Systems." Special publication 500–72. Washington, D.C.: Government Printing Office.

Nelson, T. 1974. *Computer Lib/Dream Machines.* Chicago, Ill.: Hugo's Book Service.

Nicholas, J. 1982. "The Comparative Impact of Organization Development Interventions on Hard Criteria Measures." *Academy of Management Review* 7(4):531–542.

Nine-to-Five. 1984. *The 9-to-5 National Survey on Women and Stress.* Cleveland, Ohio: 9-to-5 National Association of Working Women.

Nolan, R. "Managing the Computer Resource: A State Hypothesis." *Communications of the ACM* 16(7):399–405.

Nutt, P. 1986. "Tactics of Implementation." *Academy of Management Journal* 29(2):230–261.

O'Keefe, R., J. Kernaghan, and A. Rubenstein. "Group Cohesiveness: A Factor in the Adoption of Innovations Among Scientific Work Groups." *Small Group Behavior* 6(3):282–292.

O'Reilly, C. 1977. "Supervisors and Peers as Information Sources, Group Supportiveness, and Individual Decision Making Performance." *Journal of Applied Psychology* 62:632–635.

Otway, H. and M. Peltu, eds., *New Office Technology: Human and Organizational Aspects.* Norwood, N.J.: Ablex.

Owens, D. "Copies in Seconds." *Atlantic Monthly* (February), p pp. p. 64–72.

Packer, M. 1983. "Measuring the Intangible in Productivity." *Technology Review* (February/March), pp. 48–57.

Paisley, W. 1980. "Information and Work." In B. Dervin and M. Voigt, eds., *Progress in Communication Sciences,* 2:113–166. Norwood, N.J.: Ablex.

Paisley, W. 1985. " 'Rithms of the Future: Learning and Working in the Age of Algorithms." In R. Hayes and G. Strong, eds., *The Information Economy of California.* Berkeley, Calif.: University of California and California State Library.

Panel on Impact of Video Viewing on Vision of Workers. 1982. *Video Displays, Work and Vision.* Washington, D.C.: National Academy Press.

Panko, R. 1984. "38 Offices: Analysing Needs in Individual Offices." *ACM Transactions on Office Information Systems* 2(3):226–234.

Pasmore, W. 1980. "The Comparative Impacts of Sociotechnical System, Job-Redesign, and Survey-Feedback Interventions." In D. Katz, R. Kahn, and J. Adams, eds., *The Study of Organizations,* pp. 523-530. San Francisco, Calif.: Jossey-Bass.

Pava, C. 1983. *Managing Office Technology.* New York: Free Press.

Perlin, N. 1985. *Beyond the Personal Computer: An Introduction to Office Automation.* White Plains, N.J.: Knowledge Industries Publications.

Perrow, C. 1967. "A Framework for the Comparative Analysis of Organizations." *American Sociological Review* 32:194–208.

Perrow, C. 1970. *Organizational Analysis: A Sociological View.* Belmont, Calif.: Wadsworth.

Perry, R. 1985. "Relational DBMS Takes Off." *Computer Decisions* (February 12), pp. 106 ff.

Peters, T. and N. Austin. 1985. *A Passion for Excellence.* New York: Random House.

Peters, T. and R. Waterman, Jr. 1982. *In Search of Excellence: Lessons from America's Best-Run Companies.* New York: Harper and Row.

Pfeffer, J. and G. Salancik. 1978. *The External Control of Organizations: A Resource Dependence Perspective.* New York: Harper and Row.

Pierce, J. and A. Delbecq. 1977. "Organization Structure, Individual Attitudes and Innovation." *Academy of Management Review* (January), pp. 27–37.

Pincus, J. 1986. "Communication Satisfaction, Job Satisfaction and Job Performance." *Human Communication Research* 12(3):395–419.

Pirow, P. "Why Some Systems Don't Provide Solutions." *Systems, Objectives, Solutions* pp. 89–94.

Pondy, L. and I. Mitroff. 1979. "Beyond the Open Systems Model of Organization." *Research in Organizational Behavior* 1:3–39.

Popular Computing. 1985. "Special Report: Desktop Publishing." *Popular Computing* 5(1):56 ff.

Porter, M. and V. Millar. 1985. "How Information Gives You Competitive Advantage." *Harvard Business Review* (July/August), pp. 149–160.

Pugh, D., D. Hickson, C. Hinings, and C. Turner. 1968. "The Dimensions of Organization Structure." *Administrative Science Quarterly* 13:65–105.

Pytka, S. 1986. "Copier/Printer Market to Explode by 1990." *Mini-Micro Systems* 19(1):111–115.

Reimann, B. 1980. "Organization Structure and Technology in Manufacturing: System Versus Work Flow Level Perspectives." *Academy of Management Journal* 23(1):61–77.

Reimann, B. and G. Inzerilli. 1979. "Technology and Organization: A Review and Synthesis of Major Research Findings." In G. England, A. Negandhi, and B. Wilpert, eds., *The Functioning of Complex Organizations,* pp. 237–274. Cambridge, Mass.: Oelgeschlager, Gunn and Hain.

Rhee, H. 1968. *Office Automation in Social Perspective: The Progress and Social Implications of Electronic Data Processing.* Oxford, England: Basil Blackwell.

Rice, R. E. 1980. "Impacts of Organizational and Interpersonal Computer-Mediated Communication." In M. Williams, ed., *Annual Review of Information Science and Technology,* 15:221–249. White Plains, N.Y.: Knowledge Industry Publications.

Rice, R. E. 1984. "Mediated Group Communication." In R. E. Rice and Associates, *The New Media: Communication, Research and Technology,* pp. 129–154. Beverly Hills, Calif.: Sage.

Rice, R.E. and Associates. 1984. *The New Media: Communication, Research and Technology.* Beverly Hills, Calif.: Sage.

Rice, R. E. and J. Bair. 1984. "New Organizational Media and Productivity." In R. E. Rice and Associates, *The New Media: Communication, Research and Technology,* pp. 185–216. Beverly Hills, Calif.: Sage.

Rice, R. E. and D. Case. 1983. "Computer-Based Messaging in the University: A Description of Use and Utility." *Journal of Communication* 33(1):131–152.

Rice, R. E. and G. Manross. 1986. "The Role of Job Category in the Diffusion of an Information Technology: The Case of the Intelligent Telephone." In M. Mc-Laughlin, ed., *Communication Yearbook,* vol. 10. Beverly Hills, Calif.: Sage.

Rice, R. E. and W. Paisley. 1981. *Public Communication Campaigns.* Beverly Hills, Calif.: Sage.

Rice, R. E. and W. Richards, Jr. 1985. "An Overview of Network Analysis Methods and Approaches." In B. Dervin and M. Voigt, eds., *Progress in Communication Sciences,* 6:105–165, Norwood, N.J.: Ablex.

Rice, R. E. and E. M. Rogers. 1980. "Reinvention in the Innovation Process." *Knowledge* 1(4):490–514.

Robey, D. and R. Zeller. 1978. "Factors Affecting the Success and Failure of an Information System for Product Quality." *Interfaces* 8(2):70–75.

Rockart, J. and L. Flannery. 1983. "The Management of End User Computing." *Communications of the ACM* 26(10):776–784.

Roethlisberger, F. and W. Dickson. 1939. *Management and the Worker.* Cambridge, Mass.: Harvard University Press.

Rogers, E. M. 1978. "Reinvention During the Innovation Process." In M. Radnor, et al., eds., *The Diffusion of Innovation: An Assessment.* Report to the National Science Foundation. Evanston, Ill.: Northwestern University.

Rogers, E. M. 1983. *Diffusion of Innovations.* 3d edition. New York: Free Press.

Rogers, E. M. and L. Kincaid. 1981. *Communication Networks: A New Paradigm for Research.* New York: Free Press.

Rogers, E. M. and J. Larsen. 1984. *Silicon Valley Fever.* New York: Free Press.

Roitman, D. and J. Mayer. 1982. "Fidelity and Reinvention in the Implementation of Innovations." In C. Blakely (chair), "Adoption, Implementation and Routinization of Organizational Innovations." Washington, D.C.: Symposium at the American Psychological Association Conference.

Rosen, A. and R. Fielden. 1982. *Word Processing.* Englewood Cliffs, N.J.: Prentice-Hall.

Rosenthal, S. 1984. "Prose 'n Style: An Overview of Writer's Workbench." *Unix Review* (August), pp. 46 ff.

Rousseau, D. 1977. "Technological Differences in Job Characteristics, Employee Satisfaction and Motivation: A Synthesis of Job Design Research and Sociotechnical Systems Theory." *Organizational Behavior and Human Performance* 19:18–42.

Rousseau D. 1979. "Assessment of Technology in Organizations: Closed Versus Open Systems Approaches." *Academy of Management Review* 4(4):531–542.

Salancik, G. and J. Pfeffer. 1977. "An Examination of Need-Satisfaction Models of Job Satisfaction." *Administrative Science Quarterly* 22:427–454.

Salancik, G. and J. Pfeffer. 1978. "A Social Information Processing Approach to Job Attitudes and Task Design." *Administrative Science Quarterly* 23:224–253.

Salton, G. and M. McGill. 1983. *Introduction to Modern Information Retrieval.* New York: McGraw-Hill.

Sargent, J. 1984. "Typographical Communication—A Powerful New Tool for the Office." *The Office Automation Reference and Buyer's Guide.* Brookfield, Conn.: Butterfield, pp.A–39–A–41.

Schultz, R. and D. Slevin, eds., *Implementing Operations Research/Management Science.* New York:Elsevier.

Scott, G. 1985. "From Gutenberg to Franklin and Wang." *Linkup* (June), pp. 13 ff.

Scott, J. 1982. "The Mechanization of Women's Work." *Scientific American* 274(3):166–187.

Shapiro, E. 1984. "Text Databases." *Byte* (October), pp.147–150.

Shaw, J. 1980. "An Information Processing Approach to the Study of Job Design." *Academy of Management Review* 5(1):41–48.

Sheposh, J., V. Hulton, and G. Knudsen. 1982. *Implementation of Planned Change: A Review of Major Issues.* San Diego, Calif.: Navy Personnel Research and Development Center.

Silverman, D. 1971. *The Theory of Organizations.* New York: Basic Books.

Simon, H. 1960. *The Shape of Automation.* Englewood Cliffs, N.J.: Prentice-Hall.

Simon, H. 1973. "Applying Information Technology to Organization Design." *Public Administrative Review* 33(3):268–278.

Simon, H. 1979. "The Consequences of Computers for Centralization and Decentralization." In M. Dertouzos and J. Moses, eds., *The Computer Age,* pp. 212–228. Cambridge, Mass.: MIT Press.

Smith, M. 1984. "Health Issues in VDT Work." In J. Bennett, D. Case, J. Sandelin, and M. Smith, eds., *Visual Display Terminals: Usability Issues and Health Concerns,* pp. 193–228. New York: Prentice-Hall.

Smith, R. 1983. "Computer Setup Lets Offices Do Printing Chores." *Wall Street Journal,* March 31, 1983, p. 22.

Staehle, W. 1982. "Technological and Organizational Change in Office Work: The Case of the Visual Display Units." In G. Mensch and R. Niehaus, eds., *Work, Organizations and Technological Change,* pp. 179–190. New York: Plenum.

Steinfield, C. 1986. "The Social Dimension of Computer-Mediated Communications." In M. McLaughlin, ed., *Communication Yearbook 9.* Beverly Hills, Calif.: Sage.

Stevick, G. 1986. "Menu of White Collar Productivity/Quality Improvement Tools." Rockford, Ill.: Ingersoll Engineers.

Stewart, D. 1985. "The Delicate Art of Digital Type." *Popular Computing* (January), pp. 99–102.

Stolz, S. 1984. "Dissemination of Standardized Human Models: A Behavior Analyst's Perspective." In S. Paine, G. Bellamy, and B. Wilcox, eds., *Human Services That Work,* pp. 235–245. Baltimore, Md.: Brookes.

Strassman, P. 1976. "Managing the Costs of Information." *Harvard Business Review* (September/October), pp. 133–142.

Strassman, P. 1980. "The Office of the Future: Information Management for the New Age." *Technology Review,* pp. 54–65.

Strassman, P. 1985. *The Information Payoff: The Transformation of Work in the Electronic Age.* New York: Macmillan.

Strauss, G. 1982. "Workers' Participation in Management: An International Perspective." *Research in Organizational Behavior* 4:173–265.

Tapscott, D. 1982. *Office Automation: A User-Driven Method.* New York: Plenum.

Tapscott, D., D. Henderson, and M. Greenberg. 1985. *Planning for Integrated Office Systems.* Homewood, Ill.: Dow Jones-Irwin.

Taylor, F. 1911. *Principles of Scientific Management.* New York: Harper.

Taylor, J. 1979. "Job Design Criteria Twenty Years Later." In L. Davis and J. Taylor, eds., *Design of Jobs,* pp. 54–63. 2d edition. Santa Monica, Calif.: Goodyear.

Taylor, J. 1980. "A Day in the Life of a WP Operator." *Words* (October), pp.26–32.

Taylor, J. 1982. "Designing an Organization and an Information System for 'Central Stores': A Study in Participative Socio-Technical Analysis and Design." *Systems, Objectives, Solutions* 2:67–76.

Taylor, J. and D. Bowers. 1972. *Survey of Organizations.* Ann Arbor, Mich.: Institute for Social Research.

Tenne, R. and B. Mannheim. 1977. "The Effect of the Level of Production Technology on Workers' Orientations and Responses to the Work Situation." In M. Haug and J. Dofny, eds.,*Work and Technology,* pp. 61–89. Beverly Hills, Calif.: Sage.

Thomas, J. and R. Griffin. 1983. "The Social Information Processing Model of Task Design: A Review of the Literature." *Academy of Management Review* 8(4):672–682.

Thompson, J. 1967. *Organizations in Action.* New York: McGraw-Hill.

Toffler, A. 1981. *The Third Wave.* New York: Bantam Books.

Tornatsky, L., J. Eveland, M. Boyland, W. Hetzner, E. Johnson, D. Roitman, and J. Schneider. 1985. *The Process of Technological Innovation: Reviewing the Literature.* Washington, D.C.: National Science Foundation, Productivity Improvement Research section.

Turner, A. and P. Lawrence. 1965. *Industrial Jobs and the Worker: An Investigation of Responses to Task Attributes.* Boston: Harvard Graduate School of Business Administration.

Uhlig, R., D. Farber, and J. Bair. 1979. *The Office of the Future.* New York: North-Holland.

Van de Ven, A. and R. Drazin. 1985. "The Concept of Fit in Contingency Theory." *Research in Organizational Behavior* 7:335–365.

VDT News. 1984. *The VDT Health and Safety Report.* (bimonthly). New York: Microwave News.

Vickers, G. 1965. *The Art of Judgment: A Study of Policy Making.* New York: Basic Books.

Vroom, V. 1960. *Some Personality Determinants of the Effects of Participation.* Englewood Cliffs, N.J.: Prentice-Hall.

Vroom, V. 1964. *Work and Motivation.* New York: Wiley.

Wall Street Journal. 1983. "Rivalry Between Word Processors and Personal Computers Heats Up." March 10.

Wall Street Journal. 1985. "Technology in the Workplace." Special Report September 6, p. 7C.

Walton, R. 1975. "The Diffusion of New Work Structures: Explaining Why Success Didn't Take." *Organizational Dynamics* 3(3):3–22.

Watt, D. 1984. "Mass Storage." *Popular Computing* (May), pp. 113–134.

Weick, K. 1977. "Organizations as Self-Designing Systems," *Organizational Dynamics* (Autumn), pp. 31–46.

Weick, K. 1979. *The Social Psychology of Organizing.* 2d edition. Reading, Mass.: Addison-Wesley. (1st edition 1969.)

Werneke, D. 1985. "Women: The Vulnerable Group." In T. Forester, ed., *The Information Technology Revolution,* pp. 406–416. Cambridge, Mass.: MIT Press.

Westin, A., H. Schweder, M. Baker, and S. Lehman. 1985. *The Changing Workplace.* White Plains, New York.: Knowledge Industry Publications.

Wetherbe, J., C. Davis, and C. Dykman. 1981. "Implementing Automated Office Systems." *Journal of Systems Management* 32(8):6–12.

Whalen, T. 1983. "Office Technology and Socio-Economic Change: 1870–1955." *IEEE Technology and Society Magazine* 2(1):12–18,29.

Wilson, J. 1966. "Innovation in Organization: Notes Toward A Theory." In J. Thompson, ed., *Approaches to Organizational Design,* pp. 193–218. Pittsburgh: University of Pittsburgh Press.

Winograd, T. 1984. "Computer Software for Working with Language." *Scientific American* (September), pp. 131–145.

Woodward, J. 1965. *Industrial Organizations.* London: Oxford University Press.

WPIS (Word Processing and Information Systems). 1981. "WP/IS Survey Indicates Growth, Greater Systems Integration." *Word Processing and Information Systems* 8(1):25–30.

Words. 1982. "In-House Consultant Column." *Words* 11(2):34.

Yates, J. 1982. "From Press Book and Pigeonhole to Vertical Filing: Revolution in Storage and Access Systems for Correspondence." *Journal of Business Communication* 19(3):5–26.

Yin, R. 1978. "Organizational Innovation: A Psychologist's View." In M. Radnor, et al., eds., *The Diffusion of Innovations: An Assessment.* Report to the National Science Foundation. Evanston, Ill.: Northwestern University Press.

Zaltman, G. and N. Lin. 1971. "On the Nature of Innovations." *American Behavioral Scientist* 14:651–673.

Zaltman, G., R. Duncan, and J. Holbeck. 1973. *Innovations and Organizations.* New York: Wiley.

Zimmerman, J., ed. 1982. *Technological Woman: Interfacing.* New York: Praeger.

Zmud, R. 1978. "An Empirical Investigation of the Dimensionality of the Concept of Information." *Decision Sciences* 9(2):187–195.

Zuboff, S. 1982. "New Worlds of Computer-Mediated Work." *Harvard Business Review* 60(5):142–152.

Index

Adaptability and organizational environment, 2

Adaptation: causes of, 46–47; communication, 143–44, 154–56, 169; conceptual foundations, 45–47, 216n12; difficulty in achieving, 181–82; encouragement, 91, 151; factors predicting operator, 157–59; from standard or mainline form of WP, 72–77; in legal firms, 142–48; influenced by supervisors, 129; information, 2, 8; interviews, 210–11; job characteristics, 124–25; job design, 140; of organizations, 48, 104; of WP services, 86, 89–91, 93, 95, 97, 99, 169; operators, 156–61; outcome of, 3, 28, 204; perhaps not good strategy, 217n5; political and career risks, 100; sharing information, 190; training, 149–50

Argument of book, 3–6

Attitudes of workers, 151

Attributes of innovations, 40–42; compatibility, 41, 60; complexity, 41, 59; dimensions, 216n9; observability or communicability, 42, 60; relative advantage, 41, 59; trialability or divisibility, 42, 60

Authors: and operators, 70–71, 144, 152–53, 170; included in WP communication, 155; managing self-image, 178

Automated information systems, 34

Boundary, 6, 8, 165–86; between operators and authors, 71–72, 120–22, 153; cultural meanings, 176; definition, 166; dimensions, 221n1; formal procedures, 71–72; liaisons between departments, 56; management by supervisors, 96, 123, 145, 166, 194; managing environmental, 203; managing internal, 202; problem: commitment to past practices, 183; problem: defining managerial focus, 184–86; problem: establishing boundaries, 179–80; problem: misreading demands, 182–83; problem: misreading interdependencies, 182; problem: understanding environment, 181–84

Boundary spanning, 92

Case study: best case of management assumptions, 122–25; Big Bank and centralized WP, 52–55; boundaries at Hard Metals, 170–72; boundaries in Government Analysis Agency, 175–79; boundaries of governmental contracting, 168–70, boundaries of WP vs. OA, 172–75; District Office and individual leadership, 55–56; high-integrated WP systems, 98–100; implementing microcomputers, 187–92; private legal work and adaptation, 144–46; public legal work and adaptation, 142–44; research